Alaskan-Yukon Trophies
won and lost

An ice pothole, a peril of the Alaskan trail.

ALASKAN · YUKON
Trophies
WON and LOST

by
G. O. YOUNG

ECHO POINT BOOKS & MEDIA, LLC
Brattleboro, Vermont

Published in 2024 by Echo Point Books & Media
Brattleboro, Vermont
www.EchoPointBooks.com

Alaskan-Yukon Trophies Won and Lost
ISBN: 978-1-64837-308-4 (casebound)
978-1-64837-309-1 (paperback)

Cover design by Kaitlyn Whitaker

THIS BOOK IS
RESPECTFULLY DEDICATED TO
EVERY LOVER OF NATURE
AND THE OUTDOORS

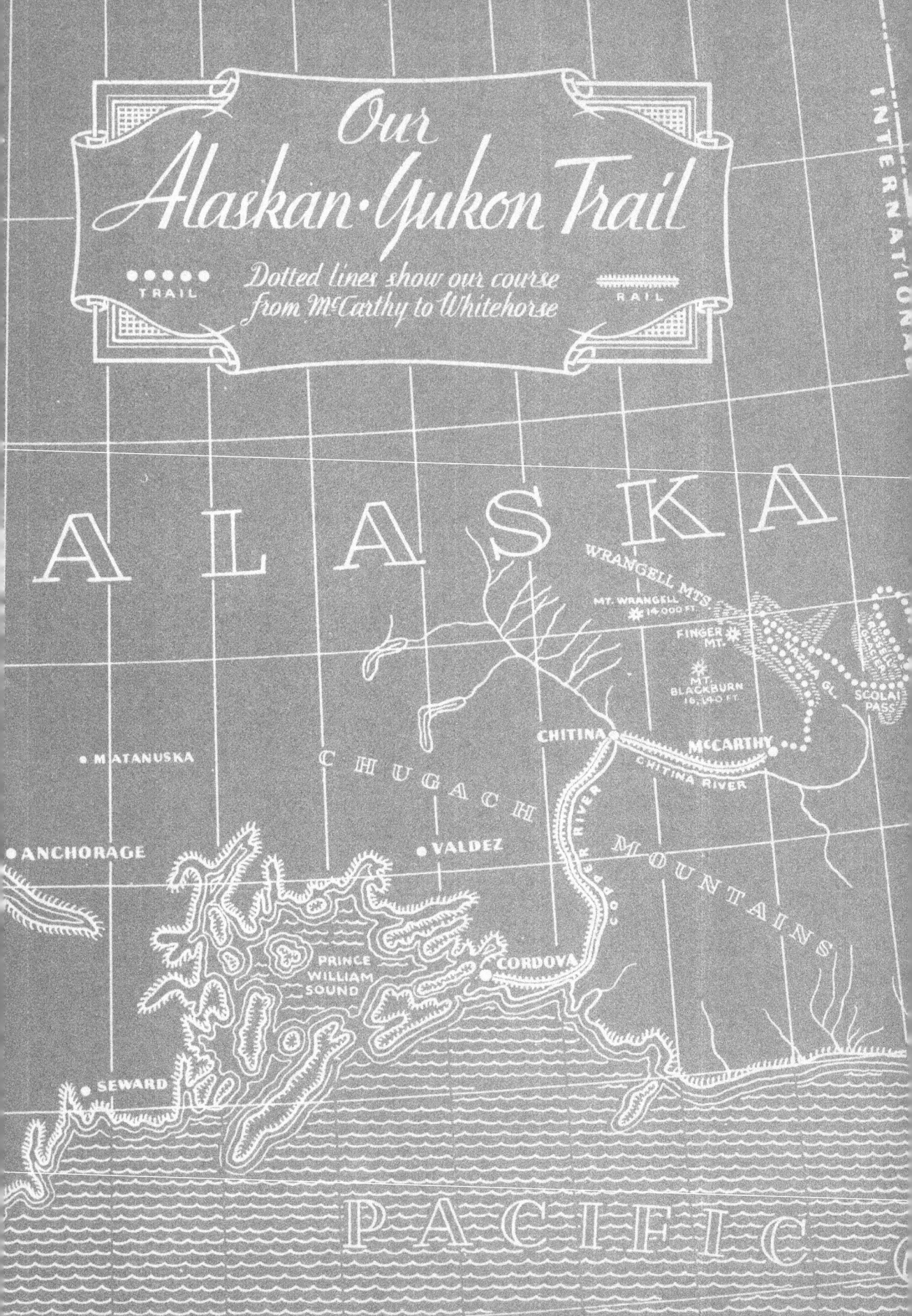

DAWSON
McMILLAN RIVER
PELLY RIVER
YUKON RIVER
YUKON
TESLIN RIVER
DONJEK R.
KLUANE R.
WOLVERINE CR.
KLUANE LAKE
JACQUOT POST
BONES' CABIN
SLIMS RIVER
WHITEHORSE
INT ELIAS RANGE
MALASPINA GLACIER
WHITE PASS
SKAGWAY
MUIR GLACIER
BRADY GLACIER
JUNEAU

CONTENTS

Chapter		Page
I	An Invitation Accepted	1
II	On Alaskan Soil	9
III	A Happy Meeting	18
IV	A Day On Nazina River	40
V	A Day On A Glacier	54
VI	A Climb For Goat	70
VII	A Distressing Accident	79
VIII	Crossing a Great Divide	90
IX	A Side Trip For Sheep	99
X	Scenes Never Forgotten	112
XI	Caught In a Storm	126
XII	On British Soil	141
XIII	Arrival At Generc River	151
XIV	Unusual Experiences	168
XV	Our Camp Menu	181
XVI	Caribou On Count Creek	191
XVII	A Day On White River	204
XVIII	Stranded On An Island	217
XIX	The Rescue	225
XX	Return To Generc River	239
XXI	Continued Hardships	249
XXII	Journey's End	262
XXIII	A Promise Fulfilled	268
	Epilogue	275

ILLUSTRATIONS

	Page
An ice pothole, a peril of the Alaskan trail	Frontispiece
Our Alaskan-Yukon Trail (map)	vi-vii
Juneau, Capital of Alaska	3
Alaska's area compared to U. S. (map)	6
Railroad bridge, Copper River	12
Child's Glacier, at Mile Forty Nine	14
Miles Glacier, at Mile Forty Nine	15
Our Alaskan-Yukon Trail (map)	21
Our party	26
Mr. Snyder and his horse	30
Dr. Evans and Old Bob	31
The author and his horse	34
Crossing an ice plain	37
Bones fording Nazina River	44
Traveling through spruce timber	47
A view of Nazina Glacier and moraines	56
Looking up the Nazina Glacier	59
On the Nazina Glacier	60
An internal moraine	61
On the ice, August 11th	63
Billie Slimpert cutting footholds	64
Crossing a natural ice bridge (two views)	67
A mountain goat	72
Author and goat on a rock slide	75

ILLUSTRATIONS *(Continued)*

	Page
Finger Mountain, with marked locations	76
Spot, the author's second saddle horse	81
Pack horse jumping a crevasse	84
Hard-going (two views)	85
Source of the Nazina Glacier	88
Waiting for horses to be packed	91
The pack train near White River (two views)	92
Moraines on Russell Glacier (two views)	95
Prince of the peaks	100
Where only a mountain sheep can go!	105
Our sheep hunt (map)	106
A ram of Boundary Mountain	111
Rock formation. Sheep camp (two views)	116
Mr. Snyder and ram	121
Mr. Snyder and goat. A silvery creek (two views)	124
Camp on Beaver Creek	129
At timber line, Mt. Nazahat	132
Loading sheep meat on saddle horses	135
Caribou swimming the Yukon River	140
A handshake across the International Line	143
Mt. Nazahat. A spruce forest (two views)	144
Many-channeled bar of the White River	144
Author and moose, at Holmes Creek	149
Volcanic ash on high plateau country	156

ILLUSTRATIONS *(Continued)*

	Page
Sandbank on Generc River; Mt. Nazahat	159
Snyder with caribou (two views)	162
Indians whipsawing lumber	165
Two mountain sheep in Alaskan setting	171
Snyder's moose and his ram (two views)	178
'Fox-feed' hauling whipsawn lumber	185
Caribou camp on Count Creek	192
Mountains near the Generc River and Count Creek	195
Dr. Evans' Count Creek caribou	197
The author's largest caribou	198
The author's second-largest caribou	201
Indian Johnnie with Dr. Evans' caribou head	202
Our fifty-one trophies	205
Eugene Jacquot drying moosemeat	208
Loading the scow in the early morning	209
Paddie guarding the scow	210
Running-ice in the White River	212
As the rapids were approached	214
The partially-raised scow	231
Breaking camp on the Wolverine	241
Jacquot Brothers' trading post	248
Indians waiting at Kluane Lake	251
Bones starting for the White River (two views)	269
The attempt to recover the trophies (two views)	271

FOREWORD

In the early 1900s, trophy hunting in Alaska was a popular activity among wealthy American sportsmen. The remote and rugged terrain of Alaska offered a unique and challenging hunting experience, and the abundance of large game animals, such as grizzly bears, moose, caribou, and Dall sheep, provided an opportunity for hunters to collect impressive trophies.

Trophy hunting in Alaska began to gain popularity in the late 1800s, as Alaska became more accessible to tourists and sportsmen. In 1896 the Klondike gold rush brought the region into sharp focus as nearly 100,000 prospectors made their way to Seattle, then by steamship to Skagway, Alaska, and ultimately inland to seek their fortune. The introduction of steamships and the completion of the Alaska Railroad in 1923 made it easier for hunters to reach remote areas of the state. The establishment of national parks and game preserves in Alaska also protectected wildlife populations, ensuring that there would always be animals available for hunting. The early Alaskan trophy hunters were mostly wealthy and influential men, including politicians, businessmen, and celebrities, who traveled with professional guides and outfitters, providing them with the necessary equipment, transportation, and local knowledge.

In 1919, lifelong hunter, fisherman, and naturalist G. O. Young joined two other men on a trophy-hunting expedition into the Alaska and Yukon wilderness. The Seattle-to-Skagway route to the interior marked the starting point for the long and demanding journey, which eventually took them to southwestern Yukon and southeastern Alaska. These spectacular unspoiled mountains, rivers, glaciers, and forests comprise one geographic region, artificially divided by geopolitical lines. Mountain goats, Dall sheep, moose, and caribou were the usual prey of the Young party.

The hunting methods used by early trophy hunters were often crude and unsporting. Many hunters used high-powered rifles to shoot animals from a distance, rather than, like Young and his companions, stalking and tracking them on foot. Some hunters even used airplanes to spot animals from the air and then landed nearby to shoot them. This practice, known as aerial hunting, would be outlawed in Alaska in the 1950s.

Despite the controversial methods used by some hunters, trophy hunting in Alaska played an important role in the state's economy and culture. The sale of hunting licenses, permits, and tags generated significant revenue for the state, and the trophies collected by hunters were often displayed in museums and private collections. Hunting was also seen as a way to control the populations of large game animals, which could cause damage to crops and property if left unchecked.

As the twentieth and twenty-first centuries have progressed, concerns about the impact of trophy hunting on wildlife populations have grown. In the 1960s the State of Alaska began to regulate hunting more strictly, imposing limits on the number of animals that could be taken and requiring hunters to report their kills. In the 1970s the federal government passed the Marine Mammal Protection Act and the Endangered Species Act, which provided additional protections for wildlife. Today, trophy hunting is still legal in Alaska, but it is tightly regulated and closely monitored by the state and federal governments. Hunters are required to obtain permits and tags for the animals they hunt, and they must follow strict guidelines on hunting methods, bag limits, and reporting. While trophy hunting remains a controversial practice, it continues to be an important part of Alaska's cultural and economic heritage.

G. O. Young continued to hunt, fish, and enjoy the great outdoors for decades after his Alaskan campaign. In later years he was known to pursue his quarry with a camera rather than a high-powered rifle. Like many big-game enthusiasts, Young became actively involved in conservation, and this riveting account of his journey into the northern wilderness manifests the seeds of that activism.

PREFACE

This volume covers an expedition made into the interior of Alaska and the Yukon Territory by a party of three men, of which the author was one. The objects of our trip have been stated in the first chapter and will not be repeated in this introductory statement.

The events of this expedition stand out in the memory of the writer so prominently and the scenery so magnificently, that this narrative has been written independently of the writer's notes, accurately made each day, which have been consulted for the purpose of verification only. The one predominating desire has been that all our experiences be related as they actually occurred, and all observations be recorded as they were made.

As a further precaution against any inaccuracies which might inadvertently appear, and fearing there might be some conflict in our memories or impressions, the manuscript was submitted to the other surviving member of our party with the request that he make suggestions and corrections. With the exception of one minor detail, which necessitated a letter to our outfitter before the writer was convinced and was willing to make the suggested change, the manuscript received his unqualified endorsement.

The photographs, with a few noted exceptions, were selected from a considerable number taken by the author. The kindness of the publishers of Robert W. Service's poems is also acknowledged, for their permission to use a number of Service's verses, taken from *The Spell of the Yukon* and *Ballads of a Cheechako*.

G. O. YOUNG

Chapter I

AN INVITATION ACCEPTED

*"Let us probe the silent places, let us seek
  what luck betide us;
Let us journey to a lonely land I know.
There's a whisper on the night-wind, there's
  a star agleam to guide us,
And the Wild is calling, calling . . . let us go."*

IT WAS a bright morning in July, as we stood at the ship's rail and watched the great throng hurrying to and fro on the piers of the Alaskan Steamship Company in Seattle, Washington. Great trucks and wagons loaded with fruits, poultry and other perishable freight forced their way through the crowd and alongside the vessel where their loads were taken aboard by the mechanical lifters, at almost the last minute before departure. Soon the last remnants of the ship's cargo were loaded, and, as if by magic, everything became comparatively quiet. A number of belated passengers hurried up the gangplank; the great sirens blew loudly, and it was not long until the *Alameda* was steaming out of Puget Sound on her sixteen hundred mile voyage to the Land of the Midnight Sun.

The ship's passengers were made up largely of people from Alaska and the Yukon Territory. Many of them were returning from "down below" or "outside" as the northerners expressed themselves when referring to the United States or to their native homes in other countries. In addition there were many tourists on pleasure trips to various towns along the southern coast of Alaska.

For four days and nights our steamship made her way through the straights and sounds of the "Inside Passage" before Skagway was reached. At times she squeezed through channels so narrow that the spruce forests on the Canadian mainland on our right and on Vancouver Island—and later Queen Charlotte Island—to our left seemed to be within a stone's throw. The mountains are bold, steep and craggy, usually rising directly from the water's edge, while the forests consist largely of fir and spruce which extend from the shoreline to an almost uniform height above the sea. Some of the mountains are timbered to their tops, while the summits of the higher ones are bare and usually covered with perpetual snow and ice.

Perhaps nowhere are conditions, taken as a whole, so favorable for an ocean voyage as along the "Inside Passage" from Seattle to Skagway. Protected from the ocean's waves, as this passage is by the archipelago of innumerable islands which fringe the Pacific Coast, one encounters water as smooth as that of a large river while the scenery is perhaps unsurpassed in beauty, within the limitations of ordinary travel, anywhere in the world.

Streams varying in size from narrow rivulets, resembling long white threads in the distance, to good sized creeks, course their way in serpentine fashion down the almost and sometimes entirely perpendicular sides of the rugged mountains. Some of them form series of cascades, others cataracts where the water drops many hundreds of feet and sometimes directly into the edge of the ocean. All of the streams are white in appearance. Those originating from springs and ordinarily clear water are churned to foam in their abrupt descent, while those having their source in the glaciers or snowclad mountains are a milky white.

Our first stop was at Ketchikan, a two days voyage from Seattle. As a large cargo of freight was to be unloaded an opportunity was given the passengers to go ashore where we visited some of the large salmon canneries—places of great interest, and inspected the Indian Totem Poles which could be seen in large numbers.

On the afternoon of the next day we arrived at the docks of the Gastinau Mining Company where freight was unloaded. Through the courtesy of the genial mine Superintendent, many of the ship's passengers were supplied with passes and permitted to go up the incline and through this ten million dollar plant. From far back and down into the bowels of the big mountain they bring out the low grade ore, which contains only a small amount of gold, not sufficient in itself to pay for the cost of operation, but along with the silver and lower grade ores we were informed that it has yielded a very good return upon the investment.

On the evening of the fourth day we cast anchor at Juneau, a mining and trading town picturesquely situated on a narrow ledge between the sea and the base of the mountain which rises

AN INVITATION ACCEPTED

Juneau, Capital of Alaska

abruptly to a height of almost one mile above the town and the sea. Juneau has been the seat of government of Alaska since 1906 and is now considered its largest and most substantially built town, having a population of three thousand people.

I now realized I had reached the land of my dreams. From boyhood I had been interested in Alaska and the far North. My interest was increased when at various times I heard a relative, Dr. S. Hall Young, pioneer Presbyterian missionary, author and lecturer, describe this wonderful country when he made occasional visits to his native State during his fifty years of Alaskan Service. At such times I took advantage of every opportunity to seek information concerning this interesting country.

In later years I had decided that just as soon as possible I would visit Alaska and undertake an expedition into the interior, not only for the purpose of seeing and learning something about that country, but to hunt big game, and if successful, bring home some good specimens for mounting as trophies. One serious question which came to my mind was that of finding a companion for this trip. I disliked the idea of going alone, and knew that an agreeable companion would add much to the pleasure, while the cost would be much less proportionately. I thought that somewhere in this broad land there were persons who would be interested in such a trip if I could only locate them, and in the course of time wrote a short article and sent it to a magazine for publication, incidentally referring to my contemplated trip.

In the meantime, and unknown to me, a physician by the name of A. H. Evans, whose home in southern Texas was so close to Mexico that only the Rio Grande River intervened; and a banker by the name of J. C. Snyder, who resided in Metamora, Illinois, had been planning a big game hunt somewhere in the far North. They had never met each other personally, but through a third person they had become acquainted by a correspondence carried on for a year or two previously. Their plans were made, which included a spring bear hunt by Doctor Evans, after which Mr. Snyder was to join him in their general hunt.

Before departing from his home in Eagle Pass, Texas, Doctor Evans took note of my article in the magazine and added a postscript to a farewell letter written to Mr. Snyder, calling his attention to same and suggesting that he communicate with me. My first information concerning these gentlemen and their contemplated trip was a brief letter from Mr. Snyder advising that he and a Doctor Evans from Texas had arranged for a big game hunt in Alaska and the Yukon Territory and having read my article they thought I might be interested in joining them. He suggested that if I were interested to write immediately giving him information concerning myself—that is, age, hunting experience, ability and endurance to withstand the hardships that one would naturally expect to encounter on such a trip, together with references. If satisfactory, he would do likewise and would give me information concerning their plans.

I was favorably impressed with the letter but did not think it possible for me to arrange my affairs so as to be able to join them on such short notice and so informed Mr. Snyder. I wrote him, however, not to consider my reply as final and at the same time gave him such information concerning myself as I thought he would be interested in and asked him to do likewise and also give me details regarding their plans. A prompt reply was received and I was surprised to find that to some extent their plans coincided with those I had in mind. He stated that they had contracted with an outfitter by the name of Bones who resided far back in the Yukon Territory. Provisions had been made for the addition of a third man should they care to increase their

AN INVITATION ACCEPTED

party to three. The understanding had been, however, that notice of the addition of such third man should be sent to Bones in sufficient time to reach him at the town of White Horse when he would arrive there for mail and supplies some time in June, or when the snow had melted sufficiently to enable him to cross the mountain passes. Mr. Snyder stated that I would have to decide at an early date and even then it would be too late to take chances on a letter reaching Bones and that it would be necessary to send a cablegram.

Information was also given me as to the contract price, which was far in excess of what I had expected it to be; but Mr. Snyder had commented upon the reputed reliability of the outfitter and his splendid equipment. He stated that a few hundred dollars difference in the cost of a trip of this kind was small in comparison with the satisfaction of knowing we would be in the hands of a reliable man who knew the country and the haunts of the various kinds of game to be hunted, and who would furnish first class guides.

I debated the matter in my mind from every angle. These men were absolute strangers to me and I had no time in which to investigate them. We might be of different temperaments altogether. One of them was already in the Yukon but Mr. Snyder knew little about him, except that he was a doctor. Judging from a picture sent him, Mr. Snyder thought him to be a man of about his own age, which was forty-five or perhaps, as he stated—"just a little older." It appeared to me that we should know something more of each other before undertaking an expedition of such magnitude. On the other hand I reasoned that sportsmen who make trips of that kind are almost invariably lovers of Nature and the out-of-doors and experience had taught me that such men could usually be relied upon. I thought of the advantage there would be in one of our party being a physician; not that I thought there was any more, nor in fact as much danger of sickness in that country as at home. On previous hunting trips to points far removed from civilization, in various parts of Canada, I had always supplied myself with a good assortment of remedies (although seldom, if ever, used) and being a pharmacist, myself, was in position to administer in case of ordinary illness. But, on this contemplated trip I was aware of the great danger of accidents which might result in broken bones.

ALASKAN-YUKON TROPHIES

Securing reliable outfitters and guides was a serious problem as there were doubtless few men in that country equipped to outfit hunting and exploring parties. Some of these lived far back in the interior and received their mail only two or three times

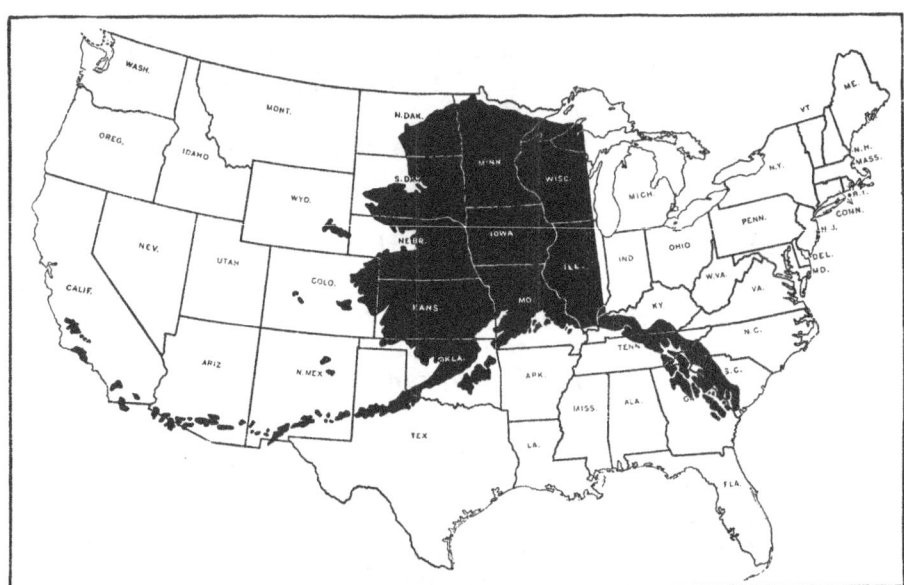

Alaska's area in relation to that of the United States. Map, courtesy of U. S. Dept. of the Interior.

a year. From my information it was advisable to begin negotiations with them at least one year in advance and even then it was likely that only two or three letters could be exchanged in the meantime.

Here was an opportunity to join a party whose members had attended to all correspondence and details necessary in the arrangement of the trip. Therefore, after weighing the matter carefully in my mind, I ventured so far as to write Mr. Snyder advising him that I was seriously considering the trip and suggesting an exchange of photographs at which time I forwarded mine. About the same time I received the following telegram:

"You must decide on Alaskan trip and if going, wire $500.00 to the credit of Morley E. Bones, Canadian Bank of Commerce, White Horse, Yukon Territory.—J. C. Snyder."

AN INVITATION ACCEPTED

Again I pondered. The matter of forwarding $500.00 as an initial payment upon my part of a contract in which I had not entered, nor had any voice, was not a small one. These men were in a measure strangers to each other, entire strangers to me, and until a few days earlier, unheard of by me; while the party to whom the money was to be cabled was a complete stranger residing in a foreign land, so I delayed acting.

Three days later Mr. Snyder's photograph was received and with it a letter in which he confirmed his telegram and wrote,—"I received your photograph, and if I mistake not, I make out an emblem in the lapel of your coat which appeals to me. I am sending my picture in return and you will note that I wear the same emblem." In this letter he expressed the hope in a very earnest manner that I would join them. I opened the envelope containing the photograph, studied the face for a few moments, and after consulting my wife, who encouraged me to accept the invitation and make the trip, I went to the telegraph office and transmitted the money and the message, as Mr. Snyder had directed.

I had reflected that the addition of one man would necessitate another guide and perhaps four additional horses—a saddle horse each for the additional hunter and guide and two pack horses to carry the extra food and supplies that would be essential. There had been some uncertainty in my mind as to whether the outfitter would be in position to properly take care of me, but I was relieved later on, when a message was received from the Bank at White Horse, advising that Bones had been there and that he would arrange for my addition to the party.

I left my home in West Virginia on July 15th, and endeavored to dismiss from my mind all business cares, with the determination of enjoying myself to the fullest extent during my absence. There had been a battle against time in an effort to arrange my personal affairs preparatory to leaving. The trip across the continent was made by way of that splendid railway system,—the Canadian Pacific; and I reached Vancouver, British Columbia a week later having stopped over a day or two while enroute. At Vancouver I boarded one of the Canadian Pacific steamers for Seattle. United States vessels bound for ports in Alaska north of Skagway do not stop at Vancouver, nor at other Canadian ports; nor do vessels sailing from Vancouver go farther north than Skagway. It is, therefore, necessary that passengers traveling over the

ALASKAN-YUKON TROPHIES

Canadian Pacific Railroad to its western terminus at Vancouver go south to Seattle in order to get a United States Steamship for more northern points in Alaska.

    In our correspondence Mr. Snyder and I had agreed to meet in Seattle and had designated the hotel at which we would stop. We had not made reservations in advance and due to the city's crowded condition at that time, I was unable to secure accommodations at the hotel designated, and was advised that Mr. Snyder was not registered there. I then started out to find my unknown friend and not until I had visited almost every hotel in the city did I succeed. As I entered the lobby of the hotel where he had located, I saw a man rise from his chair and immediately recognized him as being Mr. Snyder, while he also recognized me, as a result of the exchange of our photographs. With Mr. Snyder were his wife and two young daughters, Eula and Lois, aged about eleven and seven, respectively. They were to accompany him to Cordova, Alaska, after which they would return to Juneau and then to Skagway, where they would remain until our return in the fall from the interior.

CHAPTER II

ON ALASKAN SOIL

*"You've read of the trail of Ninety-eight, but its woe
no man may tell;
It was all of a piece and a whole yard wide and the
name of the brand was 'Hell'."*

BEFORE leaving our homes Mr. Snyder and I had forwarded to Governor Thomas R. Riggs a remittance in payment of our Alaska hunting licenses and had requested that they be forwarded to McCarthy, our outfitting point. Desiring additional information concerning Alaska's game laws Mr. Snyder proposed that while freight was being unloaded we take advantage of the opportunity to pay a short visit to Governor Riggs.

It was Sunday evening and thinking that we would find him at his home, we called at the Executive Mansion and were cordially received by the Governor with whom we spent a pleasant half hour.

"Who is going to outfit you?" inquired the Governor.

"A man by the name of Bones living in the Yukon Territory," replied Mr. Snyder.

"What? Morley E. Bones!" exclaimed the Governor, with a smile—evidently in surprise and apparently very much interested.

"Are you acquainted with Mr. Bones?" we asked.

"Yes, indeed; in fact almost everyone in all this North Country knows or has heard of Morley Bones. You will find him to be quite an unusual character."

"What is it about this man that is so unusual?" we asked. "We have inquired from several of the ship's passengers, who live in the Yukon, concerning him. Some of them know him personally; others know of him, but they have all referred to him in about the same manner that you have—nothing detrimental, but in a vague sort of a way that has left some uncertainty in our minds as to just what kind of man he is. Perhaps you can enlighten us. Is he entirely reliable and a good hunter?"

"Absolutely reliable and a man whose word can be depended upon under all circumstances; in fact, one of the best outfitters in the North Country; a good hunter, thoroughly familiar with the country and I presume as good a judge of the dangerous glacial waters of the interior as can be found anywhere. You will find him to be a very queer man, a man who is hard to describe; but you will soon learn to understand his peculiar manners. In fact, you will be very much interested in him and I am certain you will get along with him nicely."

We were awakened next morning by the noise of the hoisting cranes and platform trucks as the large consignment of the ship's cargo was unloaded on the mammoth pier of Skagway's harbor, at the head of the Lynn Canal. This canal is a true fiord, extending back from the ocean for a distance of a hundred miles and having an average width of six miles, with magnificent mountain scenery on either side. It is subject to violent winter storms but is never closed by ice and is, therefore, navigable during the entire year. Skagway during the Klondike stampede was one of the most noted towns in the world. It was there that the stampeders landed and took up their trail across the Chilkoot and White Passes afoot, the former being thirty-five hundred feet above the level of the sea which is almost directly below, and the latter twenty-eight hundred and eighty-eight feet; while the mountains on either side of the passes are from five to six thousand feet high, their height being more pronounced because they rise abruptly from the sea, there being no foothills. It was across these famous passes during 1897, '98 and '99 that thousands of gold seekers traveled in endless procession with their packs on their backs. Many there were who never returned. Their bodies were strewn along the trail to the present town of White Horse, a hundred and ten miles distant in the Yukon Territory, or lost in the icy currents of the Yukon River, in their effort to reach Dawson City, located about five hundred miles below.

Upon leaving Skagway that afternoon we retraced our course down the Lynn Canal, traveling south to Chichagof Island, then through Cross Sound and out into the Pacific Ocean proper. Many of my readers will recall the sinking of the Canadian Steamship *Sophia* on October 25, 1918, at which time three hundred and seventy-three persons, including the crew, went down with the vessel on Vanderbilt Reef, in the Lynn Canal, not a single person having been rescued. That evening as we passed by the sunken vessel, both her masts protruding above the water, there was a feeling of sadness upon the part of all of us as we thought of the seventy bodies that still remained in her hull, nine months after the disaster, while three hundred and three had been removed.

As we approached the ocean the waves became much larger and a number of passengers retired early as they were already attacked by seasickness. I remained in my stateroom writing until a late hour but was obliged to leave my door open to admit an abundance of fresh air, as when closed I also experienced a slight sensation of seasickness. Upon completing my writing I walked out on the ship's deck. Not a light was to be seen in any of the staterooms and I observed that I had the entire deck to myself. I enjoyed the quietness of the hour and leaned over the railing listening to the big waves as they broke against the bow of the vessel. We were now so far north that it did not become dark until about eleven o'clock and it really was not dark at that time as the reflection of the sun could be seen. At midnight I was able to read coarse print without the aid of artificial light. I went to the rear of the deck where I stood watching the wake of the ship far back in the distance, although there was no moon. At one o'clock in the morning I noticed that it was getting much lighter, and soon afterwards the approaching sunrise intermingled with the gray dawn of the morning presented a lurid scene such as I had never witnessed. I would have enjoyed gazing upon it longer but realized that it was long past time to retire.

Upon rising that morning we found that for the first time we were far from the sight of land. Very few passengers appeared at the breakfast table and a less number at lunch, while this group was still further reduced when the dinner gong was sounded at six in the evening.

During the entire journey the weather had been perfectly clear but this was a gloomy day with much mist and cloudiness. Until this time all had been life and gaiety on the ship but the few people to be found on deck were mostly those accustomed to making the voyage and not seriously affected by the rough waters of the North Pacific.

That day a number of whales were seen. Schools of large fish, evidently king salmon, frequently leaped high out of the water. Wild ducks were numerous and I never tired of watching the seagulls as hour after hour and even into the twilight they kept along with the vessel, often sweeping down to the water's surface for a bit of garbage that had been thrown overboard.

ALASKAN-YUKON TROPHIES

The railroad bridge which spans the Copper River, at Mile Forty Nine, north of Cordova, Alaska.

In the evening the high peaks of the St. Elias Range, which parallels the coast for several hundred miles, loomed up in the distance. Mt. St. Elias, one of the loftiest mountains in America, (18,024 feet), was seen quite plainly. At seven-thirty that evening the few of us who were still able to be on deck, made out through the mist and cloudiness of the dreary evening, Cape St. Elias, and we were told that after passing that point we would find smoother water, which was joyful news to me. At the time of passing the cape, and for the fifth time since leaving home, I turned my watch back an hour, making a total difference of five hours in time.

Contrary to the information previously given that the water would become smoother after passing Cape St. Elias, it became rougher. The waves beat relentlessly against the side of the ship and at times splashed over the deck. For a time it was a relief, when crossing a trough in the water we had a few calm moments, but I soon ceased to welcome those moments because immediately following the waves invariably attacked us with increased violence.

Before retiring I discovered to my dismay that a thief sometime during the evening, had entered my stateroom and stolen my camera. I reported this to the ship's officers who promised me all the assistance possible. Arising at four-thirty the next morning I renewed my search, but without success. I had little chance of recovering the camera, as I had no clue on which to work and little time at my disposal.

We steamed into the harbor of Cordova at five-thirty that morning—which was July 30th, having been six days enroute from Seattle. Cordova is located on Prince William Sound and is said to be the busiest town in Alaska, being the coast terminus of the Copper River and Northwestern Railroad which extends two hundred miles into the interior to the Bonanza Copper Mine at Kennecott. We found that a train would leave for the interior the following morning, but as our outfitter was not expected at McCarthy until several days later, we preferred remaining over at Cordova. That night we visited a well patronized picture show and upon leaving the building at almost eleven o'clock we were surprised to find small children still playing on the streets as it was not yet dark. We found a number of large stores with stocks well adapted to the needs of that country and at prices very little higher than we had paid in the States. We regretted that we had not waited until our arrival there to obtain such supplies as we needed. While in Cordova I was the guest of Mr. and Mrs. V. G. Vance, neighbors and schoolmates of my boyhood days. Their hospitality and attention during our stay added very much to the comfort and pleasure of our entire party.

On the morning of August 3rd, Mr. Snyder and I departed for McCarthy, leaving Mrs. Snyder and the girls to return on the next south bound vessel for Juneau. Our railroad fare to McCarthy—a distance of one hundred ninety-one miles—was twenty-four dollars and sixty-five cents, or almost thirteen cents a mile.

Soon after leaving Cordova we made the acquaintance of the genial conductor who stopped the train long enough on the famous two million dollar steel bridge which crossed the Copper River at Mile Forty Nine, to enable us to get a hurried view of the glaciers and make two or three exposures. While in Cordova I had purchased a new camera to replace the one stolen from me. I had noticed that one of those in the photographer's stock had a defective shutter, which made me somewhat suspicious and after selecting another one which appeared to be in perfect order I purchased a film, made some exposures and had them developed to make certain that the machine had no defects. Upon attempting to take some pictures from the doors of the baggage car at Mile Forty Nine I discovered that the shutter of my new camera would not work. The photographer had evidently shifted the kodaks about and had delivered the defective one to me, after having the film developed. He was aware of the fact that I would not return that way, and no doubt had taken advantage of the opportunity to get

Childs Glacier, at Mile Forty Nine, west of the railroad bridge.

rid of the defective machine. It was provoking to say the least, but the conductor told me I might possibly obtain another camera in McCarthy.

Notwithstanding my misfortune, we used the few moments at our disposal to look upon those wonderful glaciers. The Childs on the west side of the bridge is one of the most active glaciers in the world. It faces the Copper River for about three miles, rises about three hundred feet above the water line and, if I remember correctly, extends back a distance of about seventy miles. At all times when the weather is warm, one hears sharp reports followed by low rumbling sounds resembling thunder, as the glaciers crack and mammoth slabs of ice, equal in height to a three or four story building, fall from the high walls into the river below. The Miles Glacier is located on the east side of the River and huge slabs of ice almost continually break off from the lofty heights of the glacier's perpendicular face, falling directly into the water and forming high waves which apparently are not diminished in size until they break against the shores of the opposite side of the river.

They float about until caught by the swift current and are carried down this great river to the ocean forty-nine miles below. The steel bridge referred to is famous because of its figuring so prominently in Rex Beach's book, *The Iron Trail*, and furthermore,

Miles Glacier, at Mile Forty Nine, east of the railroad bridge.

from the fact that thousands of tourists visit this bridge each year for the purpose of seeing these two mammoth glaciers.

The Copper is one of the large rivers of Alaska, although not a long river as compared with some of the others. It is not navigable for large boats as it is frequently divided into a number of channels. The river bar is said to be fifteen miles wide from bank to bank at one place on account of these numerous channels. The precipitation along the coast, as well as for some distance back in the interior, is very great, which results in heavy snowfalls during the long winter months. Great avalanches of snow and ice find their way into this river and are carried down and launched along the streams, which make it very difficult and expensive to keep the railroad open for traffic—especially after the ice begins to move out during the late spring.

Quite slowly we made our way, the speed of the train perhaps not exceeding twenty miles an hour at any time until Chitina, a town of two hundred and fifty inhabitants, was reached at five o'clock that evening. We had been nine hours traveling a hundred and thirty-nine miles, but the time had passed rapidly as every mile of the distance was filled with interest, and the scenery surpassed any we had seen thus far. The conductor announced the train would remain there over night and that we would proceed on our journey at seven o'clock the next morning. Because of the dangerous and uncertain character of the country traversed by this railroad, passenger trains are not regularly operated except during the daytime.

That evening Mr. Snyder and I walked down to a lake close by and watched the salmon which could be seen in large numbers in the clear water. We went around the lake to its outlet where we found hanging beside an Indian's cabin large quantities of salmon which were being dried for use as winter food for his dogs. We walked up the railroad track to a tunnel and to the top of the hill over the tunnel, from which we commanded an excellent view of the surrounding country. We could look down on the great Copper River; also the Chitina and Klotsina which empty into the former, apparently only a quarter of a mile apart, although we afterwards learned that the distance was really a mile and a half. The mountains and rivers of that country are on so large a scale that one can form little idea as to distances until he has been there for some time and has acquired this knowledge by actual experience.

Across the river was a comparatively small mountain and apparently just beyond it and around a curve in the railroad loomed up a snow-covered peak. We remarked that if we had sufficient time at our command we would walk around the track to its base, as we would have judged the distance to be four or five miles. Upon returning to the little hotel and commenting upon the beautiful scene we had beheld, we were told the snow-covered peak was Mt. Blackburn, one of the largest mountains of the country, and that it was sixty miles distant. We listened with interest to the story related to us of some young men from an American university who had come to that country for the purpose of ascending Mt. Blackburn. After securing an outfit and starting out, they had given up without even reaching its base.

This rugged mountain was conquered, however, by a woman—Miss Dora Keene of Philadelphia. Her first attempt was in 1911, but she failed on account of having an insufficient outfit. The next year, in 1912, she attempted it again, taking with her seven men as helpers and packers. Three of them turned back at the end of two weeks; two others a week later, while the sixth man retreated within a few hundred feet of the top. The only man who had the courage and endurance to stay with Miss Keene until the summit was reached was a German from Cordova, by the name of Handy. The elevation of this mountain is sixteen thousand one hundred and forty feet, or more than three miles.

We did not know when we entered the small frame hotel that evening that it would be the last roof we would sleep under or the last bed we would sleep in until late that fall.

After leaving Chitina the next morning, we were never out of sight of Mt. Blackburn during the entire forenoon; it always appeared to be quite near, yet the closest point to the railroad was about forty miles. Of still greater importance was Mt. Wrangle, an active volcanic mountain which was at all times visible during the morning's travel. It appeared to be about ten miles distant but the railroad conductor informed us it was sixty miles from the railroad, and even at that distance it presented an impressive view as we watched the black smoke belching from its snow covered summit.

During the forenoon we crossed a railroad trestle that spanned a gorge, which was two hundred and thirty-eight feet in depth. It is one of the points of special interest along the Copper River and Northwestern Railroad.

Chapter III

A HAPPY MEETING

"The lonely sunsets flare forlorn
 Down valleys dreadly desolate;
The lordly mountains soar in scorn
 As still as death, as stern as fate."

WE arrived at McCarthy about noon and no sooner had we alighted from our train than we observed two men approaching. One of them was an elderly man who proved to be Doctor Evans; the other — whom I immediately recognized — as I had seen his picture in some of the outdoor magazines, was Charles H. Baxter of White Horse, Yukon Territory, who had outfitted Dr. Evans on his bear hunt. This was a happy meeting, indeed, especially for Doctor Evans and Mr. Snyder, who had met for the first time after a correspondence of two years. In fact, the circumstances under which the three of us had become acquainted and finally met each other appeared to me to be somewhat romantic. It reminded me of the plan sometimes resorted to in advertising for a wife, then meeting and marrying without previous acquaintance or courtship. Now, that the three of us had met for the first time, we felt we were united in the bonds of good fellowship and with bright prospects for a very enjoyable trip ahead of us.

Not until our arrival did Doctor Evans know that the postscript, which he had written in his farewell letter to Mr. Snyder before leaving his home in Texas, had resulted in a correspondence between us and my decision to accompany them. He had not had an opportunity to receive mail since leaving White Horse more than two months earlier. Immediately he took note of the small emblem which each of us wore and promptly produced a card showing him to be a member of the same fraternity. We considered this to be quite a coincidence. He stated, "Well, boys, you will have no hot sands to cross on this trip but they will be more than made up for by the great fields of snow and ice which you will cross and you will have to 'hold on to the rope' on many occasions as you have never done before."

A HAPPY MEETING

Doctor Evans was much older than we had understood him to be. He told us he was past sixty-three, later admitting he had purposely evaded Mr. Snyder's question concerning his age, and sent him a picture that had been taken many years before. He stated he was aware of the fact that a younger man might hesitate to make such an expedition with a man so far advanced in years. However, we regarded him as a very unusual person, indeed, to undertake at his age a trip such as he had just completed, yet he was as anxious as either of us to get started on our general hunt—notwithstanding much of the distance would be over the same trail which he had so recently traveled.

Mr. Baxter informed us that they were camped a mile above the village and suggested that we join them instead of going to one of the small hotels—an invitation which we gladly accepted. That afternoon we were interested in hearing Doctor Evans relate some of his experiences. Seven grizzly bears had been killed by him,—two of them young cubs, which had been taken at the time of killing the mother. Following their departure from White Horse it had rained almost incessantly until after July 1st and they had been obliged to remain in their tents much of the time. We obtained much information from the Doctor and Baxter concerning the character of the country and the prospects of securing game. Doctor dwelt at some length upon the wonders of the great glaciers and moraines we would see and stated that while he had read much concerning Alaska's glaciers, he had had no conception whatever of their magnitude and grandeur until he had traveled over them. His description of what was in store for us made us all the more anxious to get started.

I think it advisable at this time to acquaint my readers with our plans, and to give a brief account of Doctor Evans' and Morley Bones' movements prior to our arrival. Parties going in for the purpose of hunting the territories tributary to the Donjeck and Generc Rivers, in the Yukon Territory, usually go to Skagway, Alaska, where they debark; then by rail across the White Pass to White Horse in the Yukon Territory, from which point they are outfitted. This necessitates an overland trip with pack horses for a distance of three hundred miles before desirable hunting country is reached. At the conclusion of their hunt the same overland trip is usually made in returning to White Horse. Parties intending to hunt in the country tributary to the headwaters of the White River in Alaska, usually go to Cordova, where they debark; then by rail to McCarthy—as Mr. Snyder and I had done—from which point they are outfitted. They make the trip into the White River country with pack horses, then back over the same trail.

As far as we could learn only one hunting party had departed from this custom. Mr. Thomas Corcoran of Cincinnati in the summer of 1918 had gone in by way of White Horse with a pack train, having been outfitted by Charles Baxter. Upon completing his hunt the horses were returned to their winter feeding grounds with the guides, while Mr. Corcoran was taken down the White River by Mr. Baxter, in a boat built from whipsawed lumber, arriving at the mouth of the river on the fifth day. They camped there until they could signal one of the wood burning steamers operated between Dawson City and White Horse on the Yukon River. On one of these boats they traveled up the river to White Horse, a distance of about four hundred miles. In this way they avoided the long overland trip returning with the horses.

Doctor Evans and Mr. Snyder had first communicated with Mr. Baxter with the view of employing him for the expedition. A contract had been prepared by Doctor Evans and forwarded to Baxter, but he had contracted with a San Francisco party before it reached him. Further correspondence had resulted in the Doctor's decision to take a spring bear hunt with Baxter before he started on the general hunt with the San Francisco party. Baxter agreed, however, to try to secure the services of Morley E. Bones, whom he recommended very highly. Upon submitting the original contract which Doctor Evans had sent to Baxter, Bones agreed to its terms, with slight modifications, and the contract was signed and delivered to Doctor Evans when they passed his place on their way to the Generc River.

Baxter had departed from White Horse with Doctor Evans on May 14th. They had traveled over the Government Trail to Kluane Lake, a distance of a hundred and fifty miles, where the Doctor had the opportunity of meeting and conferring with Bones. From there they had traveled around Kluane Lake and continued on back into the interior. They spent some time on the Donjeck River, after which they moved on to the Generc River, from which point they did most of their hunting for bear. Their outfit consisted of twenty-two saddle and pack horses, the latter loaded with provisions and equipment. In addition to taking supplies for use during their bear hunt, the horses

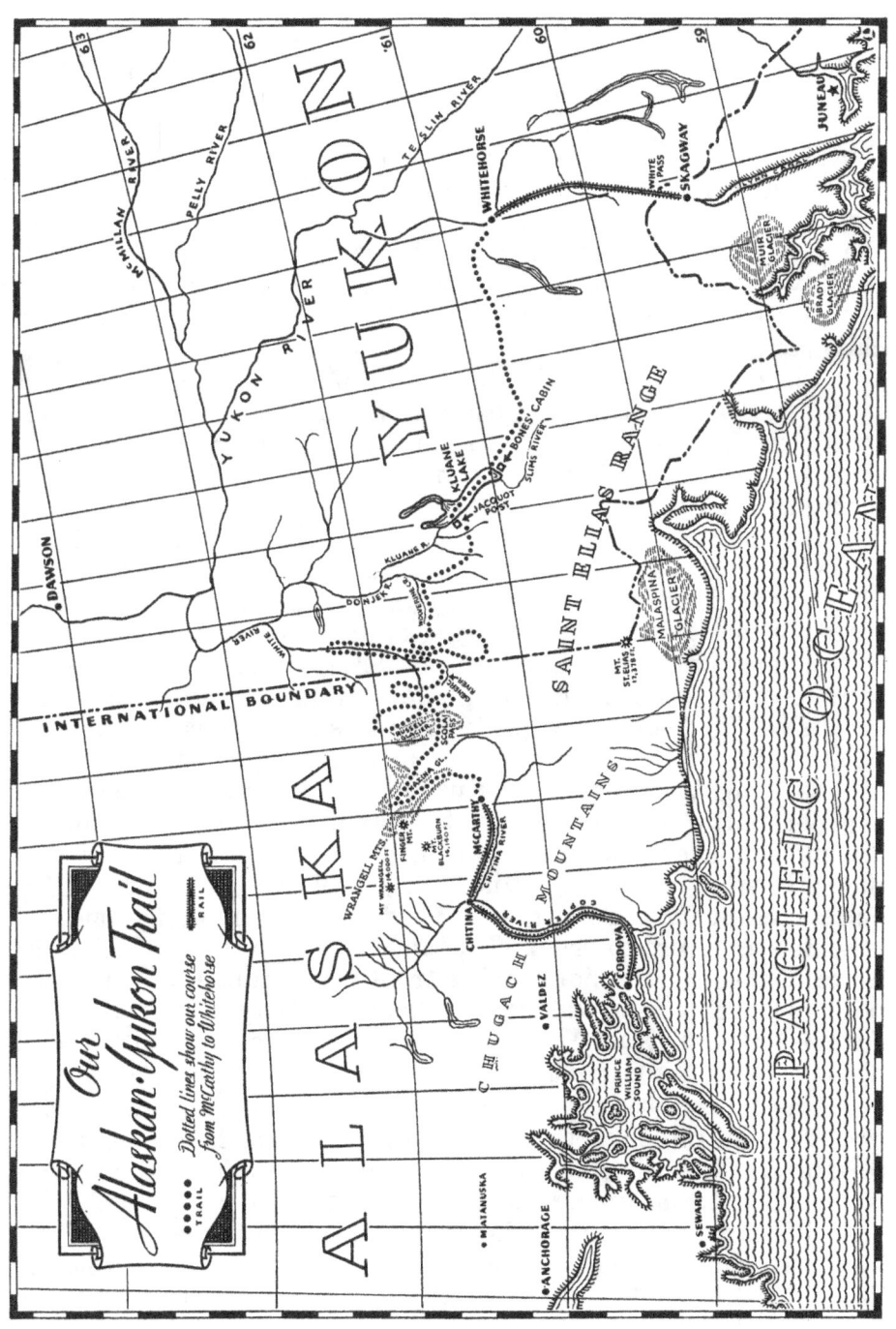

had been loaded to their capacity with extra supplies which were cached at the Generc River for use by Baxter when he would return there in the fall with the San Francisco party. During the time Baxter was engaged with Doctor Evans hunting bears along the Generc River, his men had improved their time by whipsawing lumber which they stacked for use in building a boat when they would return in the fall, a saw having been taken in on one of the pack horses for that purpose. Leaving the Generc the middle of July they had come to McCarthy, where Doctor had awaited Mr. Snyder's arrival, and Mr. Baxter the arrival of the San Francisco party.

Bones was to leave his home in sufficient time to meet us in McCarthy soon after August 1st. Before starting he had gone to White Horse for supplies. Upon his arrival there he was informed by the Canadian Bank of Commerce of my message advising that I would be a member of the party and that the initial payment on the contract price had been placed to his credit in the bank. The distance from his home at Kluane Lake to White Horse and return is exactly three hundred miles; and as we afterwards learned, more than two weeks had been required to make the round trip. Before leaving for McCarthy it had been necessary to procure an additional guide as well as additional horses because of my joining the party, and this had delayed him somewhat; but it was only a few days until accompanied by his men and with eighteen horses, they were on their way. His course in a general way was that taken by Baxter and Doctor Evans in the spring. They had only a dim trail to follow and much of that not discernible to the untrained eye. Their way was over difficult mountains and great glacier fields with many dangerous and treacherous rivers to cross. The time necessary to cover the distance of about five hundred miles from White Horse to McCarthy, with the pack train, was greater than the actual time required for me to travel from West Virginia to McCarthy, a distance of about five thousand miles.

The plans of both the San Francisco party and our own varied greatly from those of other hunting parties that had visited that territory. We wished to see as much of the country as our time would permit, and make the trip as diversified as possible. Instead of leaving our ship at Skagway, and going in over the White Pass, Mr. Snyder and I had continued north to Cordova, then by rail to McCarthy. Rather than outfitting in the latter place, going

A HAPPY MEETING

into the White River country and afterwards returning to McCarthy, we had arranged for our outfitter in the Yukon Territory and he was to meet us in McCarthy. We had purchased licenses to hunt both in Alaska and the Yukon Territory and the open season for some kinds of game being somewhat earlier in Alaska, we were to start hunting goats at the headwaters of the Nazina River in a very few days after starting out. From that point we were to cross the divide going to the headwaters of the White River where we would first hunt sheep. We would then hunt all kinds of game along the White River and its tributaries until we reached the International Boundary Line, when we would cross into the Yukon Territory and continue down the White River, stopping to hunt on the way, until the Generc River was reached.

Bones also planned to cache the supplies which he had brought from White Horse at some convenient point along the Generc River. It was his intention upon our arrival there in the fall to establish a base camp at the location selected for the cache. From there we would make numerous side trips and while doing so our cook and horse-wrangler would whipsaw lumber from the trees of the forest and from this lumber a boat would be built. At the conclusion of our hunt, Bones would take us down the White River to the Yukon River as Baxter had taken Mr. Corcoran the year before. We would camp at the mouth of the White River, with the view of signaling and securing passage on the first up-bound Yukon steamer for White Horse. Our contract with Bones included passage on the steamer, and terminated on his delivering us and our trophies at White Horse. In the meantime his guides would be sent with the horses to the place of his residence at Kluane Lake.

Baxter's contract with the San Francisco party was almost identical with the contract between Bones and ourselves. They were to start out on the same general course immediately upon their arrival at McCarthy. By building boats both parties expected to save several days' time. Furthermore, we expected that the trip down the White River—an estimated distance of two hundred miles—then up the Yukon, about four hundred miles by steamer, would be far more interesting than an overland trip with the horses from the Generc River to White Horse, a distance of about three hundred miles.

ALASKAN-YUKON TROPHIES

We spent the greater portion of the next day "seeing the sights" of McCarthy, a town with a population of perhaps three hundred. Most of the one-story buildings were of logs. We found several well stocked stores; in fact many of the retail stores in Alaska carry stocks equal to some of the wholesale establishments in our more populated centers. This is necessary as they are a long distance from their source of supply and transportation facilities are uncertain. McCarthy furnishes the supplies for the Bonanza Copper Mines located at Kennicott, four miles above, which are said to be the largest copper mines in the world. It is also the source of supply of the several gold operations located nearby, as well as for the individual prospectors who work the creek beds in that land of gold, in search of the precious dust; therefore, it is quite an important trading place and a typical frontier town.

We had observed in the coast towns of Alaska that pennies were not used or circulated, the five-cent piece being the lowest standard of value. At McCarthy we found that nickels and dimes were not in general use, the twenty-five cent piece or "two-bits," being the lowest standard of value. A cigar, an orange or a dish of inferior ice cream, made as it was from evaporated milk, sold for "two-bits." A bottle of ginger ale such as we are accustomed to buying for twenty-five cents, was sold at any one of the several soft drink emporiums for "eight bits," or one dollar. We were informed the town subsisted largely from the patronage of the employees of the copper mines above, who, especially after pay day, spent their money recklessly and with no other thought than to have a good time as long as it lasted. We were surprised to find that the village supported an ice plant, notwithstanding an immense glacier, containing no doubt millions of tons of ice, extended to the limits of the village, although the ice from it was probably unfit for domestic use. Labor is an object in that country and we were told that ice could be manufactured cheaper than clean natural ice of good quality could be collected. A small wagon drawn by four dogs was used for delivering the ice to the residents of the village. Alaskan "hootch" appeared to be very much in evidence and in all we considered it the "widest open" frontier town we had seen in many years.

Bones did not arrive that evening, causing us to become somewhat impatient as well as uneasy. However, the time passed pleasantly in Baxter's camp. There were Frank Sketch, the horse-

A HAPPY MEETING

wrangler—a quiet sturdy man of few words; "Al" Voss, the cook, a congenial fellow; and last but by no means least, Mike Knowles. Mike was a recent addition to Baxter's force, having been employed at McCarthy to accompany them when the San Francisco party would arrive. He was a stalwart, goodnatured Irishman who could make one laugh under any circumstances—in all a jolly party.

Upon going to the village the following afternoon, we were informed that a man had just arrived from the Nazina River, twelve miles distant. He reported that he had observed a pack train coming down the river bar on the opposite side and it was thought to be Bones and his party. We were told that if they succeeded in crossing the river without accident, they should reach McCarthy that evening. Mr. Snyder and I returned after supper for the purpose of having the village cobbler fill the soles of our new army shoes with hob nails for mountain climbing. The cobbler had just driven the last nail when someone came in with the information that the pack train could be seen coming down Sour Dough Hill. Soon the large husky and malamute sled dogs, which were enjoying their summer vacation and which were so numerous, began howling loudly. We hastened outside and it seemed as though all of the residents of the village, together with the barking dogs, were gathering to see the sight. A large pack train attracts much attention even in that country.

I wonder how many of my readers can recall the greatest thrill of their lives. The writer can do so quite readily. It was from the time that I first saw this outfit winding its way down the mountain trail until they arrived in the village. It was a novel sight, indeed, and one such as I had never witnessed before. One by one the horses had come into view. A man riding a white horse was in the lead. By that time Baxter had arrived on the scene, and he told us the rider was Morley Bones as he was able to distinguish him by the manner in which he leaned forward in his saddle. As they came closer we noted that the next horse was a small bald-faced roan with a large pack on his back; then a black horse with only a riding saddle; then another roan carrying a pack; then another man on horseback who we afterwards observed was an Indian; two more roans with only riding saddles; another loaded pack horse; a second Indian riding a black horse; several more pack horses of various colors; while the last pack horse carried a large cookstove on one side counterbalanced by a

OUR PARTY. Left to right: Indian Paddle, Eugene Jacquot, Indian Johnnie, Billie Slimpert, Dr. Evans, Mr. Snyder and Morley Bones. Jumbo, the large malamute dog, in the foreground.

load of about equal weight on the other side. A man who proved to be our cook brought up the rear, mounted on a fine looking bay horse. Ten or twelve of the horses wore bells, some of which were quite large and made a sound proportionate to their size. Slowly they wound their way down the zigzag trail, the cayuses carrying their heads close to the ground as is their custom; and as they crossed the little bridge and came into the village, the bells clanging and the dogs barking and yelping ferociously, they presented a scene I shall never forget. As Bones drew rein, Baxter addressed him.

"Hello, Morley."

"Hello, Charley," replied Bones.

"How long you been on the way?" asked Baxter.

"Oh, about twenty days."

"Have any trouble?"

"No, none worth speaking of. You have any trouble since leaving last spring?"

"No, except it rained nearly all the time," replied Baxter.

"Any horse feed close by?"

A HAPPY MEETING

Whereupon Baxter told him there was good ground a mile above on which to erect his tents and that the Indians could drive the horses to a gulch still farther up where an abundance of wild pea vine* could be found for horse feed.

The greeting between these hardy men of the North—the one having started from White Horse in the spring, while the other had traveled from Kluane Lake to White Horse, then back and from there to McCarthy, a total distance of more than six hundred miles—was no more than the greeting one would ordinarily receive from an acquaintance when alighting from a train after completing a trip from New York to Chicago in a luxurious pullman. Little incidents such as getting horses down in glacier crevasses and in quicksand, or having them washed down stream when crossing dangerous rivers and being obliged to unpack and dry their loads, as were incidentally referred to upon returning over the same trail, were not worth speaking of. They are men of few words.

By this time the tired horses had broken line and were beginning to bunch up as is their custom. Bones called to the men to line the horses up and "get going." I proposed to Mr. Snyder that we take advantage of the opportunity of a ride back to camp by mounting two of the saddle horses. He replied that he was not going to risk his neck by undertaking to ride a strange cayuse and that I had better walk back to camp with Baxter and him. However, I could not resist, and as the pack train passed by, I selected a sorrel near the rear of the line. Stopping him I started to tighten his girth, but upon seeing the other horses pass by and losing his place in the line, he became restless and would not stand still. All the others had passed, except one of the Indians, who brought up the rear. A bystander came forward with the admonition, "You want to be sure the girth is tight before you try to ride one of these d - - d cayuses." Together we held the horse and tightened the girth. I sensed the fact that probably I should have taken Mr. Snyder's advice. I mounted the horse and then the fun began. For a little while he reared and plunged in rodeo fashion, but I managed to stick to him, after which we continued on without difficulty. (I later learned this horse had been ridden only once.)

Upon reaching our camping place, we had an opportunity to inspect our outfit at close range. The horses were strong, ac-

---

*Not a vine as the name would indicate, but a small leguminous plant which grows on the gravel bars, and locally called "pea vine."

tive and in good condition. Pack saddles, riding saddles, bridles—in fact the entire outfit—had the appearance of having been well taken care of, but I thought the men were about the roughest looking lot I had ever seen. However, as we watched them, we saw by their movements, as they went about unloading the tired horses and putting up the tents, that they were familiar with their work. They had not had an opportunity to shave and were badly tanned from the effects of the sun's reflections on the great fields of glacier ice which they had crossed. After shaving the next morning and putting on clean clothing they presented a quite different appearance.

We were first introduced to Bones. He was a native of California and during 1888, when quite a young man, had gone to southern Alaska. He had trapped and prospected for several years and later was one of the first to penetrate the unknown wilderness of the interior of the Yukon Territory, where he has since lived, prospecting, trapping and hunting; first, as a guide and later as an outfitter. He had the reputation of being a hard worker and a very conservative man, whose word could always be relied upon. In appearance he did not differ a great deal from the mental picture I had formed of him. Most noticeable was his long bushy hair we had heard spoken of, and which had been referred to in a book we had read concerning that country. Later he told us he had thought of having his hair cut the fall before, but concluded to wait until spring as it was somewhat of a protection against the cold weather. When spring arrived, he had decided to let it go until fall, as it was some protection against mosquitoes. When we left him at White Horse in the fall he was still undecided whether he would have it cut at that time or wait until the following spring.

Bones was a well-built man about five feet seven inches tall and was past fifty years of age. He had a loud and unusual tone of voice which once heard would never be forgotten. We soon observed that he talked very little, but when he spoke—which was always in a slow deliberate manner and with much emphasis on some of his words—he always commanded attention. As I studied the face of this man whose word or promise was considered as good as the gold nuggets from the creek beds of that country, I tried to figure out what there was about him that was so unusual, aside from his long, bushy hair and his slow and emphatic manner of speaking. We were to know him more intimately in the weeks ahead.

A HAPPY MEETING

After being introduced to Bones and conversing with him for a few minutes we were agreeably surprised when he introduced the white man as Eugene Jacquot, telling us that he was to be our cook. We considered this the best news we had heard thus far. On our way to Alaska Mr. Snyder had remarked that we would be fortunate, indeed, should we find upon meeting Bones that he had employed as the cook for our party one of the two brothers by the name of Jacquot, living in the Yukon Territory. These two Frenchmen, Louie and 'Gene, had come to America as young men. They had been employed as cooks on the diners of the Santa Fe Railroad, in the Fred Harvey Restaurants, and in some of the leading hotels of the west. During the gold rush they had located in Dawson, Yukon Territory, and later, had taken up their residence in the wilds of the Kluane Lake country, where they were neighbors of Bones; that is, they resided far down the lake while Bones—their nearest neighbor—lived at the end, thirty-five miles away.

We were then introduced to Johnnie Frazier and Paddie Smith, the Indians, each of them being squarebuilt husky fellows who thought themselves to be about twenty-eight or thirty years of age. They lived in the summertime at Champagne Landing on the Dezadeash River, sixty miles from White Horse, while they spent the fall and winter months roaming about with their families, hunting and trapping. It was their first trip with an organized hunting party. Both of them could speak English fairly well—at least to the extent of being readily understood—while they were far above the average Indians of that country in intelligence. Paddie could both read and write.

Bones and Gene Jacquot spent the following day buying supplies and getting them to camp. Two additional horses were purchased, bringing our total number up to twenty.

Bones was not familiar with the locality where we would hunt goats, and he had only a limited knowledge of the country in general which we would pass through during our first few days of travel. Neither of the Indians had ever been in that section of country before, nor had they any experience in traveling over large glaciers, except as they had come through on their way to McCarthy. For this reason Bones thought it advisable to hire someone at McCarthy who knew the country and who was an experienced packer or horse-wrangler, as they are generally known. William Slimpert made application and was employed.

ALASKAN-YUKON TROPHIES

Mr. Snyder requested the tallest saddle horse.

A horse-wrangler on an expedition of this kind must be experienced in handling horses, know how to properly pack them and how to make the many different kinds of hitches that must be used. Slimpert had had much experience along this line, having gone to Alaska and the Yukon in '98. Since that time he had prospected, hunted, trapped, and freighted supplies back into the interior—with pack horses in the summer and dog teams in the winter. He had had charge of large numbers of horses for the contractor during the building of the Copper River and Northwestern Railroad. He knew Rex Beach personally, as well as many of the characters referred to in the "Iron Trail" and other of Rex Beach's books. He told us that notwithstanding these are books of fiction, the stories related therein, generally speaking, are based upon actual occurrences. He could talk on almost any subject pertaining to that country; and having a wonderful memory and always being willing to talk, we found him very interesting and a source of much information.

Mr. Snyder and I had forwarded to the proper authorities in the Yukon Territory a hundred dollars each in payment of our

A HAPPY MEETING

Yukon hunting licenses and had directed that they be sent to McCarthy. Upon applying for them at the post office they were delivered to us, properly made out. It may be of interest to note here the cost of a license and the limit of game that was allowed in each of the territories in which we were to hunt. In Alaska a license cost fifty dollars for residents of the United States or its possessions, and one hundred dollars for residents of foreign countries.

Bag limit: 2 Bull Moose (The moose must be killed north of the 62nd Degree of latitude); 3 Bull Caribou; 3 Mountain Sheep (rams only); 3 Billy Goats.

There is a limit to the number of bears that can be killed in certain portions of Alaska.

Dr. Evans and Old Bob.

ALASKAN-YUKON TROPHIES

Yukon Territory: Cost of License, one hundred dollars, except to English Subjects, which is fifty dollars.

Bag Limit: 3 Bull Moose; 6 Caribou; 3 Mountain Sheep (rams only); 3 Billy Goats.

There is no limit on bears.

However, in the Yukon Territory only one moose and three caribou could be exported. Bones stated that this was on account of a conflict between the game laws and the export regulations.*

Early the next morning all hands began packing up. There were enough supplies to start a small grocery store. As I recall there were over four hundred pounds of flour, about a hundred pounds of sugar, two hundred and forty pint cans of evaporated milk, and considerable quantities of corn meal, breakfast foods, jams, jellies, relishes, bacon and various other supplies sufficient to last until we should reach our cache on the Generc River some five weeks later. In addition there were a large dining tent and two sleeping tents, one for the hunters and one for the guides. There was a cook stove of about the size used in the average home; a heating stove to be used in our tent should it be required; cooking utensils of various kinds, white enameled table ware, a folding dining table, three very comfortable folding chairs for the three hunters—and folding stools for the others—also the personal belongings we had taken with us.

Mr. Snyder and I had left our clothing that had been used in traveling, in our trunks, which had been sent back to Skagway in Mrs. Snyder's care. My personal outfit appeared to be almost a sufficient load for one horse; in fact, realizing this, I had not taken a sufficient amount of ammunition. I called Bones' attention to my outfit which was contained in a strong heavy khaki-colored canvas bag made after the style of a United States mail bag, with staples and locks. He examined and stated it would hardly make a good top pack and that he had outfitted men taking twice as much with them, although many of the items included had been unnecessary. He requested that all of our cartridges be turned over to him to be packed in one special paniard box, or alforgha, as the combined weight of our ammunition was considerable.

Everything had to be classified so as to make a properly balanced load for each horse, which was in proportion to his

---

*I am pleased to hear that the laws in the Yukon Territory have been changed in this respect, and that the bag limit has been substantially reduced.

A HAPPY MEETING

strength and endurance. The loads ranged from two hundred to two hundred and fifty pounds each. Two or three of the strongest horses carried loads slightly in excess of two hundred and fifty pounds. They endeavored to place almost a hundred pounds on each side of the pack saddle, leaving such items as duffel bags, blankets, tents, cooking utensils or other light and bulky materials as a top pack. Once the load was properly divided with certain packs assigned to designated horses, so much time was not required thereafter in packing.

The passenger train from Cordova arrived on its tri-weekly trip at noon that day and with it the San Francisco party, who were brought to Baxter's tent. It consisted of Messrs. H. O. Harrison, Ben Crouch, Phil Lyons, all hunters, and Mr. J. H. Hornell, who had accompanied the party as a photographer and who had a moving picture camera with him; also Roy Lozier from Elk, Wyoming, who had acted as a guide for some of the party on previous hunting trips in the Rockies and who on account of his unusual ability had been brought with them in that capacity. He had the reputation of being expert in running dangerous rivers and it was planned that he should assist Baxter in running the White River at the conclusion of their hunt.

My readers will observe that I have devoted considerable space in outlining the plans of this party; and in referring to Baxter and his men, as well as to his outfit, since they figured quite conspicuously in our experiences before reaching the coast in the fall. In fact, it is altogether likely that had it not been for three of these men, some additional lives would have been demanded as toll from that Arctic Land because of our having stayed within her domains after the cold blasts of winter pierced her bosom. Baxter had everything in readiness and they began preparations with the view of starting as soon as possible.

During our stay in McCarthy we had met the genial and good natured Captain J. P. Hubric. "Cap" as he is familiarly known in that section, is also an outfitter for big game hunters and had contracted to take out that year two brothers from Boston by the name of Mitten. While waiting for Bones' arrival, we, together with Baxter, had been entertained by him and Mrs. Hubric at their cozy little home in McCarthy, where we were served one of the most elaborate meals that it has ever been my good fortune to enjoy. "Cap" Hubric possessed quite a reputation as an outdoor photographer. He had a good collection of pictures

The smallest saddle horse was assigned to the author.

A HAPPY MEETING

to show us and was kind enough to take up the defective camera sold to me in Cordova, supplying a perfect one of the same size and style in its place,—for no consideration other than sufficient postage for returning it to the Eastman Company in exchange for a perfect one. This was my third camera since leaving home.

On completing a farewell letter before our departure, I told Bones I had promised my wife that before leaving McCarthy, which was our last post office, I would write some instructions to be followed in an effort to locate me in case of serious illness in my family. I stated I would like some instructions from him as to what procedure should be taken if it were necessary for them to communicate with me, or with any of our party, and received in substance the following reply:—

"Now, Mr. Young, you had just as well tell them to forget it. There are few men who know enough about the country to undertake a trip back where we are going. Almost anyone who would attempt it would want a partner; horses would, therefore, be necessary not only for their use but to carry provisions to last them on the trip, and, as you know, the few people in Alaska and the Yukon, who have horses and outfits are employed long in advance by hunting parties. Even if there was someone who would attempt to make the trip, he would stand little chance of locating us. If he should succeed, it would likely require several weeks to find us and get any of you back to the coast and the chances would be that you would have to wait several days or a week upon your arrival there for a south-bound vessel. In the meantime, whoever was sick would likely be dead and buried or would be up and around again, so, as I have stated, you had just as well write and tell them to forget it."

This did not sound encouraging, but I could do nothing else than close my letter with the information that Bones had given me and with the advice that, no matter what might happen at home, they should not try to communicate with me; furthermore, they would not likely hear from me again until after we had reached White Horse, which should be about October 1st, when I would wire them.

It was about the middle of the afternoon on August 8th when Bones announced that all was in readiness, and gave the command to start. It was a welcome signal as we were anxious to be on our way. Now that the long awaited hour had arrived there was a thrill of excitement mingled with pleasure when we mounted our horses and fell into line on our way to the village below. Mr. Snyder had requested the tallest saddle horse in the lot on account of the advantage he would have in crossing deep waters and to him a tall black mare was assigned. Dr. Evans had requested a safe, sure-footed horse and one that would stand quiet when mounting or dismounting, and to him "Old Bob," a very peculiar looking horse, had been given. He was a pinkish roan with a bald face, white feet, and white mane and tail, and was said to be between twenty-five and thirty years of age. Of this horse more will be said later. A five-year-old roan, the smallest saddle horse in the lot, was assigned to me. He was one of the most active in the entire outfit but I realized I would be placed at a disadvantage in deep water.

As we passed through McCarthy, it seemed as though all its population, as well as its howling dogs, were out to see us off. We crossed the bridge taking the trail up Sour Dough Hill, over the same course that Bones had come down two days before. We traveled in single file. I afterwards observed that it was impossible to make those cayuses travel in any other manner, even when on a wide river bar or where the trail was sufficiently wide to permit it. At times some of us wished to engage in conversation and would endeavor to ride side by side, in an attempt to do so; but invariably one of the horses would force its way forward or drop to its accustomed place. The disposition of these horses to travel in single file was often of much advantage as any attempt to do otherwise would result in their getting into quicksand or deep water in crossing fords, into crevasses when crossing glaciers, or crowding each other over cliffs when on some of the high mountain trails.

The twelve mile ride over Sour Dough Hill that evening was an enjoyable one as the weather was ideal and not a cloud to be seen. A forest fire had swept over that section several years before, leaving only the thinly scattered dead spruce trees, while the underbrush had been replaced by wild flowers of many colors. The altitude was not so great here as to interfere with the rapid growth of vegetation during the warm sunshine of the long summer days. A tall wild plant known as fireweed—a very homely name for a plant having so pretty a flower—grew in abundance. At times no other plants or vegetation could be seen, aside from this great expanse of purple flowers which presented a very pleasing sight as the horses wound their way in single file along the

A HAPPY MEETING

Crossing an ice plain. Here, travel was comparatively easy, but the native pack horses proceeded with their habitual caution.

narrow trail, the tops of their canvas covered packs showing slightly above and in contrast to the bright colors of the flowers.

In descending the mountain on the opposite side from McCarthy a sudden halt was made; a horse was down—one of the two that had just been purchased and which had recently been shipped into that country from Oregon. They were not accustomed to the mountain trails or to carrying heavy packs on their backs. Two large tin pans, one to be used as a dish pan and the other as a bread pan, had been on top of the pack of the horse that had fallen. In the fall both pans were loosened and rolled down the mountain, but after the horse had been unpacked and had regained his footing, they were recovered.

Suddenly, we came into full view of the wide bar of the Nazina River and in the distance we could see the many sand colored channels like living things, running in swift serpentine fashion along the wide bar. Upon reaching the foot of the mountain, we stopped for the night, camping by the side of a creek, the water of which was so cold that we were obliged to drink it sparingly. One by one the horses were relieved of their heavy loads and driven up the creek bed to find feed. The ten-by-fourteen dining tent, as well as the nine-by-twelve mosquito tent to be used by us three hunters, was erected. The additional tent carried for use by Bones and his employees was not put up, for, as long as the weather was clear and the nights not extremely cold, they preferred to spread their blankets in the open wherever their fancy might choose.

While waiting for supper Mr. Snyder and I walked down to the bank of the river close by and watched for some time the peculiar colored water as it ran at flood tide. In most parts of the world, floods follow continued rains and recede with warm clear weather, but not so in that glacier country. Since the water supply is largely furnished by the melting of the glaciers and of the snow on the mountains, the streams are highest during the warm days of June, July and early August. Nearly all the rivers and creeks that are fed by glaciers are swift running streams and rise or fall quite rapidly. After a cool day these streams are almost clear, or perhaps a milky color and with only a normal amount of water flowing. When the sun comes out bright and warm, they increase in volume until the flow is many times as large in the late afternoon as it is in the early part of the day. They change to a sandy or reddish color, carrying much sand, silt, volcanic ash, or other deposits, depending upon the nature of the soil over which the water passes. These creeks and rivers overflow their banks, spreading over the bars and undermining and carrying with them trees in great numbers, and sometimes good-sized boulders. The trees are carried down the swift current, and as the water recedes they are deposited over the wide sand and gravel bars. As the summer sun loses its power toward evening, the creeks and small rivers soon run down, while the large rivers that are fed by them, continue to rise for some time afterwards. If they are not too far distant from their source of supply, they also are well run down toward morning, as the nights are always cool and usually cold. The rivers are at their lowest tide from morning until noon, thus more easily forded at that time. As they drain the great icefields, their waters are so cold that no person or ordinary animal can exist in them very long; therefore, it is impossible for a horse to swim very far in these currents. In making fords they are frequently carried down the stream, the current rolling them until they are washed ashore at some bend, or to a shallow riffle where they gain a footing. In such

A HAPPY MEETING

waters there is danger of the rider being drowned, should he be drawn underneath his horse by the force of the current.

Upon returning to the tent, we found supper ready; and after enjoying our meal and pipes, we crawled into our blankets and soon were sound asleep, although it was some time before dark.

Chapter IV

A DAY ON NAZINA RIVER

*"The nameless men who nameless rivers travel,
  And in strange valleys greet strange deaths alone;
The grim, intrepid ones who would unravel
  The mysteries that shroud the Polar Zone."*

AT SIX o'clock August 9th, we were awakened by Gene, the cook, shouting, "muck-a-muck." We did not understand the meaning of this, but it was only a few minutes until he put his head in our tent with the advice that breakfast was ready. We soon learned that muck-a-muck is the Indian name for food and from then on, it was used exclusively by our cook when announcing that a meal was ready. It was always a welcome announcement, especially when the prefix "hi-u" was used, as in the language of the Indians of that country this means large, or plenty, therefore, "hi-u-muck-a-muck" meant plenty of food.

The horses were located without much difficulty. The horse-wrangler always arose about four in the morning and started out to find them. It was his custom to make a cup of coffee and eat a few bites before starting, for as a rule there was not much certainty as to when or where the horses would be found. A corral was always made by tying cinch ropes together and stretching them around a number of trees, bushes or rocks, so as to form a horseshoe-shaped enclosure. As the horses approached the camp, everyone upon hearing the sound of the bells, turned out and rendered assistance in heading them off and driving them into this corral, where they were caught, haltered and saddled. A very complete blacksmith's outfit was carried along as it was necessary almost every morning to tighten or reset a shoe. We were told that one of the prerequisites of a cook on an expedition of this kind was the ability to shoe horses, in addition to his regular duties; at least this was one of Gene's morning tasks before the horses were packed.

Located only a short distance below was a prospector's cabin. Its lone occupant, who had paid us a visit the evening before, returned next morning and observing I had a camera requested that I take his picture, which was done. He stated that his family lived in Texas and that he had not seen them for many years but occasionally received a letter from his sons. They had grown to manhood since he had left home and he desired the kodak picture to send them. In conversation with Mr. Snyder and me he mentioned that fourteen men had lost their lives in attempting to cross the various channels of the Nazina River during the few years he had lived there, several of which had been at the fords we were about to cross.

Mr. Snyder and I walked down to the river and while it had fallen very much during the night, it still appeared quite dangerous. Without implying any discredit to Mr. Snyder, I have never been associated with anyone on outing trips who had such a horror of deep and dangerous waters — a fact which he freely admitted. He impressed me soon after making his acquaintance as being a very safe and conservative man in every respect (which is usually characteristic of bankers) and never believed in taking any unnecessary chances. I had observed since our arrival at the Nazina River that the worry upon his part on account of our being obliged to cross these waters, was detracting very much from this pleasure.

Doctor Evans and Mr. Snyder had purchased oiled "Slickers," consisting of a coat and overalls, the latter being tied tightly around their ankles which permitted their riding into water without getting wet. I had not supplied myself thus as I knew they would add to the weight and bulk of my pack and would be an additional bother when used, although it was a mistake upon my part not to have done so.

When all was in readiness for the start, Bones approached Mr. Snyder and me and in his loud tone of voice said, "The river is still running pretty high this morning, but unless the channels have changed their courses of two days ago, I think we can cross them. You must watch yourselves, as no man nor horse can swim very far nor last very long in these cold waters. Keep your horses 'into' the right course and don't let them get started down stream. Always stay 'into' your saddles, unless your horses start rolling in swift water; then slide off backward, grab their tails and hold on like hell." Then, without an opportunity upon our part for any questions or comments, he turned to the Indians saying, "Put 'em in, Johnnie; whip 'em up, Paddie; let's get started." Little consolation, indeed, for either of us, for after hearing the old prospector's statement concerning the lives that had been lost in that river, I was feeling a little shaky. I afterwards learned that Doctor Evans, who was already experienced in those glacier streams, felt very much relieved when that day's travel was over.

The horses are always reluctant about going into the cold water, especially their first ford in the morning. After a considerable amount of yelling, whipping and swearing—especially the latter, they were one by one forced off the steep bank and down into the water. Bones took the lead and it was exciting, indeed. Two or three of the younger horses failed to keep the proper course and were forced down the stream some distance. The Indians continued yelling at the horses in their native tongue and one of them ran his cayuse down the shore, jumping him off the high bank into the deep water, altogether unmindful of his own discomfort, and succeeded in heading off the drifting horses and getting them to the opposite bank.

I remained behind as I was desirous of obtaining a picture of the scene. I had my camera in readiness to make an exposure as the last horse stepped off the bank. I soon found, however, that I could not hold the camera in proper position and at the same time hold the cayuse which was rearing and plunging on account of being left behind. Finally, being obliged to give it up, I placed the camera in its case, tied it high on the horn of the Mexican saddle so as to be above the water, then mounted and rode in. I had gone only a short distance into the water when I observed that my Ross rifle was not in its scabbard attached to the right side of my saddle. I rode back and up the bank where I found it without difficulty. It had been thrown from the scabbard when I had tried to get a picture of the long line of horses in the deep water and the horse had reared and plunged. By that time the others had reached the opposite side, and having been engaged as I was, I had not noted the exact course taken, and realized that it had been a mistake to remain behind in an effort to get pictures. The others continued on without having noticed I was not yet across. Had my horse lost his footing and been carried down stream, I would not likely have been observed by them. However, I could see the point where they had landed on the opposite shore, as the sand was wet from the dripping horses. Perching myself high in the saddle, I rode in and made it over without difficulty.

We traveled up the gravel bar, Bones in front watching for a suitable place to cross the next channel. Mr. Snyder and I

A DAY ON NAZINA RIVER

wondered why he did not attempt to ford at any point. He retraced his course for almost a half mile, then beckoned us to return to him. We were not yet familiar with the quicksand we had to contend with. Notwithstanding we had been accustomed to the out-of-doors all our lives, we had many things to learn in that strange country where everything is so different. We would have ridden into that apparently safe channel at almost any place and thus into quicksand.

A knowledge of those glacial waters is acquired only with years of experience. Anyone who is familiar with them is referred to as a "good reader of water," and a man who does not possess this knowledge is referred to as one who "cannot read waters." The bottoms of those glacier rivers were not visible during the warm summer months, but Bones could tell almost instantly where there was gravel or where there were sand bottoms; never attempting the latter, and often riding ahead of the outfit or retracing his course for some distance, then signaling to us when he had found a possible ford. We later found that Gene Jacquot and Billy Slimpert were also experts in this respect. I tried very hard during the entire trip to acquire a knowledge along this line, watching the waters and their banks very closely,—especially the places selected as crossings, in an effort to ascertain how they arrived at their conclusions. While I did gather a few points, as did my associates, yet we confessed in the end we had not gained much of a reputation as "readers" of dangerous waters.

Again Bones rode in first and at a point which to us seemed least desirable as a crossing. I decided to ride in directly behind him. He was headed downstream but when about half way across he changed his course upstream and almost at right angles. Inexperienced as I was, I did not ride to the exact point where he had turned up stream so abruptly but instead, cut across a distance of a few yards in what appeared smoother water and instantly the front feet of my horse went down, the cold water running into my saddle and filling my high laced boots. I quickly turned my horse (or perhaps the horse, being more experienced than I, turned largely of his own accord) into the course Bones had taken. I then realized I had much to learn.

All safely over, we continued crossing channel after channel and gradually worked our way up the river bars. One of the channels, especially, was quite wide and the water very swift, although not deep. I was bothered with head swimming, so much so that it

Bones rode ahead to test a channel of the Nazina River for the presence of quicksand.

was difficult to keep my course in the water, and especially in the wide channels. Once, after making a crossing, I noticed a commotion in the rear and saw that the brown horse which had fallen on Sour Dough Hill the day before, had changed his course somewhat and upon stepping into soft sand had gone down. Two of the men were soon at his side and jumping off into the water removed his pack and carried it to the shore close by, after which the horse was able to get up and be repacked.

Again during the forenoon this horse went down in the same manner, and as before, the men were quickly at his side. Billy held his head out of the water to keep him from drowning while Gene took the pack off his back. In doing so, the two dish pans became loosened, and being caught by the swift current, were quickly carried away. One of the men ran down the shore in an effort to overtake and rescue them, but they were soon out in the middle of the channel and lost to our sight. This was bad luck, indeed. Gene stated it would be impossible to get along without at least one pan, as he had nothing else with him sufficiently large to mix bread in. There seemed to be nothing to do but to return to McCarthy after others. His only hope was in being able to secure one back at the prospector's cabin. If unsuccessful, he expected to return to McCarthy yet that day, where he would spend the night expecting to overtake us at the Nazina Glacier two days later. Fortunately, he was able to find and purchase the one large pan which the prospector possessed, and to overtake us about the middle of the afternoon.

A DAY ON NAZINA RIVER

Six or seven channels were finally crossed. It required almost four hours to travel a distance of only two and a half miles, but we made good time for several hours thereafter, traveling up the gravel bar of the river which varied from one to two miles in width, from bank to bank. At one point we left the river bar and traveled two or three miles through the spruce timber, during which time we crossed a beautiful stream of clear water. As we rode along the high banks, I noticed a number of large salmon in a deep pool. They presented a beautiful sight, red in color and in the sunlight having the appearance of bright gold. Taking my Ross rifle, Gene and I climbed down the bank and upon firing several shots they arose to the surface stunned as if dead. Gene plunged into the cold water up to his waist securing two king salmon, weighing perhaps eight or ten pounds each; and discarded several "dog salmon" which are undesirable as food. I noticed it was not long until the stunned fish flopped over and returned to deep waters.

These wonderful fish are found in the clear water streams throughout that country, many of them traveling hundreds and even thousands of miles from the sea to their spawning beds. Some of the creeks seem fairly alive with them. Those that survive deposit their spawn and in this manner perpetuate their race. We saw many of these fine fish which were covered with white spots, caused by the loss of scales during their long trip ascending the rough waters of the streams. After spawning they soon die. The young fish return to the sea, and these later on travel up the long rivers and to the source of their tributaries in this continuous process of reproduction. The Yukon River is more than two thousand miles long, yet these fish, in countless thousands, find their way from its mouth at the Bering Sea, not only to the headwaters of this river, but to the sources of its many long tributaries.

We had not gone far after overtaking the others until we saw our first flock of ptarmigan. These birds are about the size of the common ruffed grouse and in summer resemble them somewhat in appearance. At times they are very abundant throughout that country, but they appear to die off periodically and for a time are quite scarce. They feed in the summer on wild berries and during the winter on willow and alder buds. As winter approaches, their plumage gradually turns to white, and they are warmly feathered down to the ends of their toes. At that time of year they are quite wild, but during the summer they fly only a short distance when molested. Mr. Snyder killed several of those observed at this time. As he fired each shot, they flew to other trees or branches only a few feet away, or they calmly sat looking about them in wonder as they were fired upon, sometimes repeatedly, for hitting the head of a bird with a high powered rifle is not ordinarily possible at every shot.

The day was perfect, and the atmosphere clear which made distances deceiving. During the forenoon we had taken note of a dark spot on the face of a large rock far up the side of one of the cliffs that overhung the river ahead of us. I would have judged it to be two or three miles distant; but by noon it appeared almost as far away as in the morning. Late in the evening as we passed that point we found the dark spot, which was due to some unusual discoloration in the rock, to be as wide as the Statue of Liberty and perhaps half its height.

At four o'clock in the afternoon we reached the mouth of the Chitistone River and found it much swollen. After crossing the many channels of the Nazina River during the forenoon, we had traveled up the right side of the river bar. As the Chitistone empties into the Nazina on the same side we were traveling, it was necessary to cross the fourteen fan shaped channels which spread out over the wide bar before they emptied into the Nazina. Great quantities of gravel and silt have been carried down the Chitistone and deposited on the bar of the Nazina until the River has been crowded over against the high limestone cliffs of its west valley wall. Five or six of these channels were quite deep, but we experienced no difficulty in crossing.

Bones had brought with him from his home a huge malamute dog which he called Jumbo. It was claimed that he weighed a hundred pounds. It had been interesting to watch him crossing the waters during the day. If the ford was an unimportant one, he crossed along with the horses, but he appeared to know the dangerous waters. When they were swift, or very wide he would invariably run along the bank to a point far above, howling mournfully all the time. Plunging into the water he was always carried far down the stream, eventually landing a long distance below, after which he would run about playfully until he had recovered from the effect of his chilly bath. We all became very much attached to the dog and enjoyed his company.

At six-thirty we approached a place where the Nazina River in one great channel ran so close to the high walls on our right

A DAY ON NAZINA RIVER

that there was not sufficient space for passage. Immediately below, the river divided into a number of channels and these in turn into smaller channels. Only where a large river, such as this, spreads itself out into numerous channels, dividing its volume of water into many smaller streams, is it possible to effect a cross-

After the river bar, several miles of spruce timber.

ing. The glacier-fed rivers of that country are constantly changing their courses. Knowledge gained in making crossings one day may be of little value when the same crossings are attempted a few days later. The swift waters, especially at flood tide, are heavily loaded with gravel and silt brought down from above, and deposited on the river bars. The water cuts away the banks, carrying the sand and gravel down until a bend or an obstruction is met, where they are deposited. This continues until the current is retarded and its course changed. Then it starts overflowing its bank at some point, the volume of water gradually becoming larger, until within a few hours an entirely new channel is formed. This natural phenomenon is in constant progress during the warm days of Alaska's short summer.

Slimpert had spoken of this dangerous ford and trouble had been anticipated, as we knew the water would be running at flood tide by the time we reached it. There were six main channels, any one of which offered all the excitement one might care for in attempting a crossing, as well as eleven smaller channels. We had had nothing to eat since our six o'clock breakfast and being tired and somewhat weak from hunger, I feared I would be seriously affected with head swimming in fording the channels that lay before us. Those of my readers who have experienced this dizziness or "head swimming" in crossing swift waters can understand how unpleasant and at times how serious it is. It is a sensation of being carried on the surface of the water at the same rate of speed that the water is running, but in the opposite direction. The faster the water is running, the more rapidly one appears to be moving. It is best illustrated by the common experience of being on a railway train which is at a standstill while another is passing, and being deceived into thinking that we, ourselves, are in motion. Men of wide experience told us that often when attempting dangerous river crossings, they have been compelled to retrace their course and make a second start before trusting themselves to pick a crossing. Many of the river disasters of that country have been caused by men "losing their heads" in the water.

After making our first two or three fords in the morning, I had resolved I would not again tarry behind or in the rear, but would go into the water at once. When one has a difficult task to perform, there is a certain amount of satisfaction in going about it and accomplishing it promptly. Just so in crossing these dangerous waters, there was a certain amount of satisfaction in reaching the opposite shore safely, where one could turn and watch the remainder of the procession as the horses floundered through the deep waters. Furthermore, experience has taught me that when confronted with danger which cannot be avoided, it should be met without hesitancy or without thought of fear, which is almost certain to develop if one hesitates or is inclined to give way to his feelings.

While the men were consulting among themselves concerning a crossing, we took advantage of the time to change the leather scabbards containing our rifles. Our extra guns had been taken apart and rolled up with our bedding, but from the start each of us carried a gun in a leather scabbard attached to the left, or "near" side of the saddle. Before making our first crossings in the morning our guns had been changed to the right or down stream side of our saddles so that the scabbards would not fill with the sandy water as it rolled against the up stream side of the horses. As the water would strike our horses on the opposite

A DAY ON NAZINA RIVER

side at these crossings we took the same precautions by changing to the left side and buckling them high on the saddles.

Billy rode in first leading the brown horse, as he was afraid to trust him in the treacherous waters. With feet drawn from the stirrups and perched high on the saddle, I followed directly behind. I fixed my eyes on the horse ahead in an effort to keep in the exact course, but we had not gone far when it was apparent our horses had been swept from their feet and we were being carried away. From boyhood days I had owned horses and was accustomed to horseback riding but on this occasion it was with great difficulty that I kept my balance and remained on the cayuse. I grabbed the horn of the saddle and quickly lowered my feet into the water and into the stirrups, hugging them tight against the horse in an effort to hold on. The admonition Bones had given me that morning came into mind quite vividly. "Stay 'into' your saddles," he had said, "unless your horses lose their footing and start 'rolling' then slide off backwards" etc. My horse had certainly lost his footing, yet he was not rolling and as long as Slimpert remained in his saddle I knew that I should do likewise. I looked upward only to find that the mountains appeared to be passing swiftly by. Our horses seemed to be making some headway, but slowly compared to the speed at which it appeared that we were being swept into still more dangerous waters. I closed my eyes for a moment but upon opening them the effects were the same. Soon I saw Slimpert had reached the shore. I urged my horse on, and before I realized it he made a plunge out of the water and up the bank. I looked about and was so dazed that for a few moments everything in sight appeared to be running away. I again closed my eyes for a minute. Upon opening them I looked at the water and was surprised to find we had come almost directly across and that the other seventeen horses were following in our course. Never before had I been so seriously attacked in this way, and some of the others were more or less affected in the same manner. I knew I must overcome this and while the next crossing was being decided upon I gave the matter some thought. While I knew it was brought on to some extent by an empty stomach and fatigue, yet I thought it was due partly to having allowed myself to give way to the sensation, instead of exercising sufficient will power to prevent it; and I resolved I would not allow it to occur again.

ALASKAN-YUKON TROPHIES

At the next ford I fixed my gaze upon an object in the distance, glancing down at the man in front of me only as often as was necessary to keep in the proper course, and I made it over with only slight sensations of dizziness. In crossing the next channel I firmly impressed upon my mind the fact that the water was running to my left, while in the sensation of being carried away it appeared that I was being swept to the right, or upstream. With this thought fixed firmly in mind I began looking directly at the water, trusting myself to do so for a few moments only. By practicing this mental exercise thereafter, even though it was often in places of danger, I gradually overcame this sensation until I afterwards experienced little difficulty in this respect.

Five of the main channels had been crossed without serious difficulty; the sixth was reached and appeared to be more difficult than any we had encountered. Another "council of war" was held, a crossing decided upon, and Slimpert rode in first. He had not gone far when the front feet of his horse struck quicksand and went down so quickly that Slimpert was immersed in water to his hips. Having a tight rein the horse was quickly turned, enabling him to get a footing on solid bottom. In the meantime, the brown horse which he was leading, stepped forward into the sand and Slimpert lost hold on his halter rope as he attempted to turn him. Quickly the horse was caught by the current and washed into deep swift water. Over and over he was rolled, sometimes the horse being on top and sometimes the pack.

It was indeed an exciting scene. Observing a bend in the river two or three hundred yards below, it occurred to me that the current would wash the horse to the shore at that point. I ran my horse down the bar and seeing the horse in the water was being swept toward the shore, I quickly dismounted and ran to the water's edge just ahead of him. Fearing the cut sand and gravel bank would not sustain my weight should I approach too close to the edge, I threw myself on the ground, and reaching out grabbed the horse's halter. However, not securing a good hold, the force of the water wrenched him away and he was swept onward. By this time Indian Paddie had overtaken me and succeeded in getting a firm hold upon him. As the horse had been carried down the current I resolved in my mind that if we were able to rescue him, I would personally see to it that the dishpan was placed on the back of a more trustworthy animal. As Paddie

A DAY ON NAZINA RIVER

held on to his halter the water washed him within reach, whereupon I quickly cut the strings and rescued the dishpan.

By that time the others had reached the scene and assisted in holding the horse's head above the water, the surface of which was perhaps eighteen inches lower than the bank on which we stood. Bones climbed out on the horse and removed the load which included Doctor's duffle bag containing his personal belongings. A lariat rope was removed from one of the saddles and tied to the strong leather halter. Repeated efforts were made to pull him out of the water but without success. At Bones' request Doctor Evans brought his saddle horse, "Old Bob." He had been trained to pull by attaching a rope to the horn of his saddle and it was remarkable the load he could haul in this manner as was witnessed on several occasions thereafter. The end of the lariat rope was attached to his saddle and his girth tightened. Bones then mounted him and the horse pulled as though he had been in harness. All of the men assisted by pulling on an extra rope that was attached. It looked as though we would certainly disjoint the horse's neck. Several attempts were made but we could not command sufficient force to draw him up the bank.

Presently we discovered the horse was badly cut about the head and neck while it appeared that one of his eyes had been put out. It looked like a hopeless case. The horse could not live much longer in that icy water and even then appeared to be almost dead. It was cruel to torture him further by attempting to pull him up the bank. Another plan was suggested and tried. Farther down the stream we could see that the cut bank gradually sloped off into a sandy, almost level beach. The horse was pushed out into the current, while the men held tight to the ropes in an effort to keep his nostrils above water. Upon reaching the sandy beach the Doctor's saddle horse was again brought into use and he was rescued from the water without much difficulty. It was some time before we could get him to his feet, after which the Indians forced him to walk about for a half hour in an effort to get his blood in circulation, never allowing him at any time to lie down.

The horse being rescued, the next question was to get across this and remaining channels. We were tired and hungry and some of us were wet to our waists. The long eventful day was drawing to an end and as the sun was low, we shivered with cold as we waited for the Indians to revive the horse and the guides to decide upon a crossing. It appeared impossible to proceed but we could not remain on that barren little island. The men decided that we should try it again at a point a little farther up the stream. Gene Jacquot suggested a course and was willing to take the lead.

The pack horses were "tailed" together in groups of two or three. This is a plan that is adopted when short turns or corners must be made in the water. The front horse of the group is led; the horse behind is tied to this horse's tail by his halter rope and every horse that is added to the group is tied in this manner to the tail of the horse in front of him. This insures their keeping in the exact course of the leader as a few feet variation or an attempt to cut across when making a turn often results in experiences such as we had just encountered. This channel was much wider than any we had yet crossed although not as swift as some of them, which accounted for its depth and so much sand in the bottom.

Leading two "tailed" horses, I followed directly behind Gene. Riding into the water he headed downstream for a short distance then out into the flood. He then proceeded diagonally up stream for perhaps twenty-five yards, after which he crossed to the opposite bank in a zigzag course. It required close observation upon my part to turn those corners in the deep water at the exact places that Gene had turned and at the same time bring my two horses to the same points before they were allowed to turn. At one time the rear horse of the two I was leading attempted to cut across and stepped into water over his back, but being one of the old trusties, he quickly recovered himself.

After getting over, I watched with interest as the others followed in the same course—Bones, Slimpert and the Indians each leading groups of two or three horses. We marveled at the skill displayed by the men in selecting their course in the sandy waters and especially Gene's skill in leading the way. All over safely, we felt very thankful we had been able to make these dangerous crossings successfully, and especially this latter one. We were told we would have no more large rivers to cross until fall, by which time, the warm days would be ended and there would be no flood tides. This was quite a relief as it seemed our greatest dangers were over, but others of a different nature awaited us.

A matter of much regret upon my part was the fact that I did not succeed in getting any desirable pictures of our pack train in deep waters. Failing in my first attempt in the early morning, I had hoped for a more favorable opportunity later in the day.

A DAY ON NAZINA RIVER

This did not come as all was confusion and excitement at all crossings where the water was sufficiently deep to have made interesting photographs. It was impossible to hold my horse and at the same time operate the camera when the others had gone ahead, and there were no trees or other objects along the wide bar to which a horse could be tied. Neither did I ask Mr. Snyder nor Doctor Evans to assist me as it was dangerous for any of us to remain behind and lose sight of the course taken by the others in the water. Every man had his hands full looking after himself and it appeared to be an inopportune time to bother with pictures. Several times after making the crossings I quickly dismounted and attempted to make exposures of the horses that were following in the deep waters but it happened that the light was not in my favor and I was unsuccessful. Only those who have had experiences in crossing these muddy, cold glacial streams can have any conception as to what they are like.

The few remaining channels were of little importance and at nine o'clock we reached the camping place Slimpert had had in mind, where wood and horse feed were plentiful. The Indians secured some balsam of fir from trees standing close by and applied to the fresh wounds of the unfortunate horse. While our supper of salmon and ptarmigan was being prepared and the Doctor's personal belongings being dried by the fire, I asked Bones if the brown horse purchased at McCarthy had a name. He replied that so far as he knew, he did not. I requested the privilege of naming him and it being granted he was from that time on known as "Dishpan." But in naming him I specified that the dishpan or anything else of value was not to be placed on his back thereafter, and it was agreed. "Dishpan" carried only a light load thereafter, and not being sufficiently hardy to withstand the Alaskan winter, died soon after the termination of our trip. Upon retiring at midnight Mr. Snyder and I agreed it had been the most exciting day of our lives—but there were many more to follow.

Chapter V

A DAY ON A GLACIER

*"There where the mighty mountains bare their fangs
  unto the moon,
There where the sullen sun-dogs glare in the snow-
  bright, bitter noon,
And the glacier-glutted streams sweep down at the
  clarion call of June."*

THE day's journey after our exciting experiences on the Nazina River was a short and very enjoyable one. The weather was perfect and as we had no large waters to cross we were able to ride along leisurely admiring the wonderful scenery that surrounded us. At times the river bed narrowed until little room was left for us to pass between the edge of the water and the canyon walls which towered hundreds of feet above,—sometimes not only perpendicular but often leaning over our heads. Numerous streams of clear water gushed from the mountain sides, at times in cascades; at other times falling over high precipices. Again they emerged from holes or cracks far up the sides of the canyon walls—perhaps outlets of natural reservoirs or small lakes located in the benches of the mountains far above—for many of them spouted out with much force. Some met with no obstructions whatever as they descended to the river bed below. Many of the streams were a milky white, coming as they did from the numerous glaciers that filled the gorges or overhung the snow clad mountains.

During the forenoon one of the Indians remarked that another pack outfit was following us perhaps six or eight miles in the rear. He had been able to detect them with his naked eye. We strained our eyes but not until we had brought our binoculars into use could we make them out. We concluded it was Baxter and his party.

About noon we came in sight of the great Nazina Glacier which we were approaching. We continued to a point where the Nazina River emerged from its source under this glacier, where we left the river bed and traveled along the side of the big ice

A DAY ON A GLACIER

field and close to the foot of the mountain to our left. We had been told there is more or less danger in traveling these river bars. Great quantities of water are often backed up by the ice gorges that form. When sufficient force has accumulated these ice dams give way, the water then rushing down with terrific force, and making a clean sweep of everything in its pathway. A pack outfit caught between the walls of the canyons would have little opportunity to escape.

We reached our camping place at two o'clock in the afternoon. In traveling through country of this kind horse feed is the first consideration, as it cannot be taken along. In fact, had our horses been loaded with grain and nothing else, the amount which they could have carried would have been sufficient for their subsistence for a few days only, if other food had not been available. Bones stated only three or four of the older ones in their outfit had ever tasted grain or cut hay. They lived largely on the wild pea vine which grows along the river and creek beds of that country and preferred it to any other kind of food. Little grass was seen in the river bottoms, but it was sometimes found at or above timber line. When the wild pea vine could not be found, the horses browsed on the small willows that usually grew along the edges of the creek beds, although they constituted very poor food for a hard working animal.

Most of the horses used by the outfitters of Alaska and the Yukon Territory were originally wild cayuses, captured in Oregon or other western states, and shipped North. We were told that many of them are unable to endure the extreme cold; but if they survive the first winter, they usually become acclimated and are able to shift for themselves. I was very much interested in these cayuses from the beginning, notwithstanding some of them were often very provoking—leaving their places in the line and having to be rounded up, turning their packs and otherwise making trouble,—but one becomes familiar with the peculiarities of each individual animal. I learned the names of all of those in Bones' outfit, as I did those of Baxter's twenty-two cayuses, before we reached the first outpost of civilization that fall.

The distance traveled in a day and our camping places at night depended altogether on horse feed. The availability of firewood was also a factor in the selection of camping sites, although unimportant as compared with horse feed. Even in sections where there was no timber the Indians could usually find sufficient

A view of Nazina Glacier and moraines, from high on a mountainside.

small, dry willows with which we could do a limited amount of cooking. When we were in regions where we could see some distance ahead, the men could often tell in advance by the appearance of the country, where wild pea vine would likely be found. Sometimes upon reaching a place where horse feed was plentiful our day's journey was cut short, the men knowing it would be impossible to reach another camping place that day. More often was it necessary to travel until late at night to find feed for the horses. When large glaciers were approached we were obliged to start early in the morning so as to get over them in a day, as it would be a serious matter to spend a night on a glacier with a pack train. In this instance we could not proceed farther, but spent the remainder of that beautiful Sunday afternoon camped by the side of the great ice field that we would encounter the following day.

After supper I climbed to the top of a high ridge which lay between our camping place and the glacier. It was the shore line moraine of the ice field and extended along the edge of the glacier as far as the eye could see in both directions. I stood for some time in amazement. Was it a reality or was I dreaming? From mountain to mountain, a distance of six or eight miles, there was nothing to be seen but ice. As far up the valley as I could see there was nothing but ice; mountains of ice, hills of ice, and valleys of ice.

At no time in my endeavor to give a true and graphic account of our trip do I find myself so helpless as in attempting to write a few lines concerning these wonderful glaciers and their moraines. The subject of glaciers had always been a very dry one to me. I had read of them and had heard them described but had always welcomed an opportunity to change the subject of conversation. Therefore, while I do not expect to be able to interest my readers to any extent, on this subject of glaciers, I cannot refrain from making a few passing comments.

I had seen glaciers along the beaten trails of the tourists but they were as toys compared to the Alaskan glaciers; and since viewing them there is nothing else that I have ever seen or read of that is so wonderful and to me so interesting. I cannot conceive why I should have shown so little interest before. The glaciers of Switzerland are known throughout the world, yet the entire glacial area of that country is not equal to some of the single larger glaciers of Alaska. For perhaps a thousand miles they extend along the slopes of the Pacific Coast Range, some of the larger ones of the central portion having areas of many hundreds of square miles. That portion of Alaska and the Yukon, and reaching down into British Columbia, is one great field of ice and snow, much of which has never been penetrated by man. Thousands of small glaciers, which are really arms of this great system, extend from one to fifteen miles or more in length, filling the crevasses and mountain valleys. A large number of them reach to the ocean and may be seen by those who travel along the coast. The discharge from many of them on their west and southwest slopes forms creeks and great rivers that flow into the ocean. On the north the Tanana, the White, and other large rivers, the waters of which flow to the Yukon and then into Bering Sea, have their source in these glaciers.

Greatest of these Alaskan glaciers is the Malaspina, a vast elevated plateau of ice, fifteen hundred square miles in area. It is fed by Alpine glaciers some of which in their course flow over cascades, falling hundreds of feet in their descent from higher areas. The Valdez, Seward, Russell, Nazina, and the celebrated Muir are a few of the large glaciers of that country.

One may visit these great ice fields and gaze upon them in awe but cannot understand nor appreciate them to their fullest extent until he has traveled over them, or several of them, as we had the opportunity of doing on different occasions,—at times for whole days. The law of gravitation applies to glaciers as well as to all other objects; therefore, most glaciers travel downward from a few feet to several hundred feet annually. The Miles and the Childs, which are said to be the most active glaciers in the world, travel at the rate of about a quarter of a mile each year, but ordinarily these big ice fields do not move forward more than a few feet or yards annually.

The moraines of these glaciers were almost as interesting to me as the glaciers themselves. These are the accumulation of earth, rock, and gravel upon the surface and along the edges of a glacier or ice field. I observed that all glaciers located in valleys carried with them large moraines at their edges or shorelines. In their downward course these ice fields undermine, or cut away the bases of the mountains and carry with them on the edges of their surface great quantities of earth and gravel. In addition a considerable amount of earth and gravel accumulates on the edges of these ice fields as a result of spring thaws and

A DAY ON A GLACIER

Looking up the Nazina Glacier. The dark lines are internal moraines, formed by the inside shoreline moraines converging above.

rains. Most of the earth is in time washed away leaving only stone and gravel. This affords protection to the ice underneath, while the exposed surface between these moraines gradually melts away under the rays of the summer sun, leaving a valley of white, exposed ice between the ridges of gravel-covered ice. These ridges, or moraines, vary in height from a few feet to a hundred feet or more, on the Nazina Glacier.

Glaciers converge just as rivers or valleys converge and as a glacier has two lateral moraines,—one on each side—when two glaciers descending adjacent valleys, converge, the two inner lateral moraines unite into one medial moraine, which is carried downward on the surface of the glacier. The same thing may be repeated again and again as various lateral glaciers unite with the main ones. As a result some five or six moraines were found running parallel with and on the Nazina Glacier. In the distance they appeared as large dark streaks in contrast with the exposed white ice which lay between.

The call of "muck-a-muck" was made at four o'clock the next morning as we had a long and dangerous day's travel ahead of us. The horses were soon located and we were able to make an early start. Slimpert took the lead and we were soon winding our way up and over the rough surface of the first moraine, then

On the Nazina Glacier.

down to the white ice below. What a sensation it was! At first we were afraid to remain on our horses and likewise afraid to walk. Of one thing we were certain; namely, that there was no danger of the ice breaking through, as it was one solid mass from mountain to mountain and hundreds of feet thick. It was not long until the sensation of fear had passed to some extent and we felt more at ease in our new surroundings.

We proceeded up the valley of white ice for some distance, then across another moraine to a valley of ice beyond. Traveling soon became more difficult. We were at times down in deep gullies, at other times on high ridges and hills of solid ice. Sometimes it was so rough and the surface so uneven that it was impossible for the horses to proceed until foot-holds, or steps, were cut in the ice with the double-bitted ax and miner's pick which we carried for that purpose. Soon a horse was down in a small crevasse and had to be unpacked and assisted to his feet. After continuing in this manner for a while we were able to cross another moraine, and presently came into view of a wide plain of white ice. For several hours thereafter travel was comparatively easy. Narrow cracks and crevasses extended diagonally across the ice plain and uniformly about a hundred feet apart and parallel with each

A DAY ON A GLACIER

other. These did not interfere with our progress as it was an easy matter for the horses to step over them or jump the wider ones.

The surface of the ice was not slushy as I had expected it to be in the summer time—on the contrary, it was hard and brittle. Many small streams of clear running water were crossed. The ice which formed the creek beds varied in color from a beautiful emerald green to that of a blue veined onyx effect. The surface of a large ice field corresponds to a considerable extent with that of land as ordinarily found. There are ridges, hills, valleys, plains and sometimes mountains. There are heights of ice just as there are heights of land and from these divides rivulets and small creeks course their way in the summertime uniting at the intersection of the various valleys of ice, just as they do in valleys on land. The streams eventually find their way into some of the cracks, and in the course of time wear away the perpendicular walls of ice, forming what are known as "pot holes." These are usually round, funnel shaped at the top, from ten to thirty feet in diameter and sometimes many hundreds of feet deep.

A number of reservoirs and small lakes were passed, the water as clear as crystal. I thought of the millions of gallons of pure, cold water that were contained in those natural reservoirs of ice, none of which could possibly be contaminated to the slight-

An internal moraine, and beyond it can be seen another valley of exposed ice.

est degree, and which could be utilized to such advantage for domestic use if they were within the reach of civilization. Yet, it occurred to me if they were so located, they would soon cease to be pure and uncontaminated. At times when looking down at the side walls of these reservoirs or into the pot holes, or against the fresh surface of some ice cliff that had recently broken off, a variety of colors was presented that surpassed in beauty any rainbow I have ever seen—sky blue, dark blue, many shades of green, crimson, turquoise, lilac and others,—all delicately blended in perfect harmony.

I was so interested that I remained behind studying and admiring the surroundings of that strange lonesome country. How I wished it might be possible for some of my friends to be with me to enjoy that wonderful scene, even though it might be for a few moments only. As I lingered I heard unusual noises and strange sounds about me. I rode in the direction from which one of these sounds appeared to come. Dismounting I walked about, leading my restless horse, until I located the crevasse from which this particular noise emanated. After listening to it for a few moments, I continued to another crevasse. Lying down on the ice and placing my ear close to the narrow opening, I heard strange gurgling sounds that came from the subterranean river hundreds of feet below. I did likewise at other places and they called to mind stories of ghosts and spirit lands that I had heard when a child. I wished to make further investigations and to take some pictures but found it impossible to do so without assistance. I was unable to quiet my horse which charged and plunged frantically as he was detained in that weird and unusual place, while the party proceeded on in the distance.

It was some time before I could overtake the others, as any attempt to make speed over the numerous cracks and crevasses would have been dangerous. The surface soon became more uneven and the crevasses larger and more numerous. No trail had been left on the hard ice by the horses and it required much zigzagging about upon my part in an effort to get around these crevasses. After overtaking them I thought it advisable not to linger behind thereafter.

By that time we had encountered some very rough going. It was not long until we found we would be unable to proceed farther, which necessitated retracing our steps to a point where the moraine to our right could be crossed. After this we traveled up

A DAY ON A GLACIER

the valley of white ice on the right side of the moraine we had just crossed, but later we were compelled to recross into the valley we had so recently left.

Since our horses were rough shod, they were able to travel on the hard ice without slipping, but it was impossible for them

Waiting until footholds for the horses could be cut in the ice, August 11th.

to ascend the gravel covered moraines unless the grades were quite easy. When they attempted it, one would think they were shod with roller skates as the smooth gravel under their feet slipped, or rolled on the solid ice beneath.

After proceeding for a time we finally reached a point where we were shut in completely by the steep moraines on each side of us and several wide and deep crevasses in front. Some of them extended across the valley of ice from one moraine to the other, while there were numerous large pot holes no doubt several hundred feet deep. The men scattered out on foot in an effort to find a passage but returned without having been successful. Presently a short natural bridge of ice was found extending across the crevasse above the base of the moraine to our right, and it was decided to cut a passage over this surface of connecting ice. Everybody went to work taking turns with the pick and ax.

Billie Slimpert cutting footholds for the horses.

At this point I wish to digress from my narrative and introduce the most interesting horse in the entire lot,—Pinto, a roan, and by far the smallest of our horses—his weight being not over eight hundred pounds. In appearance one would have judged him to be a one-year-old colt, yet he was about fifteen years old and for many years had been used on hunting expeditions. He was the leader and the boss of the entire lot, his place always being in the lead of all the other pack horses. When going into deep water, in ascending almost impassable mountain trails or other places of danger, the other horses usually waited for Pinto to take the lead. Because he could stand more and was willing, he was worked harder than any other cayuse on the trip and with the exception of the stove horse, Skookum, carried on an average the heaviest pack in the entire outfit. When a permanent camping place was reached in the fall, he was used often as a saddle horse in order to give the others a rest. Notwithstanding this, at the end of our hunt he was in the best condition of any horse in the lot.

A DAY ON A GLACIER

The trail in the ice having been cut, Bones directed that Pinto be brought up and allowed to cross. Cautiously he picked his way along the trail of ice, his nose close to the surface, carefully selecting every step he made. Bones ordered that everyone should keep quiet while the horses were crossing the trail as otherwise there was danger of their becoming excited, losing their footing and dashing into the deep chasm below. Several of the old trusties were then allowed to follow unassisted, while the younger horses, and especially Dishpan, were led across. A second large crevasse which extended the full width of the valley of white ice, was encountered a short distance above, and another and even more dangerous crossing, had to be cut in the ice. At least two hours' time was consumed in traveling a distance of two or three hundred yards. All safely over, we continued.

During the afternoon it began raining and became much colder. We were traveling lengthwise of the great glacier and in the direction of Finger Mountain, so called from the fact that a tall pinnacle extends upward from a point on its extreme summit like the index finger of the hand. It was our purpose to pass by this mountain, leaving it on our left and to continue upward and across the glacier to the base of a mountain on the opposite side. Slimpert stated we would find a camping place there which was used in the wintertime by men who freighted supplies with dog teams to the Chisana (pronounced Shu-Shan-a) gold fields beyond. He stated we would likely find a small supply of wood there for cooking purposes, as well as grazing for the horses.

We were to do most of our goat hunting on Finger Mountain; therefore, we had been on the lookout for goats on this mountain from the time we had first come in sight of it. As we traveled along, I located one, as I thought, far up the distant mountain side. I told the Indian of my find and he laughed heartily, exclaiming, "Him no billy goat; him little patch of snow; all same I show you billy goat in little while, maybe!" My eyes were not as yet trained to judge the deceptive distances of that country, nor was I experienced in climbing mountains such as these; therefore, I had little knowledge of the real distance of that patch of snow against the mountain side. Had there been trees or other familiar objects in sight which would have enabled me to make a comparison, I probably could have gotten a better conception of the actual distance. I would have judged the "finger" on the top of the mountain to be four or five feet in diameter and ten or twelve feet in height. I observed at close range, a few days afterwards that it was many times that size.

Later on one of the Indians announced he had located goats. The pack train was stopped and everyone began straining his eyes to find them, except the other Indian who made them out instantly. Not until their location had been pointed out and our high powered glasses brought into use were we able to discover them. They were as white as snow and twelve or fifteen in number—feeding on what appeared in the distance to be barren ground, just below a high ledge of rock. It was my first sight of live wild goats in their native haunts. We then tried to make them out without our glasses but it was some time before we could do so. I could hardly believe my eyes, as they appeared like white mice so far as size was concerned. I then looked at the patch of snow I had first seen and was not at all surprised at the Indian's laughter.

The weather became very disagreeable. Later on the rain turned to a sleet that was almost snow. Again we encountered very rough going and towards evening arrived at a point where it appeared impossible to proceed. As the men looked about for passages, Indian Johnnie pointed out two goats against Finger Mountain, the foot of which at that point was not more than a mile distant. They were perhaps a quarter of a mile apart and quite low down. Upon looking at them through our binoculars, they both appeared to be billies and Mr. Snyder insisted upon trying to get a shot at one of them. As we would be there for some time hunting a passage over the rough ice, Bones told him to take Johnnie and make an attempt, while Doctor Evans decided to take Paddie and try for the other one. I remained with the horses while Bones, Slimpert and Gene started in different directions to find a passage. Later I ventured to leave the horses long enough to climb to the top of a nearby moraine from which point I watched all of the men with much interest. Slowly Doctor Evans ascended the steep mountain in the direction of the goat that he had selected. Presently I discovered this goat was working his way up the mountain, stopping to feed as he went, but at a rate of speed much faster than it was possible for the Doctor to travel. I had no way of signaling him to let him know that his climb would be for naught. To the left, I saw that the other goat retained his position, but I could not see Mr. Snyder nor the Indian as they worked their way up a gully. In opposite directions I watched

A DAY ON A GLACIER

Left: Cutting trail across a natural ice bridge. Right: Little Pinto, leader of the pack horses, was the first to cross.

the other three men climbing about over the rough ice and moraines. At times it was necessary for them to retrace their course when they found they were blockaded and could not proceed farther. Noticing that the horses were becoming restless, I returned to them and after that it required some effort to keep them herded together. Being tired and hungry they became more and more restless and there was danger of their crowding each other off into the "pot holes," or crevasses. It was very cold and when not engaged with the horses I danced about to keep warm, as my clothing was wet from the continued rain and sleet. Far up the mountain and at the head of the glaciers, I could see it snowing steadily, and I contrasted that day, which was August 11th, with the heat in which my friends back home no doubt were sweltering.

Presently a shot was heard, followed by others and, upon making use of my glasses, I saw the billy which Mr. Snyder was after making his way at a good rate of speed up the mountain. Upon reaching a rock cliff he did not turn but continued up the steep sides without interruption and disappeared from sight. Mr. Snyder told me later that when almost within shooting distance, a marmot saw them and by his continued whistling warned the goat of danger. The goat started running and the long distance shots fired at him were without effect.

Shortly afterwards I heard a crash as though the entire mountain was giving way. Some distance to the right in the course that the Doctor had taken, but beyond him and far up toward the mountain's top, I saw that an avalanche of ice and snow had broken loose from an overhanging glacier. Down the mountain it thundered, leaving a barren path behind, finally plunging into a deep gully which extended diagonally down the mountain. What a lonely barren place that entire section of country was, not a tree nor even a bush in sight! Far removed from civilization one would expect perfect quiet, but not so. Now and then noises almost equal to cannonading, at other times low and rumbling, were heard. The great ice field seemed to be like some living monster which was endeavoring to devour us in its gaping crevasses, while up the mountain sides portions of the overhanging ice continued to break loose from their lofty heights. It appeared to be a great workshop where the forces of Nature were constantly active.

One by one the guides returned with the advice that it was impossible to proceed farther in the direction we were traveling. A consultation was held and they appeared at a loss to know what to do. It was almost night and the cold rain and sleet continued. The horses were tired and we knew the packs should be off their backs. Finally it was decided to retrace our course and try to get over to the foot of Finger Mountain with the hope of finding horse feed and a camping place at its base. Upon starting a signal shot was fired for the purpose of attracting the attention of Mr. Snyder and Doctor Evans so they would meet us farther down the glacier. Doctor, finding that the mountain was too much for him, had turned back some time before. We traveled down the glacier about two miles, Mr. Snyder and Doctor Evans having joined us in the meantime, and gradually traveled over towards the base of the mountain. One of the men who had gone ahead returned to report that he had found a large basin between the base of the mountain and the shoreline moraine, which would make a very good camping place. He also stated that someone was already camped within the basin.

A DAY ON A GLACIER

It was nine o'clock when we arrived there and while it was a cloudy night, we were able to get the tents up and supper over before dark. It was the first time we had been off the ice since early morning. We found it far more comfortable here than on the glacier as we were protected by the rim of the basin from the cold wind which continually blew up the ice field. The other party consisted of an expedition sent out in the interest of a Los Angeles museum and was headed by Doctor Edward D. Jones of that city, and a Mr. McClellan and his son. The party also included a taxidermist who had been supplied by the museum. To our surprise we found that Baxter and his party had also reached the basin shortly before night and were camped against the side of the upper rim, a little ways above. There was an abundance of feed for the horses but no firewood. By searching for some distance along the edge of the moraine, however, the Indians were able to find a few dry willows—little larger than one's thumb—with which to do a limited amount of cooking. After eating our supper, which was the first morsel of food we had had since early morning, we immediately retired.

Chapter VI

A CLIMB FOR GOAT

*"You who this faint day the High North is luring
    Unto her vastness, taintlessly sweet;
You who are steel-braced, straight-lipped, enduring,
    Dreadless in danger and dire in defeat;
Honor the High North ever and ever,
    Whether she crowns you, or whether she slay;
Suffer her fury, cherish and love her—
He who would rule, he must learn to obey."*

AUGUST twelfth found us ready at six-thirty in the morning for our first day's hunt. Bones ordered Indian Johnnie to accompany Mr. Snyder, at the same time directing their course, while he took charge of Doctor Evans. Both parties traveled up the glacier for some distance, then leaving their horses, went in different directions. Indian Paddie was ordered to go with me. We started climbing the big mountain, directly back of our tent, and a half hour was required to reach a bench which extended for some distance around the mountain. Paddie carried my field glasses and camera, while I carried a new 30 special Newton Rifle, purchased in Seattle, anxious for an opportunity to try it. Upon reaching the bench, we stopped for a few minutes' breathing spell. It was not long until Paddie located a goat standing on a narrow ledge in a perpendicular cliff far above us. Making use of the binoculars we saw that the goat was an unusually large billy having good horns and well worth trying for.

Before starting that morning I consulted a small U. S. topographical map which showed Finger Mountain to be about eight thousand feet above sea level, while we were camped at an elevation of about three thousand feet. To reach the foot of the cliff on which the goat stood meant a climb to an altitude of perhaps six thousand feet. There was a rock slide approximately fifty yards in width at the top, widening out to about three hundred yards at the bottom and extending all the way from the base of the perpendicular rock cliff on which the goat was seen, to the bench on which we were standing. The mountain on each side of the slide was barren rock and so steep that no one could possibly climb it. We studied the situation for a few minutes and decided that the only possible way to get within shooting distance of the goat was up the slide. At the bottom the granite rocks were almost uniform in size, rectangular in shape and about four feet long, while their surface indicated a comparatively fresh fracture.

It looked to me like a dangerous undertaking to try to ascend the slide,—which by the way, was one of the largest encountered on the entire trip. I saw that the Indian did not want to undertake it, and thinking perhaps he considered it too dangerous to attempt, I endeavored to get an expression from him. He stated, "You no climb big slide; all same billy goat him too far; little while you get tired; can't go maybe; all same we climb on rocks, they slide, maybe; we slide too, maybe." I told him that if he considered it dangerous we would not attempt it, but that we would not hesitate on account of what he thought was my inability to make the climb. I did not know that I could succeed, but was anxious to try it. I asked him if he thought he could make the climb alone, but he did not reply. I then asked him if he would try it if the other Indian were with him and I was not there; whereupon, he replied, "Maybe so." I then told him that we would attempt it.

As we ascended the rocks gradually became smaller but most of them were nearly uniform in size at the various elevations. They afforded good footholds and travel for a time was comparatively easy. We had to use great care with every step as some of the rocks were on a balance while others appeared to be "key-rocks" and if slightly moved the other rocks on the surface for some distance up started sliding, although they did not roll or lose their relative position as one would suppose. We continued upward with great care as the rocks became smaller. Toward the top of the slide the rocks were uniformly about the size of a brick and similar in shape, while a little farther up they ran out altogether and we had nothing but loose shale. Our troubles then began. I strapped the gun on my back while Paddie did likewise with the camera and field glasses. We made progress very slowly.

Upon reaching the steepest part of the slide we found it impossible to stand and were obliged to flatten ourselves against the surface like a squirrel against a tree. The shale became finer and quite often upon being unable to secure firm footholds or handholds, we slid backwards several yards. It looked at times as though we must give it up and it would have required no per-

A splendid specimen of the mountain goat (Alaskan). Courtesy of U. S. Dept. of the Interior.

suasion to have induced the Indian to do so. I removed my gloves as I found I could use my bare hands to better advantage in clinging to the shale. We made constant use of the toes of our shoes, digging them in as best we could and in the most difficult places we used our chins as every ounce of resistance counted when changing hand or footholds.

Upward we climbed, gaining a little all the time, but very slowly. I had preferred keeping in the lead as I knew the force from an occasional stone which the Indian might dislodge above would be sufficient to cause me to lose my balance, and I tried to use great care in this respect on his account. When we would slide backward a few feet, we were careful to keep our bodies parallel with the slope of the slide. Had we started sliding in a slanting position, we would have instantly lost control.

A CLIMB FOR GOAT

We finally made it over the steepest ground, and stopped a few moments to take another look at the goat through the glasses. There he stood like some old patriarch; his white whiskers blowing in the wind, his fore feet on the very edge of the narrow rock shelf, as he looked down on us defiantly and no doubt with a feeling of absolute security. He had perhaps occupied this same position on previous occasions, when chased from his feeding grounds farther down the mountain side by other enemies. Their defense and protection is their ability to reach spots that are inaccessible to other animals except their friendly neighbors, the mountain sheep. Why should he now fear the approach of these strange objects that moved so slowly up the slide, hundreds of feet below? But alas, he had not reckoned with the high powered rifle of man!

He was at the extreme end of the shelf and could not proceed farther in that direction, nor could he go upward. His only means of escape was by winding his way down the shelf to our left and somewhat in our direction. We were not yet within shooting range, therefore, it was necessary to continue farther up the slide. We hesitated about doing so, thinking that the goat would become alarmed and start running down the shelf before we could get within reasonable shooting distance. At the edge of the slide to our left and some distance above us was a large protruding rock. We concluded to make our way to a point directly beneath the rock, thereby hoping to keep out of sight of the goat, then working around to our right again, to a point where we would be almost directly below and within shooting distance.

Before attempting this, I happened to look down and could not resist the temptation to gaze for a little while at the valley below. There was the great ice field extending up and down the Nazina Valley as far as the eye could see. Farther in the distance to our left and in the direction of the head of the big glacier, heavy clouds were visible and it appeared to be snowing. To our right the sun was shining brightly, casting shadows from the mountains to the white glacier ice below. The Indian pointed out our tents located in the basin by the side of the moraine. They looked like tiny specks, while the horses that had gone down into the basin for water looked like ants moving about in the distance. I looked at my watch and found that we had been just three hours climbing to that point and we had stopped only a few minutes on the way.

ALASKAN-YUKON TROPHIES

Until this time I had displayed at least as much courage as the Indian, but in gazing down on the scene below I had become dizzy and could not balance myself. The slide was not as steep at the point where we were then standing as it was just below or farther up near the base of the cliff. The Indian straightened up and maintained his position. I attempted to do likewise, but had to make several attempts before I succeeded. I realized I had made a great mistake by stopping to gaze on the distant valley below. I tried to crawl but made little headway. Taking my gun, the Indian strapped it to his shoulder and after repeated efforts, I finally was able to stand on my feet and follow him.

Upon reaching the boulder we made our way back towards the center of the slide, although it was a dangerous undertaking as at that point the surface was again very steep. It was necessary to go some twenty-five or thirty yards to reach a point where we thought the goat would be visible and at the same time within shooting range. We proceeded very carefully and as quietly as possible. Upon reaching the desired location we looked up at the ledge where the goat had stood, but he was not to be seen. We felt certain he must be there as he could not have passed down the narrow ledge without our having heard him. We descended the slide a few yards and upon looking up saw the top of the goat's back, but he was not sufficiently exposed to offer a shot at that great distance. We slid down a little farther whereupon a greater portion of his back became visible and I decided to attempt a shot; but a problem presented itself. How was I to shoot? I could not kneel; I could not sit down nor could I stand up, as we were then clinging to the surface by digging our toes and fingers into the shale and my fingers were by that time worn until they were bleeding.

However, the Indian soon solved the problem. He took a position below me, dug his toes and hands into the shale while I rested one foot against his shoulder. Placing my elbows against the surface, I took aim at the goat's back and fired. I was afraid the recoil from the high powered gun would unbalance me, but having a good foothold against the Indian's shoulder, I retained my position. I saw that the bullet had hit the solid rock just above the goat's back. Immediately after firing, the goat awakened from the nap he had been taking and arose. I lost no time in firing again, hitting the ledge at the goat's feet. Both had been fair shots under the circumstances, considering the distance and

The goat lodged fifteen-hundred feet down the slide.

Finger Mountain, from beyond the glacier and about ten miles distant. (1) Cliff from which goat was shot. (2) Where the author's horse was killed.

the fact that it was the first time I had used my new rifle, other than to shoot at a target. After firing the second shot, Mr. Billy stepped promptly to the edge of the shelf, lowered his head and looked down on us in a deliberate manner. I hesitated for a moment, while the Indian in an excited manner kept urging me to fire. It seemed unfair to shoot so pretty a creature, standing as he was almost directly above us and at such great height. However, we had come a long distance; we had made a hard climb, and I realized I might not have an opportunity again to get a shot at so fine a specimen. These thoughts occupied my mind for a few seconds only.

A CLIMB FOR GOAT

The goat presented a wonderful sight as he gazed down upon us, his head, neck and right shoulder showing plainly. He appeared as white as snow in contrast to the color of his surroundings. I aimed carefully at his right shoulder and fired, whereupon he plunged forward, just grazing a slight projection on the cliff only a few feet below the shelf where he stood; then down he came, turning over and over, a sight that I shall never forget. Not once did he touch the sides of the granite walls in his descent. He struck the surface of the steep slide about twenty-five yards above and to the right of us, making a report that sounded like a small explosion. He glanced off the surface and fell and rolled down the slide at a rate of speed that appeared to be almost as great as when falling through the air. It made me shudder to think what our fate would be should we lose our holds and go thundering down the slide in the same manner. The speed of the carcass did not slacken until it reached the jagged surface of the slide rock far below. It lodged perhaps fifteen hundred feet down the incline, where it was not so steep.

What an experience it was! Perhaps no hunter ever witnessed a more spectacular sight in securing a trophy. I never expect to have such an exciting hunting experience again. I felt well repaid for the hard climb and the risk that I had taken to secure this trophy.

We stopped to study the cliff and take some pictures of its base. I estimated the distance the goat had fallen before striking the slide and asked the Indian to make an estimate. He was far above the average in intelligence and conservative in any statements he made. We agreed it was fully five hundred feet. Make a comparison in your own mind; think of Washington's Monument which is five hundred and forty feet high, then think of a large goat falling a distance of about five hundred feet, then rebounding and falling and rolling together a distance of about fifteen hundred feet more down the slide.

From the time that I had stopped to look down in the valley and had become so dizzy, I had been in constant dread of the descent. I realized much of the way it would be necessary to face about with the great expanse below me in full view—and I doubted my ability to do so. However, after the excitement in connection with the killing of the goat, I found this fear had left me to a large extent. We faced about and carefully made our way downward. I found that descending the slide was much easier than I had thought it would be. We used great care in every step, sometimes flattening ourselves against the slide and easing down backwards, until we reached the granite rocks and farther down, the goat.

I had fully expected the horns to be damaged, but saw to my surprise they were intact. The Indian said it was one of the largest goats that he had ever seen. We estimated his weight to be three hundred and fifty pounds, while his horns were ten and a half inches in length. After taking two or three photographs and making some measurements, the Indian skinned and dressed him. That portion of the skin extending as far back as the shoulders was removed with the head, for use by the taxidermist, while the remainder was taken with us for the purpose of having it tanned with the hair on. The goat had landed on his hind parts when he had fallen from the high cliff and they were mashed into a jelly. The front quarters were taken for use as food.

We reached camp at three in the afternoon, having spent eight and one-half hours in the climb for the goat. We found that our movements had been witnessed not only by our horse-wrangler and cook, but by the entire San Francisco party. When ready to start hunting that morning they had observed the Indian and me ascending the slide far above them. With their glasses they located the object of our climb and seeing the great distance he would fall, in the event we were successful, they thought it worth while to remain in camp and witness the sport through their binoculars. Later on, in an article by Mr. Baxter which he contributed to a sportsman's magazine, he referred to the sight as one of the most exciting he had ever witnessed, mentioning that it would have made a wonderful scene for a moving picture, and estimating the height of the cliff from which the goat had fallen as being between five and six hundred feet.

Doctor Evans, Mr. Snyder and the guides returned about six in the evening. They had put in a hard day's work and, while goats had been seen, they were unable to get a shot.

Chapter VII

A DISTRESSING ACCIDENT

*"The lonely sunsets flame and die;
    The giant valleys gulp the night;
The monster mountains scrape the sky,
    Where eager stars are diamond-bright."*

I FOUND myself so stiff and sore from the climb for the goat that I remained in camp the following day. Upon returning from their hunt that evening, Doctor reported an unsuccessful day, although goats had been seen. Mr. Snyder had killed two billies,—one medium-sized, the head and skin of which he had brought to camp; while the horns of the other one, which was a much finer specimen, had been broken off at their base in rolling down the cliff after he had been shot. Quite naturally, Mr. Snyder was very much provoked at his misfortune after such a difficult climb to secure him.

It rained so hard the next day that we remained in our tents. The time dragged by very slowly. Firewood was almost unobtainable. Only by searching for some distance, along the edge of the moraine, were the Indians able to find some small dry willows for use in the cook stove.

The next morning dawned bright and clear and we all started to a point about eight miles distant where a number of goats had been seen two days earlier.

We crossed the shoreline moraine, traveling down the white exposed ice a distance of about one mile; then re-crossed and went to the foot of the mountain. Bones decided on a course which appeared to be the steepest of any that were seen. It was one of a number of ridges, or "hogsbacks" that extended up to the bench, with narrow, almost perpendicular walled gulches between. It was selected for its low, scrubby birch and alders growing on the crest, thereby affording footholds for the horses.

As we proceeded up the "hogsback" I allowed my horse to rest frequently, as he appeared to be getting his breath with difficulty. In doing so, those in the rear—except the two Indians—overtook me. Later as the Indians passed I endeavored to make them understand that my horse appeared to be in distress, but they continued upward. The grade became steeper. I was obliged to lean forward in the saddle, holding the bridle rein with my right hand and grasping the horse's mane just back of his ears in order to hold on, as the others had also done. The others reached the top and passed out of sight. I called to the Indians asking them to wait on me, but they gave no heed to my request or perhaps did not understand me.

By this time my horse was groaning and apparently suffering, but I could not do otherwise than to urge him on, as we could not remain there. Placing his front feet forward and tightening every muscle in his body as is their custom when making such climbs, he would take two or three jumps upward, then stop for breath. Each had kept his horse in a somewhat zigzag course—first to the right, then to the left of the narrow crest, and I was doing likewise in order to make it easier on the horse. I was well up towards the top when I observed that just ahead the grade was steeper than any place below and there was less shrubbery. The agony of the horse appeared to be increasing, and thinking perhaps he had a bad case of colic, I thought it best that I should walk the remaining distance. Furthermore, I considered it dangerous to continue to ride at that great height and on the almost barren ground above me.

Dismounting, I climbed upward the length of the bridle rein. Then, turning, I urged the horse to follow. He placed his front feet forward and, getting a good hold, made a jump or two upward. This was repeated two or three times, when he made a final jump and immediately slumped in his tracks. I grabbed a close hold on the rein, but my strength amounted to little in comparison with the weight of the horse. As he started down the steep incline I relinquished my hold and recovered balance just in time to save myself. It was not more than five minutes after dismounting, and certainly not more than five seconds from the time the animal made his last leap upward, until he was rolling and falling into the gulch far below. The carcass bounded six or eight feet each time it struck the surface of the steep incline, and the animal was undoubtedly dead before he reached the bottom. In fact, that horse may have been dead, or nearly so, when he started falling, as he had a bad case of colic. I then recalled Gene had that morning criticized one of the Indians for drawing the horses' saddle girths so tight when they were first brought in

A DISTRESSING ACCIDENT

Spot, the author's second saddle horse.

from their feeding grounds, and stated that to do so might result in their developing colic.

It was a gruesome sight, and as the horse struck with a dull thud far below, the sensation was altogether different from that experienced three days before when the goat had fallen five hundred feet from the rock cliff and rolled hundreds of feet down the rock slide. The experience was more horrible due to the fact that I had already become quite fond of this splendid horse. I thought of the Ross rifle which was contained in the scabbard, attached to the saddle, and congratulated myself on having purchased a second gun. I remembered also my camera tied to the horn of the saddle; then my binoculars, but fortunately, I had removed them from my saddle bags and they were suspended by their strap around my neck and tucked safely under my overshirt. These thoughts passed hurriedly through my mind as I gazed into the deep gorge where the dead horse lay, six or eight hundred feet below. Then I thought after all, how little the loss of the horse, gun and camera amounted to as compared with my own safety. Had I not dismounted, no doubt I would have met the same fate.

Hurrying up the mountain I reached the bench, and finally making one of the Indians hear me, told him of the accident. I then returned and went down into the gorge where the dead horse lay. I removed the camera and saw that it was broken beyond repair. (It will be remembered that this was my third camera since leaving home.) The gun was not in the scabbard nor was it in sight. I examined the contents of the saddle bags and found that my lunch, milk chocolate, gun oil and other small items were all in one mass. A pocket comb enclosed in a leather case and left in the saddle bags had been crushed until it had the appearance of coarse black gunpowder.

The Indians and Bones soon arrived. We removed the saddle and bridle with the intention of picking them up as we returned in the evening. Starting up the mountain again we looked carefully for the missing rifle. When about two-thirds the distance up we saw it lodged against some protruding rocks. One of the Indians climbed around the steep slope and secured it. I was pleased to find it was not injured beyond a few scratches. Evidently it had fallen from the scabbard near the top of the gorge, after which it slid down to the ledge where it was found.

Upon reaching my companions they were told of the accident and I was congratulated on my narrow escape. I walked three or four miles, then rode one of the Indians' saddle horses until we reached our destination.

We found a band of goats scattered in groups up the mountainside. Dividing into three parties of two each we traveled in different directions in an effort to stalk them. We had some very exciting experiences during the next two or three hours, which resulted in Doctor Evans' killing three billies, one of which had its horns damaged so badly, by falling and rolling, that it was valueless as a trophy and was left where it fell. Mr. Snyder killed one billy having a very nice head, while I killed two,—both of them having very good heads, although none of them equal in size to the large goat I killed on the first day. This concluded our goat hunt as each of us had killed our legal limit of three.

I disliked returning by way of the dead horse, and hoping to get sight of a bear, I started ahead of the others, traveling higher up the mountain side, but saw no game in my eight mile walk back to camp. The saddle, bridle and my saddle bags were brought to camp by the others, and later one of the Indians returned to remove the shoes from the dead horse.

A DISTRESSING ACCIDENT

During our absence that day Gene had made doughnuts from the fat of the first goats killed. He said that doughnuts made from goat fat dried quickly and were too brittle, but we would no doubt kill a caribou quite soon and he would mix the fat from it with the goat fat and have real doughnuts.

We did not regret leaving that basin camp the next morning, as we were anxious to reach a country where we would find wood for warmth and cooking. Being without a horse Bones assigned to me his saddle horse, Spot, so named from the fact that he had a spotted nose but was otherwise pure white. I rode him almost continuously during the remainder of the trip. Ordinarily, he was a very satisfactory horse, except for the fact that he would take sleepy spells each afternoon, and until his drowsiness had worn off, it availed nothing to urge or whip him. During his afternoon naps he was not sure-footed and would often stumble and fall. In going through timber I had to watch constantly to keep him from raking my knees against the sides of trees and saplings.

The day we remained in camp on account of rain Indian Johnnie had been sent afoot across the glacier to select a trail. With this Indian in the lead no time was lost in hunting passages and we were able to cross in about three hours. Only once did we experience trouble and that was in ascending the shoreline moraine on the opposite side. This moraine was a large one and the ascent quite steep. Directly below and at the bottom of the grade, was a large pool of water. The sides of the pool were almost perpendicular and if a horse were to fall in, he would stand little chance of getting out. Leading the way, the Indian made the ascent without accident; so did little Pinto following immediately behind. Slim, another very active pack horse, carrying a very heavy load, attempted it and when almost up the grade lost his footing. He was quickly on his feet again but unable to stand. The surface of the ice was covered with small stones and gravel which slipped or rolled under his feet. Time after time the horse gained his feet only to fall again. Each fall brought him farther down the grade and almost into the deep pool of ice water. We stood watching breathlessly for a few moments, fully expecting to see him go over the ice bank and into the water on making his next attempt. Evidently aware of his danger, he made one last noble attempt, and tho he went to his knees several times, he at last succeeded in reaching the top of the grade.

ALASKAN-YUKON TROPHIES

Pack horse jumping a small crevasse.

Realizing this was one of the most active horses in the lot and that only by his unusual strength and activity had he saved himself from the pool of ice water below, Bones knew it would not do to trust some of the other horses on the same grade. Much time was then spent in making a trail from which the stone and gravel were removed, after which steps were cut so the horses could get footholds on the solid ice. We then crossed the moraine without further difficulty.

The remainder of the afternoon we traveled up and around the side of the mountain in the direction of Skolai Creek. We arrived at a clump of spruce some time before night and camped there, as the distance to the next place where horse feed would be available was too great to be reached that day. It was an ideal camping spot, high up against the mountain side, with an abundance of feed close by. Wood was plentiful and it was a pleasure to have a camp fire to sit by until time for retiring.

Far in the distance ahead of us we could see the famous Skolai Pass of which we had heard so much and which we should reach on the following evening. From this pass the swiftly running waters of Skolai Creek made their way abruptly down the valley. Gradually this valley narrowed until, for some distance, it was a deep gorge. Again it widened out into another valley which contained a small lake, and from the mountain side where we were camped, it looked like a large emerald. Below this lake Skolai Creek continued for several miles to the Nazina Glacier, where it emptied its waters into the subterranean Nazina River far be-

A DISTRESSING ACCIDENT

neath the surface of the ice. Looking down, it appeared to be but a short distance to the great ice field or to Finger Mountain on the opposite side. I could hardly realize it had required the greater portion of the day to cover the distance, so close did it appear.

We were able to make an early start on the following morning; in fact, it was necessary that we do so as we had a hard day's

Hard-going. Left: Men and horses pick the way on an incline of exposed ice. Right: Next, they toil up the side of a steep moraine.

climb ahead of us. A report of the United States Geological Survey of that district stated that travel should be undertaken only by way of the "Goat Trail" which is up the Chitistone River to Skolai Pass. This was the route Bones and his party had traveled on their way to McCarthy to meet us. The report further stated that few people had undertaken the other route, it being dangerous and in fact a perilous undertaking with pack horses. Over this route, however, we were obliged to travel until we reached "Goat Trail." Slimpert had been over this trail several times, and spoke frequently about it. Upon leaving camp he led the way down into the valley, then up the creek for a mile or two. He told us on leaving the creek we would make our steepest ascent, and after having covered a distance of one mile, we would be at an elevation of just fifteen hundred feet above the creek,—as shown by the report of the United States Geological Survey. We found he had not in the least exaggerated this climb, and it required all the strength of both men and horses to make it.

From the time we left McCarthy I noticed numerous skeletons or portions of skeletons of horses strewn along the trail. I heard Slimpert speak of the many horses which had perished in crossing Skolai Pass and, therefore, took note of them during the day's travel,—counting seventeen skeletons. Nearly all of them were seen after reaching "Goat Trail." They were relics of the stampede of several years before into the Chisana Gold Field.

The wind blew fiercely from the pass above and at times it seemed it would unbalance our horses from their lofty trail above the deep gorge. When travel became somewhat easier, Mr. Snyder and I rode some distance ahead of the pack train with the hope of getting sight of a grizzly, but we were not so fortunate. The Fredericka Glacier was reached during the afternoon but we were not obliged to cross it. Instead we crossed the Fredericka River at a point where it emerged from the foot of the glacier. In fording it Gene's horse fell in the icy water but regained his footing without damage to himself or rider, other than a good wetting for Gene.

It was evening when we approached the Skolai Basin. This is a large natural basin formed by the Russell Glacier on one side, while the foothills of the high mountains extend almost around it on the other sides. Upon reaching the rim we descended into the basin, crossed the creek and continued up and around a small glacial lake for perhaps a mile. We camped at four o'clock in the upper end of the basin and only a short distance from the shoreline moraine of the Russell Glacier. Bones and his party had camped at this same spot when on their way to McCarthy. Knowing they would be above timber line and far removed from fire wood, they had cut a supply on the headwaters of the White River, loading it on one of the pack horses, and carrying it a day's journey across the Russell Glacier to the Skolai Pass. A portion of it was used at that time and the remainder cached until he would return with us. We located the wood without difficulty and used it in preparing our supper and breakfast the following morning.

It was very cold and the wind continued to blow with terrific force, although the rim of the basin afforded us some protection; but even so we experienced great difficulty in erecting our tents. The Indians found some scrubby, green willows growing near the moraine and several of these pieces were spliced together with cinch ropes taken from the horses' packs. By using these spliced willows, we were able to erect the tents sufficiently high to crawl under, while their edges were weighted down with stones. It was a weird lonesome place. To the west was a series of seven peaks, all similar in size and appearance and known as the "Seven Sisters." Gene stated it was to be regretted that there was not one less in our party or one more of the "sisters," in which event

A DISTRESSING ACCIDENT

each one of us could select a "sister" and spend the evening with her. He said it was Sunday and a very appropriate time for calling on ladies, but inasmuch as there were eight in our party, we would not quarrel over the ladies but would retire early.

Great glaciers of blue ice extended down from each peak to the valley below and connected with the main glacier, which lay in a semicircle around another large mountain, known as Sheep Mountain; so called from the fact that mountain sheep may usually be found on its sides. It is almost perpendicular on the south and west sides, while the top and north sides are covered with perpetual snow and ice. To our east Castle Mountain extended about five thousand feet above the basin. Skolai Creek flows almost west and in looking down that creek one could see in the distance a white streak of ice. It was the Nazina Glacier, and beyond it rose Finger Mountain. It appeared to be only a few miles away but we had traveled two days since leaving its base. Far to the north and northwest we could see a portion of the great Wrangle Range of Mountains and its adjacent ice fields.

Quoting from W. T. Young, a big game hunter of Nashville, Tennessee, I give my readers the following description: "No one but John Muir could begin to give you an idea of the beauties of those surroundings. It is worth a trip to Alaska to go through Skolai Basin and climb the foothills for a thousand feet early in the morning. There one may watch the colors come and go on the cheeks of the "Seven Sisters" as the sun plays peek-a-boo around old Castle Mountain and kisses the faces of the "Seven Sisters." While sitting there admiring the prettiest scenery in the world, you can also see with the naked eye numerous bands of mountain sheep (ovis dalli) peacefully feeding near the foot of Sheep Mountain; in fact, the atmosphere is so clear that you think you can step over and get your rams and return in a few minutes. But when you cross the valley and work your way around the edge of the moraine, you will find you have traveled several miles."

There are storms in Skolai Pass almost every day in the year. Quoting further from this writer, he states, "Clouds appear around the tops of the mountains and snow storms lash the high peaks; then the sun bursts out and drives the clouds away, only to be covered again by other waves of clouds that again charge the peaks. These waves come up from the coast, wave following wave, and appear to fight great battles against the peaks that surround Skolai Pass and usually they would be torn to pieces.

Source of the Nazina Glacier.

This is a great battleground of the elements. It is nearly always stormy on the south side of the Pass and clear on the north, as the mountains change the climate entirely. Skolai being the lowest pass in this section, it appears that the winds funnel through this pass and bring all the storms up from the coast. There they wear themselves out against the mountains and appear to rise, for as soon as you cross the Russell Glacier and get on the north side, you encounter an entirely different climate from what one finds on the south side."

It was not long after our arrival at camp until it began raining and snowing, while up the mountains we could see that the storm was more severe. We retired at eight forty-five, which was some time before dark, in an effort to get warm, as our supply of wood was sufficient for cooking purposes only. We were destined to sleep little that night. Sometimes we were awakened by the fierce wind which blew so strong that it seemed as though our tent would be torn loose from the rocks which weighted down its corners. At times when the wind subsided and we had fallen asleep, we were awakened by sharp reports followed by crashing, then rumbling noises, as the great masses of ice broke loose from

A DISTRESSING ACCIDENT

above and thundered down the mountain sides. It is impossible to describe the sensations I experienced as I was frequently awakened by these strange and unusual sounds. As I lay there trying to sleep, it seemed as though I must be dreaming or in a nightmare; at times I had feelings of fear and it was difficult to bring myself to an actual realization of our surroundings and the fact that we were really in no danger.

Chapter VIII

CROSSING A GREAT DIVIDE

*"No! There's the land. (Have you seen it?)
It's the cussedest land that I know,
From the big, dizzy mountains that screen it
To the deep, deathlike valleys below.
Some say God was tired when He made it;
Some say it's a fine land to shun;
Maybe; but there's some as would trade it
For no land on earth—and I'm one."*

I WAS glad, indeed, when morning came and we crawled from under the canvas, dressed in our heaviest clothing. Fresh snow covered the mountain sides and extended down to the basin. We all took a hand in the work in an effort to keep warm and to get an early start, as we had a long and dangerous day's travel ahead of us in crossing the Russell Glacier. One of the horses had been kicked during the night, and being quite lame, a light load was placed upon him.

The Los Angeles Museum party had arrived in the basin the evening before and camped a short distance below us. They had with them, as a guide, an Englishman by the name of Harry Boyden. He was an intelligent, courteous gentleman, stalwart and fine of appearance and we all admired him very much. That faraway land of the North had been adopted by him as the place of his abode and he had spent many years prospecting and freighting supplies into the interior. He told us he had crossed the Russell Glacier a number of times—with dog teams in the winter and pack horses in the summer—and if we cared to follow him, we would experience no difficulty in crossing. Bones had had some trouble on this Glacier on his way to McCarthy, and was pleased to accept the invitation.

All in readiness, both parties fell into line and we were soon climbing the big moraine, then out on to the white ice. The Los Angeles party had seventeen horses, while the number in our outfit had been reduced to nineteen since my saddle horse had been killed, thus making a total of thirty-six horses. It was an im-

CROSSING A GREAT DIVIDE

We wait for the horses to be packed.

pressive sight as those trusty cayuses, with heavy loads on their backs, wound their way over the great ice field. The Englishman led the way, down into the gulches, then out and over the hills and mountains of solid ice, jumping the small crevasses and detouring around the larger ones, the horses' noses well down toward the ice, carefully observing every step they were about to take.

Hour after hour we traveled, and mile after mile. Not once did Boyden hesitate or appear to be the least confused in his course. There was no visible trail to follow, no trees or other familiar objects to guide him; neither were there any land marks of any kind, although occasionally we saw a stick or short pole which no doubt had been carried for miles and stuck in a crack in the ice. Sometimes when winding around the rough surface of the moraines, we observed little piles of stone that had been placed there perhaps as guide posts. The untrained eye would not have noticed them lying as they were among many others, but men such as these were quick to see that they were placed there by the hand of man. None of these markers appeared to mean anything to Boyden as he apparently took no notice of them. During the winter when he and other freighters mushed their way with dog teams over the great ice fields, and frequently through blinding

Above: The pack train on a large moraine, and almost within sight of the White River. Inset: Where the glacier-covered mountains reach into the clouds.

snow storms, these sticks protruding from the ice doubtless were welcome guide posts.

About the middle of the day while descending the trail around a rough moraine, we suddenly met a man walking, followed by eight pack horses in single file. We were quite startled for a moment as he was the first person we had seen since our first night out and the last and only person we saw until we came out late in the fall—except the other hunting parties and Indians. He was a freighter on his return trip from the Chisana Gold Field.

"Hello, Shorty," said Boyden as they met.

"Hello, Harry, colder than hell, ain't it?"

And they continued on their way without stopping.

After he passed it occurred to us that this man might take mail to McCarthy for us. We asked Slimpert to stop him and inquire if he could wait long enough for us to write a few lines on postal cards. He replied that he would do so if we would not be long about it. Quickly locating some postal cards the hunters of each party hurriedly wrote a few lines home. None of us had expected such an opportunity,—otherwise we would have had letters written ready for mailing. We thanked "Shorty" heartily for waiting and were soon on our way again. The meeting of this

CROSSING A GREAT DIVIDE

man had been quite an event. As I looked back at him winding his way over the crest of a moraine, followed by his eight sturdy horses in the same manner that dogs follow their master, I thought what a lonely life it was for anyone to lead.

It is of interest to note that about two weeks are required to make the trip from McCarthy to this gold field and return; and the customary price for transporting supplies is forty cents a pound in the summer, when pack horses are used, and thirty-five cents a pound during the winter with dogs. One can well understand why the cheaper commodities such as flour, sugar and salt are sold in the Chisana Camps at a uniform price of about sixty cents per pound, when he stops to consider the cost of transportation from the States to McCarthy with the cost of freighting back into that country added.

Late in the afternoon we came within sight of the great White River. It derives its name from the fact that the river bar and mountain sides are almost covered with white volcanic ash for a distance of about fifty miles, giving it the appearance of snow. The river bar is almost two miles wide at the foot of the glacier where many channels emerge from beneath the big ice field. The width of the bar increases to about five miles farther down. Thanks to Boyden's thorough knowledge of the glacier, we crossed it in seven hours of steady travel, which was said to be unusually good time.

We had now crossed the greatest divide of that country, the St. Elias Range, and were on waters that flowed to the Arctic. Before us lay a section of country considered to be one of the greatest game fields on the American Continent. A vast expanse of territory lay before us, with the lofty snow-covered Coast Range to our right; the broken up volcanic mountains to our left, and a large area of country between. Dark green spruce timber extended from each side of the river bar, back a distance of several miles on the foothills, while the great mountains towered above. It presented a magnificent view.

We were glad, indeed, that we were approaching a timbered country where fire wood was available for cooking and heating purposes during the coming colder nights. On the headwaters of this river the timber was confined exclusively to small scrubby spruce, not exceeding seven or eight inches in diameter; and an occasional clump of willows and cottonwood growing along the edges of the creeks, these not exceeding four or five inches in diameter. Wild pea vine in abundance was found on the river bar, and it was with difficulty that we urged our hungry horses past the numerous patches.

The course of Doctor Jones with the Los Angeles party, after crossing the glacier, was to our left and in the direction of the Chisana Gold Field; and soon after leaving the glacier we bade them goodbye. Continuing down the river bar for several miles, we camped in the edge of timber and by the side of a creek which was so full of sand and volcanic ash that it was unfit for drinking and cooking. There being no other water available, it was necessary to make use of a canvas bucket which Bones had brought with him for a filter. We were obliged to resort to this method quite often during the next several weeks as many of the creeks were of glacial origin.

It was almost noon the following day when Slimpert returned with the horses which had wandered far down the bar. After waiting some time, Mr. Snyder shouldered his gun and summoned one of the Indians to accompany him back into the timber, saying that he might find some game. Doctor Evans decided to go also and called the other Indian. They were gone not more than fifteen minutes when Doctor sighted a good-sized grizzly feeding in an open space about a quarter of a mile from our tents. As Doctor had already killed seven bears on his spring hunt, he extended the courtesy of the shot to Mr. Snyder, who made quick work of him with his new 256 Newton rifle. We were very much surprised when they returned a short time afterwards carrying the head and skin of the bear. His fur was of a brown color, but not in prime condition owing to the season of the year.

After a light lunch Doctor Evans and Mr. Snyder took the Indians and horses, and again started out in the scrubby timber back of our camp. Bones and I made quite a circuit that afternoon. We first crossed over the bar; then traveled down the river a distance of about five miles. Numerous gopher holes were seen which had been dug into by bears. We also saw a number of caribou and moose tracks, most of them comparatively fresh, but no game was sighted.

Upon returning in the evening we found that Doctor Evans had killed a caribou. The Indian guide saw him at the edge of timber line about two miles back of our camp. It was a fairly good head, but at that time of year was "in the velvet." The horns of this caribou were so beautifully covered with this fine soft velvet

CROSSING A GREAT DIVIDE

Crossing a moraine on Russell Glacier. Thirty-six pack horses in line.

Cross-section of a moraine. The diagonal lines seen on the ice presented rainbow-like colors, with emerald green predominating. The surface of the moraine was thinly covered with gravel and stone.

that Doctor wanted Bones to try to preserve them as they were. Bones expressed some doubt about being able to do so but was willing to try. Caribou and moose shed their horns annually, usually soon after the first of the year. New horns start growing about March and are later covered with very fine soft hair which in appearance and to the touch resembles brown silk plush. Not until they have entirely shed this velvet in September, which is just before the mating season, are their horns fully developed and at their best. In moving our camp from place to place thereafter the horns were carefully wrapped and when we camped at one place for several days, they were unwrapped and hung up to dry. A great deal of time was spent in trying to carry out Doctor's wishes, but before going out in the fall the velvet had lost its beauty and had decomposed to such an extent that it was necessary to remove it altogether. This was done as easily as one would strip the bark from a hickory or chestnut sapling in the spring of the year.

The next day Bones and I went down the bar a short distance, then up a good-sized creek. We followed it to the edge of timber line, then up through the barren expanse of tundra to the foothills of the mountain. We continued up into a canyon until we were near a fairly large glacier. It was a wild looking place; the high mountains towered on either side, while above us the glacier completely filled the gulch between. Presently we discovered two rams on the apparently barren slopes to our left. We examined them through our glasses and found they were not sufficiently large to make them desirable as trophies. They were of much interest to me as it was my first sight of Alaskan sheep. As we continued we searched the mountains with our glasses and presently located a ram high up in the cliffs to our left. From his hunting coat Bones took a telescope which he often carried for the purpose of examining minutely the horns of sheep when at a considerable distance. On many occasions we found it to be a great aid. When we located game it was not always possible to judge their horns with our binoculars. With the telescope, however, Bones was able to ascertain whether a ram had desirable horns and if the points were broken. A number of difficult and useless climbs would have been made on several occasions had we not been provided with this instrument. Arranging a suitable rest for the telescope by piling up some stones on a bank, and lying down in a position where he could steady himself, Bones looked carefully and said the horns

CROSSING A GREAT DIVIDE

of the sheep were not only large, but that they had a splendid curve and perfect points. I then took the instrument and studied the animal quite carefully and with much interest. He stood on a narrow ledge in the high cliffs, casting his head about nervously, as he no doubt had caught sight of the horses when we wound our way up the creek bed. We decided to try for him and, hitching our horses securely to some large boulders and removing all surplus clothing, we began the climb.

The sun was shining brightly when we started up the mountain, but a half hour later it began raining. Farther up the canyon and above the glacier it was snowing. We climbed slowly but steadily upward, stopping frequently for a few moments' breathing spell. After climbing for an hour we reached a point where we could proceed no farther, and believing that we were within shooting range, we stopped and tried to locate the ram. It had ceased raining but the white clouds were passing rapidly in the cliffs above, and it was some time under these conditions before we could make him out, as his color blended with the clouds and mist surrounding him. When ready I took careful aim and upon firing saw that the bullet struck the ledge at the ram's feet. Instantly he stepped out of sight through a little opening in the cliff. We waited a while with the hope he would reappear. Bones said the ram had stepped through the door of the cliff into another room and no doubt had closed and locked the door behind him. After studying the situation, we concluded there was nothing to do but give him up. Our hard climb had been in vain.

Descending we saw a small ram coming down the mountain on the opposite side of the creek. Reaching a narrow bench we stopped and watched him. Bones thought he was on his way to join the two small rams we had first seen farther down the gorge, and said that if we kept out of sight, he would likely come up the mountain near where we stood. Upon reaching the creek the small ram crossed a short distance below the horses and started upwards. Bones told me to try and kill him for camp meat as the goat meat was exhausted. We walked back from the edge of the bench and did not have to wait long until he appeared over the crest, and seeing me, started running. I killed him with the first shot at a distance of about a hundred yards. He proved to be a two-year-old ram; and after dressing him, we carried the hind quarters down to the horses.

ALASKAN-YUKON TROPHIES

Looking around, we saw a number of sheep on the mountain above the glacier, but it was too late to try for them that evening. Presently we again located the large ram in the cliffs where we had first seen him. The distance was so great that it was somewhat difficult to make him out with our naked eyes, but I decided to take a shot, although I had no hope of hitting him. I raised the folding sight of my Newton rifle for a distance of a thousand yards or more, took a coarse bead and fired, whereupon the ram promptly stepped back through his little doorway to the other side of the cliff, where he had stood when I shot at him before. He returned in a few minutes, but not wishing to waste any more time or ammunition, we strapped our mutton to the saddles and started home. We did not return down the creek but traveled around the tundra, above timber line, with the hope of getting sight of a grizzly. We watched carefully, stopping every little while to search the country with our glasses, but saw nothing.

Chapter IX

A SIDE TRIP FOR SHEEP

"I've stood in some mighty-mouthed hollow
  That's plumb-full of hush to the brim;
I've watched the big, husky sun wallow
  In crimson and gold, and grow dim,
Till the moon set the pearly peaks gleaming,
  And the stars tumble out, neck and crop;
And I've thought that I surely was dreaming,
  With the peace o' the world piled on top."

AS WE returned from our sheep hunt we crossed a high point where we commanded a good view, and Bones spent some time making observations. I noticed his gaze was directed beyond a low range of mountains that paralleled the White River on its opposite side. Presently he pointed to a lake located in the foothills of a mountain range farther on saying, "I passed through that section of country in 1906 on a prospecting trip. I was walking and had with me one pack horse carrying a light outfit. It was evening when I reached the lake so I spent the night there. It is known as Ptarmigan Lake. I have never been back there since, but if I remember correctly it looked like good sheep country." He stood some time—no doubt studying the country and making plans in his mind for our hunt—then told me we would start to that lake the next morning.

It was seldom that Bones told either hunters or guides anything concerning his plans. When first starting out some of us occasionally asked him what the plans were for the following day, but we never received a satisfactory answer. He would simply state that when morning arrived, we would be advised in sufficient time to make our arrangements. Doctor Evans, Mr. Snyder and I thought that we should sometimes be consulted;—we were paying the bills and should have some say-so in making the plans. We thought there would be a certain amount of satisfaction in talking them over as we sat in the dining tent after supper enjoying our evening smoke. At one time being particularly anxious as to our course the next day, Doctor, at the suggestion of Mr.

Prince of the peaks. Photo by 'Cap.' Hubric.

Snyder and myself, had ventured to interrogate Bones receiving in substance the following reply:

"When morning comes, Doctor, you will be told in plenty of time so as to get ready."

"But," replied Doctor Evans, "We feel we should have some part in making our plans; in fact, the contemplation of our hunt for the following day is one of the pleasures of the trip, and we think we should be consulted or at least that we have a right to be advised."

"Now, let me tell you once and for all," replied Bones, "I am the man who is responsible for showing you a good time and putting you in sight of game. I propose to give every one of you a square deal. I intend to change your guides every day or so instead of letting one man have the same guide all the time. I know from experience that this is best. I also know from experience that when you leave it to hunters to make their plans and choose their guides, sooner or later there will be dissatisfaction and trouble among them, and also with the guides. Now, as I have told you, I am the man who is responsible for the success of this trip. I will make my plans. Sometimes I can't make up my

A SIDE TRIP FOR SHEEP

mind until in the night when you are all asleep; at times my mind is not fully made up until the following morning. Please do not ask me questions about it after this. You will always be told by the time breakfast is over or by the time the horses are brought in and that will give you plenty of time to get your belongings together."

I afterwards decided Bones was undoubtedly right in this respect. We soon learned that when a command was given there was no opportunity for argument. We did think, however, that it was unfair to the cook, as he was often unable to make his plans concerning baking. Notwithstanding the Jacquot brothers owned half the outfit, Gene never ventured to ask Bones any questions that were not absolutely necessary. Sometimes orders were given after Bones had finished breakfast and lighted his pipe; at other times not until the horses were brought in and saddled. With a gesture of his hand, they were in general about as follows:

"Johnnie, you take Mr. Snyder and hunt the north side of that mountain. Paddie, you take Mr. Young and hunt the southwest side. I will take the Doctor and we will hunt above timber line in this direction. Gene, you and Billy break camp." Then pointing in the distance, "You see that ridge over yonder? You see that range of hills beyond? Then you see them hills or small mountains beyond them? When you cross them, you will find a creek; keep up that creek to the edge of timber line; take the left-hand fork and when you have traveled about two miles, you will find little patches of dwarfed spruces on the right-hand side. Make your camp at the upper edge of the last patch. You will find fire wood there and plenty of pea vine just above. We will be there tonight."

One command was supposed to be sufficient for all; therefore, everyone listened eagerly and seldom asked any questions. The responsibility rested upon Gene and Slimpert to find that exact location and upon the Indians to find the camp at night. It sounded quite plain when the command was given but it did not always work out so easily in the evening, after we had traveled a circuitous route all day. Often these hills and mountains look altogether different at close range. It was sometimes difficult to determine when we arrived on the ground which was the "second" or the "third" ridge. Often there was more than one branch of the creek. Gene and Slimpert sometimes found the patches of dwarfed spruce but no pea vine close by. At other times they found the pea vine but no wood; but they were usually able to locate the spot to which Bones had referred. Once or twice they varied a little from the exact spot and Bones complained very bitterly, expressing much surprise that they should have missed it, when as he said repeatedly, "I told you in language just as plain as it was possible for me to express myself."

The Indians did not take Bones' directions so seriously. They simply traveled as evening approached in the general direction that had been pointed out; then circled about until they found the trail of the pack horses, and tracked them to camp. Upon finding the tracks the Indians could instantly judge how long it had been since they were made. If they thought Gene and Slimpert had had sufficient time to get the tents up and most of the evening work done, they would hurry on; if not, they would suggest some little knoll ahead from which point we might locate game. Aside from their tendency to linger behind on evenings when camp was to be made, we found them very willing and hard workers at all times. Perhaps they were justified in this to some extent, as their work was that of guiding. However, it was often provoking, especially when we were tired, hungry and anxious to reach camp.

On returning to camp that night we found Doctor and Mr. Snyder had hunted all day without seeing any game. Making use of the fat from the caribou killed by Doctor Evans the day before, our cook had made a large box of doughnuts. We had roast caribou for supper—all in all, a very elaborate meal.

I felt highly honored because Bones had made known to me his plans for the following day; and I whispered this information to the other members of our party, including the cook, but asked that it be held in confidence as I did not want Bones to think I had betrayed a trust. The next morning Bones gave his orders as usual, which were received with all seriousness by the members of the party. He told Gene and Slimpert to pack up preparatory to leaving for Ptarmigan Lake, while he would take the hunters and one Indian and go to the carcass of the caribou killed by Doctor Evans two days before, with the hope of finding a bear feeding upon it. The Indian led the way through the scrubby timber until a small creek was reached, when he stopped and announced that we were almost to the place. Doctor suggested that I be given the opportunity for a shot in the event a bear was found. Gladly accepting this courtesy the Indian and I left our horses with the

A SIDE TRIP FOR SHEEP

others and proceeded noiselessly across the creek bar and around the side of the hill. With the wind in our favor we crept over a little knoll until we could see that portion of the carcass which had not been taken for food, and on going close up, we found it had not been disturbed. After coming out in the fall, we learned that the two Mitten brothers of Boston, who had been outfitted by "Cap" Hubrick, happened into this locality a few days later and were successful in killing two grizzlies that were feeding upon this carcass.

Returning to our camping place we found everything was packed and in readiness to start. Crossing the numerous channels of the White River, we traveled down the river bar for a distance, then up through the timber. It was rough going as there was no trail to follow. Most of the horses used good judgment and instead of trying to wedge their way between trees and saplings that stood close together, they very sensibly went around them. The majority seemed able to determine in advance whether or not they could pass between certain trees with their packs. I was amused at one of the horses called "Skookum," which in the Indian language means "strong" or "possessed of great strength." This horse carried our ponderous cook stove on one side counterbalanced by a heavily loaded paniard box on the other. He would wedge his way between two trees and when his load would catch, instead of backing out, he would pull like a horse in harness. If the trees were small they would bend and let him through; otherwise, we had to back him out. He blazed a trail with the corners of the stove and the paniard box that one could have easily followed.

At one time that afternoon I caught sight of a cow moose which trotted away in the timber to our left. It was the first one we had seen. We traveled for several miles up the mountain grade, passing above timber line; then through a low gap in the mountain and down a creek on the other side until a small and beautiful lake was reached. By this time it was almost night and as we were about six miles from our destination we made camp. Several varieties of wild ducks were seen on the lake, while grayling fish were abundant in the clear waters of the creek. It was a beautiful camping place but there was little wood and horse feed. Being afraid the horses might return to the White River where feed was more abundant, Bones told the Indians to take their blankets and go up the creek to a point above the area where the horses were grazing, and spend the night. He told them to listen for the sound of their bells during the night and if they heard them leaving, to head them off. After eating their supper, the Indians took their blankets and a gun, and it was not long until we could see their little camp fire about a mile up the stream.

Gene and Slimpert were told the next morning to pack up and continue on to Ptarmigan Lake where they should use their judgment in selecting a good camping place. Bones planned that we should start out hunting from where we were and in the evening return there, picking up the trail of the pack outfit and following it to camp. Thus far we had not taken the trouble to prepare lunches as we had not been in one place sufficiently long for Gene to have food in readiness. Since Doctor had killed the caribou and I the small ram, we had an abundance of meat which we relished, especially the young ram. From that day on we prepared lunches, each man usually taking two sandwiches made of one or two kinds of meat; two slices of bread spread with butter and orange marmalade, and four large doughnuts. This was sufficient to keep us from becoming extremely hungry until our evening meal.

On giving orders that morning, Bones had stated that we would hunt sheep; that the Indians would accompany Mr. Snyder and Doctor and that he would go with me. I asked him if he was going to take lunch. He first stated he didn't think he would bother with it, but later changed his mind and in an apologetic manner said, "I do not care anything about the lunch but I always enjoy a smoke better when I have had something to eat and I believe I will take a sandwich to make my afternoon's smoke taste better." As a matter of fact, his "afternoon smoke" lasted the entire afternoon. The first thing Bones did upon arising in the morning, was to reach for his pipe, and he seldom took it out of his mouth until he had undressed for bed. In this respect he did not differ from most men of the North country.

Included in the pack outfit was a three-year-old horse that was broken only to carry a pack. A bridle had never been on him, nor anyone on his back. Bones thought it a good time to break this horse, so he mounted and soon had him under control. He told me to take the lead as it was very difficult to guide the young horse. I led the way toward a gap in the mountain about three miles from camp. Upon making our ascent into the gap we saw a band of eleven sheep feeding on the mountain side only

A SIDE TRIP FOR SHEEP

Where only a mountain sheep can go! Photo by 'Cap.' Hubric.

a short distance above. We were surprised to find sheep that low on the mountain. Turning so as to get our horses out of sight we cautiously dismounted. I held the horses while Bones examined the sheep through his binoculars. He said he had never seen as many fine heads in one band before. They were all rams. Three of them had fair horns; five had large ones, while the other three had unusually fine horns. Looking again he centered his gaze on one particular ram of the three largest and stated that it had a head well worth trying for as it was one of the best, if not the best he had ever seen. In the meantime the sheep saw us and started moving up the mountain, first slowly then increasing their speed as they continued. We thought best not to take chances on firing at that distance. The ground ahead of us was so steep we could not proceed farther on horseback, and there was nothing to which we could tie them. We remained quiet until they had passed over the brow of the mountain, then locating a crag of rocks on the other side of a draw, we took our horses there and tied them. A lariat rope was removed from the saddle and used in tying the horses to a large rock.

Knowing we would have a hard climb, I took my coat and heavy woolen overshirt off and hung them on my saddle. Doctor Evans was kind enough to let me use his camera a portion of the time, since mine was ruined when my horse fell off the side of Finger Mountain. I left the camera, together with our lunch, in the small canvas saddle pockets attached to the saddle. We made a circle around the mountain hoping the sheep had stopped

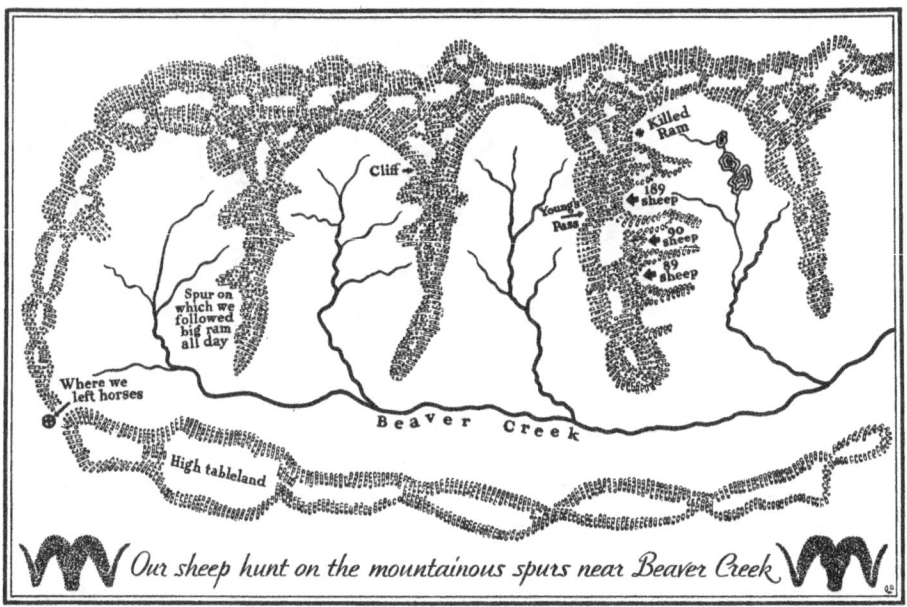

Our sheep hunt on the mountainous spurs near Beaver Creek

above and that we could head them off. Arriving at the top we found they had crossed the bench and gone up the mountain side beyond. We followed and had another hard climb to reach the top but they were nowhere to be seen. The side of this mountain was smooth, with no loose rock or slides—something unusual for that country. The top was level and formed a plateau of perhaps two square miles and was covered with green grass. Notwithstanding our interest in the sheep, we hesitated a little while to admire this beautiful spot. We had no idea of the direction the sheep had taken but we crossed to the opposite side, talking as we went. On reaching the edge of this tableland and looking over, we saw the sheep running rapidly down the mountain. Evidently they had stopped a short distance below the rim and heard our voices as we approached the edge of the plateau. We were very much provoked at our carelessness.

In front of us and perhaps ten miles distant on an airline, a high mountain range stretched from our left to our right as far

A SIDE TRIP FOR SHEEP

as we could see. Spurs, from six to eight miles in length, branched off at right angles from the main range and extended towards us. There were five or six of them and all lay parallel with each other. Their average height was almost equal to that of the main range, and much higher than the mountain on which we then stood. A beautiful stream, which we afterward located on our maps as Beaver Creek, wound its way from the direction of the low gap where we had left our horses. It flowed to our right along the base of the mountain on which we stood, and the end bases of the high mountain spurs which extended from the main mountain towards us, and at right angles to the creek. Deep, narrow valleys lay between these high spurs, and small creeks coursed their way from the head of each to the creek in the main valley below us. All of these mountains were barren and covered with slides of talus rock, appearing to be of volcanic origin. It was a beautiful sight, and we gazed with rapture upon those grand mountains; their granite and limestone slopes carved into canyons and precipices, their crests serrated in rising and falling outlines with occasional high peaks. Here and there great beds of snow and ice glittered in the bright sunlight as they overhung the precipitous sides.

As we stood admiring the beautiful scenery, we kept our eyes on the sheep. Reaching Beaver Creek they crossed and started up the end of one of the highest spurs in front of us. Bones suggested following them; whereupon I asked if he considered the horses safe on the steep mountain side where we had hurriedly left them. He replied that he did not, and that it might be best to return for them; in which event we could ride through the gap and down the slope to Beaver Creek, then continue down that creek and leave the horses at the foot of the spur on which the sheep had just started up. On the other hand, this would require much time and Bones thought we had better take no chances on their gaining too much headway and that it would be advisable to follow them immediately. He said it would be a very hard climb and asked me if I thought I could make it. I replied that I could perhaps go any place that he could, provided he did not push me too hard on the steeper places. We decided to make the attempt, and as I looked at the high spur, I secretly wished for an airplane or some other means to cover the short distance across, instead of being obliged to lose the elevation we had already gained.

ALASKAN-YUKON TROPHIES

It was perhaps more than a mile down to the creek, and after crossing it we started climbing the end of the spur. The sun was shining brightly and it was very warm. We found more mosquitoes than we had encountered at any previous time and they swarmed about us in increasing numbers as we began perspiring profusely from the labor of the hard climb. We fought them off as best we could, but they worked their way up under our hats and into our hair. Bones lowered his mosquito net which he constantly wore draped about his hat, while I produced a net from my pocket and adjusted it. This kept the mosquitoes out, but it limited the supply of air so much needed, that I was later obliged to remove it. Bones was very considerate and often stopped for a short rest and breathing spell. As we gained a higher altitude the mosquitoes became less numerous, and reaching a considerable height we found a good breeze which caused them to disappear altogether.

Fortunately there was no slide rock on the end of the spur and we were able to secure good footholds. At last we reached the top and continued along the comb for two or three miles. I will not give a detailed account of our afternoon's experience in following the sheep from one place to another. We often caught sight of them but were never within shooting distance. Other sheep were located and at times in places that were easily accessible. Bones sometimes stopped to examine them with his glasses but always advised that they were ewes or lambs, or rams having poor heads.

By the middle of the afternoon we were getting quite hungry. Water was not obtainable on the mountain and my tongue was almost parched with thirst after our long climb. I felt somewhat impatient because of Bones' dogged determination to keep relentlessly after the one band of sheep, although I did not let him know it. Later on, as I began to realize more fully the value of unusual trophies, I appreciated Bones' great efforts on this and other occasions to secure extra fine specimens. In this respect the Indians were very much lacking, especially at the beginning of the hunt. In pursuing game their one object was meat for food but they later became more interested in our securing larger trophies as they noted Bones' interest and our success.

As night approached we realized we were a long way from the horses, but Bones never let up. On and on we went until we neared the main mountain from which the spur extended. The

A SIDE TRIP FOR SHEEP

sheep did not travel along the comb of the ridge. Sometimes we caught sight of them in the distance making their way around the crags and cliffs, sometimes on one side then on the other, but always near the top. Having seen nothing of them for quite a while Bones stopped and said we had better return. He stated that we could not even then reach the horses before dark, as they were about nine miles away. After reaching them we would have to go about three miles to the small lake where we had camped the night before and then take up the trail of the pack horses, for five or six miles, to Ptarmigan Lake. We did not intend returning along the crest as we had come but decided to descend to the little creek below, and follow it to Beaver Creek, then up that creek to the low gap. It seemed almost hopeless to try to get down the mountain at that point, or any other place within the limits of our vision, as it was covered with loose slide rock for hundreds of feet below.

We went forward to a saddle or low place in the comb of the mountain ridge and selected a place where we would try to descend. We proceeded cautiously until we reached a great bed of flat slide rock on which it was almost impossible to stand. Looking about we found two or three well worn sheep paths leading diagonally down the mountain. Selecting one of these we again started down, when suddenly we caught sight of a big ram standing on a small crag at the edge of a draw which extended up and down the mountain. Instantly I raised my gun to shoot, as I saw that he was a sheep of immense size and with unusual horns, but he was too quick for me and disappeared in the draw. Bones was certain it was the large ram of the band of eleven we had been following all day, and we could then hear a number of sheep making their way up the draw. They had last been seen on the other side of the mountain and we were surprised to find them at this point. The wind was blowing toward us and as we had been out of their sight, we had approached to within a comparatively short distance without being observed. We could hear the slide rock rattling as they made their way rapidly up the mountain. Had it been feasible, we would have run toward this draw with the hope of getting sight of them, but it was impossible to cross the slide rock. Bones insisted that we retrace our steps up the mountain after the sheep. I told him I was perfectly willing to do so, but felt sorry for the horses which had been on the mountain side, without food or water since early morning. He said,

"To H--- with the horses," and I replied, "All right, they belong to you and if you are willing, I am."

We hurried upward and reached the saddle of the comb from which we had started a half-hour before, but no sheep were to be seen. We looked about for a little while, then continued on the top of the sharp comb for some distance in the direction of the main mountain. We felt certain they had gone down the mountain on the opposite side, yet we could not see them. Presently we saw the entire band of eleven making their way around the head of the basin and almost up to the point where the spur connected with the main mountain ridge. Bones told me to try a few shots with my sights raised as they were then nearly a half-mile away. Sitting down I looked at them through the sights of my gun and saw that a sheep in the distance appeared no larger than the notch in the rear sight. In the meantime Bones had brought his binoculars into use and soon picked out the large ram as the fourth sheep from the front. I fired and Bones told me he was then second from the front. I fired again and he said I was overshooting. I emptied my Newton and reloading it continued firing until the magazine was emptied a second time. Loading again I took careful aim and could see that my shots were hitting quite close. With each shot Bones announced the ram's location in the band—sometimes third from the rear, sometimes the sixth sheep back, and sometimes in other positions. Finally after firing the fourteenth shot, during which time the distance to the sheep was rapidly increasing, we saw him turn out from the band and start running down the hill, and we knew that he was hit. Presently he fell and rolled over several times; then regaining his feet, he started walking slowly around the basin toward a cliff of rock. The remainder of the sheep continued upward and finally went over the main mountain. With our glasses we could see that the large ram had been hit in the left hip and was bleeding profusely. He dragged himself into the cliff and disappeared from sight. Bones, thinking he had been fatally shot, advised leaving him 'til the following day. Under the stimulus of this experience I wanted to recover him before leaving, but Bones said it would take at least an hour to go around the basin to the sheep, and that the walking would be very difficult. He stated also that if we should attempt it, we would be obliged to remain there all night.

A SIDE TRIP FOR SHEEP

We started down the mountain in the same course as before. At one place we encountered a slide of fine loose shale perhaps three or four hundred yards in length and found easy going as it was only necessary to keep tramping and hold our balance while we slid along almost as one would in coasting. Reaching the creek an hour and a half later, we lay down and quenched our thirst since the only water we had had since morning was the drip from a small glacier which overhung the mountain top. We traveled down the creek as rapidly as we could walk until we reached Beaver Creek perhaps four miles below. The days were rapidly becoming shorter, so by nine o'clock it was dark. I dreaded the long climb in the darkness from the source of Beaver Creek to the gap in the mountain where we had left the horses. By the time we reached the head of the creek I was so tired I could hardly proceed. It would have been a very hard day even had we been provided with food

A ram of Boundary Mountain.
Photo by 'Cap.' Hubric.

and water. I was becoming weak from hunger and exhaustion, but hesitated to admit as much to Bones when we paused for rest. I had a horror of the horses being gone and so expressed myself, but he said he did not think they could get away as we had tied them securely. I expressed my pity for them on account of their long wait, without food and water, but he said that they had had it easy compared with us. Finally the constant climbing began to tell on me and at last I said to Bones, "I am all in." He remarked that within a short time we would reach the gap, and upon crossing to the horses on the other side, we would eat our lunch. Summoning all the strength I could command I made a final effort and succeeded in reaching the top. We continued through the gap and around the side of the draw to the cliff where we had left our horses—but they were nowhere to be found!

Chapter X

SCENES NEVER FORGOTTEN

"The summer—no sweeter was ever;
  The sunshiny woods all athrill;
The grayling aleap in the river,
  The bighorn asleep on the hill.
The strong life that never knows harness;
  The wilds where the caribou call;
The freshness, the freedom, the farness—
  O God! how I'm stuck on it all."

THE escape of the horses during our absence was a disappointment, indeed. I felt as though I could not travel farther without rest and food, but we could not remain there; so I forced myself on, Bones leading the way. After going about a mile we heard the nicker of a horse and, proceeding in the direction of the sound, we found the young horse feeding on wild grass. We thought the other horse must be close by and that we could find him in the darkness by his white color, but we were unable to do so.

Reaching the lake about eleven o'clock we looked about until the location of the previous night's camp was found. There was nothing to do but build a fire and remain there until daylight as it was impossible to follow the trail of the pack outfit in the darkness. The young horse was tied while we searched about for wood. It was the coldest night we had experienced and only by groping about in the darkness were we able to find sufficient wood to keep a small fire going. My clothing was damp from perspiration due to the twelve mile walk from the mountain where I had wounded the sheep, and it was not long until I became chilled with the cold. Being without my coat and heavy overshirt I huddled up to the fire as close as possible, but could not sleep as it was necessary for me to change positions frequently in an effort to get warm. Bones fared better as he had worn his hunting coat, and it was not long until he was sound asleep. It was August 24th by which time the nights were becoming colder. Frequently I went in search of wood, and this helped to pass away the uncomfortable hours of that miserable night. Finally the Northern Lights appeared and, notwithstanding my plight, the wonderful and ever changing display in the heavens held my interest and admiration.

At three o'clock it was getting light and I awakened Bones. He got up, untied the horse, and allowed him to graze about for awhile before we started. It was difficult to follow the trail of the pack horses as the ground was white with a heavy frost. The small ponds and rivulets were frozen over and ice had formed along the shoreline of the lake. The exertion of walking soon warmed me, but being stiff and sore from the hard tramp of the day before, I mounted the young horse. He was not bridle-wise, however, and I found walking much easier. Reaching the head of a creek and passing over the divide we soon came in sight of Ptarmigan Lake and could see our tents pitched on a little knoll overlooking this beautiful body of water. It was six o'clock when we reached camp, just as the others were ready to sit down to breakfast. I was so weak from exertion, hunger and exposure that I was almost ready to drop. It had been just twenty-four hours since we had tasted food. Bones said we had walked no less than thirty miles during that time. A tramp of thirty miles a day over an average trail is nothing unusual to one accustomed to long-distance walking, but most of our time had been spent in steep mountain climbing and in toeing our way along the combs of the rugged crests.

Going to the water pail to get a drink before eating I found ice in the bucket. Gene said it had frozen over during the night notwithstanding the bucket was inside the tent. A warm breakfast and a hearty welcome from our party soon revived our strength and spirits. They had been uneasy lest one of us had fallen and broken a limb or met with some other accident.

Bones was of the opinion that Spot had returned to the White River where pea vine was abundant. He, therefore, directed Slimpert and Indian Johnnie to saddle two horses, taking blankets and two days' supply of food, and go in search of the horse. I did not expect to ever again see the Doctor's camera, my mackinaw coat or overshirt, tied to the horn of the horse's saddle; or my diary and some personal items contained in the saddle bags.

After Bones had rested a short time he and Mr. Snyder took a shorter route in the direction of the mountain where I had wounded the sheep. Doctor and Paddie hunted together in the opposite direction, and I spent the forenoon sleeping. I took advantage of the opportunity during the afternoon to do some laundering. That evening Gene confided to me that he was planning a surprise for Mr. Snyder. It was his forty-sixth birthday and Gene was making a large cake in honor of the occasion.

Doctor and Paddie returned with the heads of two large rams, both of which would have been unusual specimens had the points of the horns not been badly broken.

I awaited the return of Bones and Mr. Snyder with much interest. Bones had planned to hunt the side of the mountain on which I had shot the big ram, climbing to the cliff where he had last been seen. Late in the evening they returned with a fair-sized head secured by Mr. Snyder. Bones reported that he had bad news for me. He had taken with him that day his Mannlicher rifle and said Mr. Snyder had used it to kill his ram.

Later Bones took the gun and leaving Mr. Snyder with the horses climbed the mountain for the purpose of "skinning out" my sheep, as he expressed himself. Arriving at the cliff he made his way to the point where the sheep was last seen and there he lay, dead—but suddenly he came to life! The sheep did the "skinning out" instead of Bones. Getting on his feet the ram staggered about. Bones raised his gun to shoot but found that he had forgotten to reload after Mr. Snyder had used it. He fumbled about for cartridges and discovered he had none. He was amazed at the size and curl of the ram's horns and could see that they were even larger and more perfect than he had thought them to be. Discarding his gun he quickly grabbed his hunting knife and leaped forward intending to finish him with it—so determined was he to secure this prize. By this time the ram was getting limbered up and, as Bones leaped forward, the ram did likewise. He ran around the mountain side, Bones after him, at times almost within reach. He could see that the ram was badly wounded but he gradually gained strength as he ran, and Bones had to give up the chase. He regretted his carelessness in having climbed to the cliff with an empty gun, but stated that our chances for getting him next day were good.

I did not let my disappointment interfere with the enjoyment of the sumptuous meal Gene had prepared that evening. The large cake, covered with white icing and surrounded by candles, formed the centerpiece on the table. The meal was quite elaborate, consisting in part of roast caribou with mushrooms, and roast lamb with mint sauce. It was a pleasant surprise for Mr. Snyder.

SCENES NEVER FORGOTTEN

Bones, Mr. Snyder, and I returned to the mountain the next morning with the hope of killing the wounded sheep. Presently we located him low down on the mountain side where he had no doubt come to graze. Bones and I climbed in his direction, leaving Mr. Snyder with the horses. We were unable to approach closer than two hundred and fifty yards without coming directly in his sight. The wind was blowing with such force that I knew it would be impossible to hold my rifle steady. Bones had with him his Mannlicher rifle, loaded to its capacity. I told him to have his gun in readiness and in the event I missed, for him to shoot. Holding my gun as steady as possible under the circumstances, I fired and Bones did likewise, both of us missing. Almost instantly the ram disappeared from sight in a little draw. We ran forward and saw him going out of the draw far down the mountain. We fired two or three more shots, without effect, before he disappeared a second time. We hurried around the mountain as quickly as possible but saw nothing of him, but presently discovered the ram had crossed a little valley to a second spur, which he was covering at a fair rate of speed. We followed for some distance but later gave him up, for the time being, and returned to the horses.

The three of us then rode as high up the mountain as possible and tied our horses to some boulders. Climbing almost to the top of the mountain, which required perhaps an hour, Bones left Mr. Snyder and me, sheltered from the wind, while he finished the ascent and continued along the crest of the mountain until he located the wounded ram. Soon Bones returned for us and we spent the remainder of the day following the ram, but never sufficiently close to get a shot. Three days had already been spent on this animal, therefore, we gave him up, descended to our horses and returned to camp.

Doctor and Indian Paddie had killed a fine young ram that day which, although having a small but good head, was very fat and the meat quite tender.

Billy Slimpert and Indian Johnnie returned that evening with the stray horse; and, very much to our surprise, the camera, mackinaw and overshirt—as well as the saddle pockets, with contents intact—were still attached to the saddle.

I was growing somewhat impatient at my bad luck and was hopeful of getting a good head the next day; so Bones and I started quite early in the morning. We crossed the divide and went

Above: Formations such as this are the habitat of sheep. Inset: One of the camps in 'sheep country.'

to the highest of the several mountain spurs and tying our horses securely, started our two hours' climb at the end of the spur. Considered from every standpoint, this was one of the most interesting days of the entire trip. Until this time I had not found sufficient courage to straighten up and walk along the sharp combs of the mountains, although Bones did so, apparently without fear. Sometimes he had been obliged to wait while I cautiously toed my way along the sides, holding to the crest, very much as one would walk along the sides of an old-fashioned rail fence. On this day I gradually summoned courage and finally was able to straighten up and follow in Bones' footsteps.

    I found that nearly all of the mountains appeared quite different in their contour upon reaching their summits. At times one would hardly recognize them as being the same mountains seen from a distance. This was especially true of the one on which we were traveling. The results of volcanic action were everywhere in evidence. Huge lava beds were crossed; tons of hard flint rock as black as ebony were seen—samples of which I brought home with me. Great slides of talus rock of many colors and shapes extended hundreds, yes thousands of feet down the mountain on either side. Beautiful flowers were seen here and there on the otherwise barren ground. Sometimes they were found growing at the very edge of great patches of snow and ice. At times we discovered small glaciers covering the crest and extending down on either side, like great saddles placed over the mountain. We saw numerous oblong stones, ranging from six to twelve inches in length, and covered with a soft moss that looked and felt like fine velvet. They had the color and appearance of green plush covered pincushions. Many of them were covered with tiny purple flowers growing up through the fine moss, with stems about the length of a pin, and flowers little larger than a pin head. These were probably the fruiting organs of the moss. They were sometimes so thick they almost covered the stones, the purple showing in pleasing contrast to the green moss. What a wonderful sight it was to see these beautiful and delicately tinted flowers growing on top of the wind swept mountain, in places where perhaps no other man had ever set foot and where the surface for a few weeks only is free from snow. I regretted that it was not possible to bring one of these beautiful "pincushions" home with me. I called Bones' attention to them and he said he did not recall ever having seen them before.

We picked our way cautiously around the knife-like edge of the mountain, realizing that a mis-step might result in serious accident,—perhaps death. At times we were obliged to straddle the sharp combs; at other times we toed our way along the side with our guns strapped to our backs, as it was often necessary to use both hands in holding to the sharp, serrated ridges. At other times it was impossible to proceed, and we were obliged to retrace our steps, working our way around the precipitous sides of the mountain some distance below the crest. This was especially true when we were obstructed by overhanging glaciers. When doing so, great slides of flat rock were frequently encountered and crossed with much difficulty. An obstacle which confronts one on the top of a high mountain is the wind which blows almost constantly. There were occasions when it was impossible to walk or even to hold to the crests of the high peaks—so great was the force of the wind. At such times we were forced to the shelter of a cliff or to the opposite side of the crest where we were more or less protected. From the main spurs comparatively short ones extended at right angles. Particularly was this true of the right-hand side of the mountain on which we were traveling. These short spurs formed great gorges like amphitheatres, and there was a fascination in approaching their rims where we could look down into the vast depths below.

Topping a sharp peak we came in view of the largest amphitheatre we had seen. With our binoculars we discovered below the upper limit of vegetation a large band of sheep. Most of them were ewes and lambs while three large rams, located some distance above the others, were on sentinel duty. Presently we discovered a ewe and a small ram also on sentinel duty on the opposite side at about the same height. We watched them with much interest as they turned their heads first one way and then the other, always on the alert for any sign of danger. They were safe so far as we were concerned, as the walls of the gorge were so steep no one could descend within shooting range. We counted them two or three times and found that there were eighty-nine sheep in that gorge. Continuing we passed the short spur which divided that amphitheatre from the next, and to our surprise we found about an equal number of sheep occupying a relative position to those in the amphitheatre just passed. We counted ninety in that band, of which some four or five were also doing sentinel duty above the line of vegetation. After studying them carefully with our glasses we decided none of them had a desirable head. We were impressed with the similarity of these two gorges,—the general contour, formation of the rock walls, and their color effect, being almost identical.

We followed along the main ridge for a short distance until we could command a view of the left side of the mountain. Bones said large rams were not usually found with the ewes and lambs at that time of year, but that they would not be far distant and thought we might locate some on this side. Making a careful survey with our glasses, we discovered three large rams, with splendid horns, lying sunning themselves, far down the mountain side. There were no gulleys or draws which we might take advantage of in approaching them; therefore, we had no means of getting within shooting range without being detected. Finally Bones decided to return along the crest and take advantage of a draw which extended down the mountain some distance back. He told me he would go down this draw until he was below the rams and fire a shot, which would likely start them up the mountain, in my direction. I stationed myself behind a large boulder where I was sheltered from the wind and in about three-quarters of an hour heard Bones shoot. Instantly I saw the rams spring to their feet and start running, quartering up the mountain to my right. From their course I concluded they would cross the mountain perhaps a mile beyond me. I debated in my mind the advisability of working in that direction or making a long range shot from where I stood, but decided on the latter course. When they reached a point which I thought was as close as they would come to me, I fired at one of them and saw that he was hit. They hesitated for a moment and I fired a second and third shot, but without success. I then hurried along the comb of the ridge with the hope of getting a shot at them as they topped the mountain.

During our entire trip I was impressed with the fact that an accident to one of us would not only mar our pleasure, but would interfere with or possibly terminate our expedition. As I made my way along the mountain crest, I realized caution on my part was of greater importance then a shot at the sheep; therefore, tried to use great care. At places the rocks which composed these serrated, knife-like edges were eroded and carved by the elements until sharp irregular projections protruded upward like the teeth of a comb.

Often I could proceed only by toeing along the sides with the gun strapped to my back. Presently I saw that the crest was widening into a tableland, perhaps a half-mile in length, which broadened to an almost equal width. Surprised to find a level area on top of this mountain, I made all possible haste across the barren, rock covered surface to the opposite side, and looking down, saw a low pass in the mountain, used as a sheep crossing. Commanding a good view I soon discovered the rams had crossed and were already far down the precipitous side of a still larger basin than any we had seen. I saw only two of them and concluded the wounded one had been unable to proceed. Upon going down into the saddle I observed many trails on either side, all converging into one well-worn trail which crossed the pass. By this time I was more interested in this great amphitheatre than I was in the rams that had already passed out of reasonable shooting distance down its slopes.

ALASKAN-YUKON TROPHIES

I was startled at the scene which lay before me and as I studied the surroundings, saw that I was standing on the rim of what had been the crater of a volcano. Projecting spurs formed a large circular basin, perhaps two thousand feet deep. Crags sculptured by the elements descended in vertical cliffs many hundreds of feet, and from the foot of these cliffs loose slide rock extended down the barren sides hundreds of feet farther. The variegated colors of the cliffs and slides gradually blended into soft green pastures still farther down, and the entire basin opened into a green valley beyond. In the valley three beautiful lakes glistened in the sunlight, all of them drained by a stream of clear water which appeared in the distance as a silver thread. On the other side of the valley dark green, scrubby spruces extended up the mountain and gradually ran out. Farther up and to the right large glaciers overhung the mountain top; and from them muddy colored streams, running at flood tide, emptied their waters into the clear stream of the valley. In the distance I could see the great contrast in the colors of the water.

The basin below contained strata of granite, grey and white limestone, and deep orange colored formations; while other strata were a beautiful rose color—all of them blending with the dark colored rock of the shadowed area below and the soft green of the pastures still farther down. A small glacier overhung the crest a short distance from where I stood, with its color in sharp contrast to the rich red of the iron stained cliffs directly beneath. I stood just below the crest of the mountain where I was protected from the wind. Not a sound reached my ear, except the trickle of the water from the ice and snow close by, where I quenched my thirst. The sky was cloudless; the whole landscape appeared to be hushed and still, and a deep peace breathed over the entire region. I experienced a sense of loneliness as I gazed upon that immense chasm and the multitude of towering heights beyond; but it was a joyful loneliness brought about by the silence and the indescribable desolation. I felt a great desire that all my friends and comrades of the outdoors, and everyone who loves Nature, might share with me the deep emotion and pleasure of that moment, and hoped the picture of it would never leave me.

In the green pastures below I discovered many sheep, which added much to the impressiveness and wildness of the scene. Scanning the basin with my glasses I saw it was by far the largest band we had found. Some of the sheep were feeding peacefully

Mr. Snyder, and the ram which rolled some distance down the slide.

at the upper edges of the grassy slopes, while others were doing sentinel duty farther up and in positions which would enable them to notice any approaching danger. I sat down and watched them for a half-hour and saw that the two rams continued down, but instead of joining the others, stopped some distance above and stood like statues. I thought of trying to climb down to within shooting distance, but was in doubt as to whether the descent could be made. Suddenly, and without any apparent cause, I heard a crashing noise, and looking in the direction from which the sound came, saw a large stone start rolling down the slope. I was interested to see what effect, if any, this would have on the sheep. The two rams, not having recovered from their recent fright, ran wildly down the mountain, but the others took little notice of the stone as it landed in a small gorge above them. No doubt they regarded it as a natural occurrence. About this time I looked up and saw Bones coming down from the edge of the high tableland into the saddle. When he reached me he stated that I had badly wounded one of the three rams fired upon, and that it had made its way to the foot of a cliff to lie down. He suggested, therefore, that we return that way. I then called his attention to the sheep in the basin below and after watching them for awhile we made two or three careful counts and found there were a hundred and eighty-nine, making a total of three hundred and sixty-eight sheep we had seen in the three adjoining basins. There were several large rams among them, all of which were separated in groups to themselves. We tried to devise some plan whereby we could get within shooting distance of the large rams, but were obliged to give it up as it was impossible to descend the steep slopes. Even so we could not have approached within shooting distance without attracting their attention. Bones suggested that I fire two or three shots at a point below the sheep with the hope that they would not locate the direction of the sound and upon hearing the bullets strike below them, would start up the mountain. I did so and it had the desired effect, as eight of the large rams, in a group to themselves, started climbing directly toward us, while the others stood at attention. It looked as though the rams were coming to the pass where we stood, but they stopped. I fired again and both groups started slowly up the mountain, only to stop again as if undecided. I fired a third shot and by that time their minds were evidently made up and they started the long ascent, the rams directly towards us and the

SCENES NEVER FORGOTTEN

others to our right and up what appeared to be the steepest walls of the basin. Leaving the line of vegetation the ewes and small rams were soon working their way up the rock slides, then up the barren rock walls above, which seemed impossible of ascent.

The hour that we watched them stands out in my memory as one of the most interesting experiences in my life. They traveled in single file, led by an old ewe. Now and then she would hesitate for two or three minutes to "stop, look and listen" as she probably believed in safety first. When she stopped the entire procession halted and they all looked nervously about. The moment she started the others did likewise, moving in single file and as close to each other as they could walk. In the distance they appeared to stick to the sides of the barren mountain like flies to a wall. Their course was in a zigzag manner instead of directly upward. Through our glasses, however, we could see that the course chosen by the old ewe was along well defined trails. On the rock slides or up the stretches of shale these trails were well worn, but among the cliffs or on solid rock they were not visible. I thought of the many years that this same trail had been used by sheep in times of danger or when crossing to the opposite side of the mountain.

The hundred and eighty-one sheep looked like a long flexible white line bending and twisting its way among the cliffs. Quite often they formed the letter "S." Sometimes when sharp angles were turned they formed the letter "Z"; and at one time as they passed over an overhanging crag and down the other side, they formed a perfect horseshoe. As they neared the top we concealed ourselves behind a rock, about fifty yards from the pass, where we thought they would cross. When the leaders reached the top they hesitated for some time, as if undecided in their course. What a wonderful picture they made as they stood there silhouetted against the sky line not more than fifty yards from us; and how greatly I regretted I did not have a camera! On this and numerous other occasions I realized that a second camera on an expedition of this kind is as essential as a second gun. Doctor Evans had very kindly allowed me to carry his Kodak a portion of the time, but it seemed that when the greatest opportunities for securing unusual pictures were presented I was always without it. Mr. Snyder had a small camera with him but only a limited number of films. We unanimously agreed that if we should make another trip to this country, the selection of an adequate number of cameras would receive greater consideration than the selection of guns.

The sheep stood motionless except that they occasionally turned their heads about as if undecided in their course. Not a large ram was among them, so we did not molest them. At first

Left: Mr. Snyder inspects a goat which fell to his rifle. Right: A silvery creek marks the bottom of a rugged valley.

it looked as though they would cross the saddle and come directly by the rock which concealed us, but presently they started up the divide to the tableland above, where they stopped on its edge for a short time, then passed out of sight.

We next turned our attention to the group of large rams which had stopped far below us. Going to the edge we looked over and saw them start running up the mountain to our left. We were at a loss to understand the cause of their fright as we had not made the slightest noise and felt certain they had not seen us. We then noticed that the sun cast our shadows down the mountain side, which had frightened them and caused them to run toward the left side of the amphitheatre. Seeing that they were traveling briskly, we hurried along the crest expecting to head them off when they reached the top, but we had a high peak to cross and were a little too late for they had crossed the rim into the next basin—although they were yet within long range shooting distance. We had traveled on the left side of the mountain comb so as to keep out of their sight and to avoid casting shadows below. The wind was blowing so hard on that side of the ridge that my hands were soon numbed with the cold and, as I raised my gun, it was with difficulty that I operated it. I fired three shots at the ram with the largest head. At the third shot he fell and rolled a short distance down the slide, then over a cliff, and out of sight. In the meantime the other rams started running around the amphitheatre and disappeared from view behind some crags. It would have been impossible for us to descend on the flat slide rocks down the almost perpendicular walls of the basin, had it not been for the well worn sheep trails which we used. Reaching the cliff we found the wounded ram had regained his feet, so I fired again and he rolled several hundred feet, landing on a ledge below. I did not shoot again, for since he was lying lengthwise toward us, I was afraid the bullet might strike his horns. Furthermore, I was already alarmed over the possibility of running short of ammunition and did not want to use a cartridge unnecessarily. After watching him for a few moments, we saw he was dead.

The sun was quite low and we thought it inadvisable to descend to the ram that evening, so we retraced our course to the top of the spur, then around the ridge to the well worn sheep crossing in the saddle, which Bones designated as "Young's Pass." It was too late to return by way of the cliff, where Bones earlier in the afternoon had last seen the wounded ram. We began our descent at that point, taking advantage of one of the numerous sheep trails leading down the slide. We were two and three-quarter hours walking from the Pass to the horses—an hour and a half of that time being required to descend the mountain. It was long after dark when we reached the horses, and we had to ride about six miles to our camp on Ptarmigan Lake, the last two miles being through thick scrubby timber. A matter of much interest to me was the ability of the cayuses to retrace their course at night. It was very dark and we could do nothing but let them find their way, which they did apparently with as much ease as a dog would follow a scent. It was midnight when we reached camp, but Gene arose and prepared supper, which included cold ptarmigan.

Chapter XI

CAUGHT IN A STORM

*"Have you seen God in His splendors, heard the text
    that nature renders?
    (You'll never hear it in the family pew.)
The simple things, the true things, the silent men who
    do things—
Then listen to the Wild—it's calling you."*

THE morning following the sheep hunt Pinto was taken along, as we felt certain there would be two good heads to bring in. We left the horses well up toward the head of the creek, close to where we had descended the previous evening. Soon after starting up the mountain we sighted eight fine rams feeding in a cove at the head of the creek, perhaps two miles distant. Bones inspected them for some time with his telescope and concluded they were of the band of eleven rams we had followed during our first day's sheep hunt. I was entitled to kill one more ram in Alaskan Territory, so we decided to try for one of the larger heads in this band. Their location was only a short distance up the mountain and our chances of approach were quite favorable—but the unexpected often happens in hunting big game. We went back to the creek bed where the color of our clothing blended with that of the rock and gravel, and cautiously made our way to within a quarter of a mile of the rams, when we discovered a band of twelve or fifteen small sheep feeding at the head of the creek directly below the rams. We thought we would be detected by the small sheep before we could get within shooting distance of the rams, but there was no other means of approach. Crouching low we moved on as quickly as possible, but we did not go far before they saw us and started running around the cove, while the rams immediately headed up the mountain. Notwithstanding the fear of running short of ammunition, I fired ten or twelve shots, but with little hope of success at that great distance. After they disappeared over the skyline, we gave them up and returned to start our long climb up the mountain.

It was the hottest day experienced on the entire trip and we could see heat waves as they were reflected from the barren rocks

CAUGHT IN A STORM

above us. There is a general impression that it is continuously cold in Alaska, but this is not true. There are days when the heat is almost unbearable; and this was one of them, as the sun shone directly on us from a cloudless sky. I had left my coat and heavy overshirt with the horses, and it was not long until I was forced to unfasten my clothing, so as to admit as much air as possible. We found the loose earth and shale had thawed only a few inches below, while the ground underneath was still frozen hard. It was difficult to obtain footholds as the surface gave way with almost every step, exposing the frozen ground and, occasionally, small areas of ice beneath. Presently we found a sheep trail, which made the ascent easier, until a cliff of rocks was encountered. At first we did not think it possible that sheep had gone up and down this cliff but upon investigation there was every evidence they had done so. In order for us to get up, Bones would climb a short distance and I would hand him the guns, and then follow. We repeated this operation several times until the top of the cliff was reached, all the time keeping in the sheep trail as shown by hair on the rocks and by other distinct signs.

At this elevation we noticed quite a difference in the atmosphere. There was a stiff breeze and it was much cooler. Farther up we could see clouds gathering rapidly. In a few minutes it started to rain, and it was not long until it was coming down in such torrents that we were as wet as if we had fallen into a river. Reaching "Young's Pass" Bones thought it was unnecessary for both of us to go down into the gorge to get the head of the sheep killed the evening before, and told me he would go alone. I knew I could not wait there in the cold wind and told Bones I would climb to the flat, and go to a large rock which I had seen the day before where I would be sheltered from the wind. I watched Bones make his way down the steepest part of the gorge, and then I climbed toward the level area above. Soon I was overtaken by a violent hail storm, and the large stones beat down on me with such terrific force that I became alarmed. Presently it changed to snow and I found myself in such a blinding snow storm that I considered it dangerous to proceed up the sharp crest, so waited until it abated. When starting again, I found it difficult to proceed because of the strong wind which chilled me to the bone. What a contrast it was to the extreme heat from which we had suffered in the valley, and for some distance up the mountain, only two or three hours before! Quite naturally one becomes very warm and perspires freely when making such climbs and after reaching the top soon becomes chilled, and feels the need of additional clothing. However, I disliked being burdened with a single ounce of unnecessary weight, as ounces become pounds on such occasions. Ordinarily, I chose to suffer the discomforts of high altitudes rather than the inconvenience of carrying extra clothing on such climbs, but on this occasion I found myself in a bad way. Hurrying across the flat mountain top, I sought the shelter of the rock, but the wind blew with equal force on all sides. I jumped about in an effort to keep my blood in circulation as the cold was almost unbearable. It was not long until it ceased snowing and I could see the fog lifting from the valley on each side. It was a beautiful sight and looked like a vast body of water, the rolling fog resembling large waves, while the crests of other mountains about me appeared as islands on the opposite sides. When the fog reached the top, it was so dense I could see but a few feet away. I knew that if it continued it would be difficult for Bones to find me or for us to get off the mountain that evening, but it soon lifted and the atmosphere became clear. My discomfort was great, as my wet clothing clung closely to my body, while my teeth chattered from the cold and exposure. The time dragged by slowly; one hour passed, then two, and I could not help feeling some fear that Bones had met with an accident while descending the amphitheatre in the blinding snow storm.

Noticing the wind was drying my outer clothing, it occurred to me that if I would remove them, my undergarments would soon become dry. I realized that it would be quite cold, but preferred enduring this increased discomfort for a little while, rather than wet clothing during the entire evening. With fingers numbed by the cold I removed my outer garments, and going to a level place, ran and jumped about in an effort to get warm, while the wind was drying my exposed undergarments. Suddenly it occurred to me that if Bones were to catch sight of me in my present condition, he would be justified in thinking I had become demented! I went up to the large rock, and getting my field glasses, looked in the direction Bones would come. I was surprised to see him standing at the farther edge of the flat—his glasses raised to his eyes—and looking toward me. Seeing that I was watching him, he returned them to the pocket of his hunting coat, and as he stooped over and raised up, I saw that he

CAUGHT IN A STORM

A beautiful campsite on Beaver Creek.

had the sheep's head. Before he reached me, my underclothing was dry and I had finished dressing. When he approached I saw that he was laughing heartily. He stated that on reaching the flat he had noticed a white object moving about in the distance; that it did not look like a sheep, yet he could not figure out what it was. With his glasses he discovered the nature of the object, but could not yet understand why I would be moving about in such a plight. Quite naturally this experience was related in camp and was the cause of much amusement thereafter. However, I shall say in passing, that I paid dearly for the experience, as I contracted a heavy cold—the only one in all my hunting and camping experience.

Bones found the sheep where we had left it the evening before. It was a good head, and with a single exception, one of the largest secured on the trip. The horns were thirty-seven inches in length, with about two inches broken from each of their ends. They had good curves and unusually heavy bases. Bones had a difficult time getting up the mountain with the head, as it weighed, with its scalp, fully thirty-five pounds; and together with his gun made an unhandy load. However, he had worn his hunting coat and had not suffered from the exposure. We retraced our course of the day before along the comb of the mountain, and descended to the cliff where Bones had last seen the other sheep which I had wounded. Fortune was with us again for there we found him lying dead. His horns were not as large as those of the other one, but were well shaped and not broken at the points. We skinned him from the shoulder to the head—as is the usual custom—and since it was almost dark, each of us took a head and started down the mountain.

I was in high spirits. Only those who have suffered such discomforts; dangerous climbs over lofty mountains; going without food; lying out all night, and experiencing exposures such as I had during the past week, can appreciate the rewards of such persistent efforts. There is no other animal on the American continent so wary and so hard to procure as the mountain sheep. When their heads are seen on exhibition in museums or elsewhere, it is reasonable to assume someone has put forth great efforts, undergone hardships, and perhaps risked life and limb to secure them.

When we reached the horses we fastened the heads to Pinto's saddle and started to camp. Two or three times while going through the scrubby timber the young horse which Bones was riding seemed undecided as to his course in the darkness. Bones did not attempt to guide him but rode with a loose rein, depending upon the horse to retrace our course of the morning. As the horse continued to hesitate and look about as though undecided, Bones lost patience and cursed him in his usual manner. Little Pinto—evidently disgusted—finally ran in front of him of his own accord, put his nose to the ground, and after scenting about in the manner that a dog searches for a trail, started off in a trot, never hesitating until camp was reached at midnight. It was another exhibition of the unusual intelligence of this horse.

I was pleased the next morning to hear Bones give orders to move camp from Ptarmigan Lake to a point more convenient to the mountain spurs, where it seemed most of the sheep were to be found. He and I had been going early and late for several days, with little sleep or rest, and much of the time had been spent traveling some five or six miles to and from camp. He ordered one of the Indians to assist in moving the camp and the other one to accompany Mr. Snyder, while he went with Doctor Evans and me.

Crossing a marshy place on the mountain side that morning, my horse mired down so quickly, with his left front foot, that he fell. I did not have time to jump or remove my feet from the stirrups; and in falling, my left leg was caught under him. He plunged about for a few moments trying to get up but was unable to do so. I disengaged my right foot from the stirrup and tried to get out from beneath him, but could not. In the meantime Bones hurried forward and was soon at the horse's head to keep him quiet, fearing he might cripple me in his struggles to get up. Using all the strength I could command, and with Bones' assistance, I finally succeeded in extricating myself from beneath the horse, and my uncomfortable position in the mire. As the ground was quite soft where the horse fell, being composed of quicksand and volcanic ash, I was none the worse for my experience, other than a good wetting on my left side. Removing the boot and woolen socks from my left foot, I poured the water from the boot; and wrung out the socks, then tying them to the horn of my saddle, I rode with one bare foot while they were drying.

We located two rams during the day. After stalking them for some time, we succeeded in reaching a position above them, within easy shooting distance. Crawling forward Bones looked down on them and advised that only one had a good head, the other having only one horn. Rising quickly Doctor began firing, whereupon the ram started running, but he succeeded in bringing him down at the third shot.

We found our camp that evening, located between the foothills of the mountains, and by the side of a beautiful stream of clear water. Scrubby spruce trees extended a short way up the hills and all in all it was the most desirable camping place we had found, for we had an abundance of wood.

We changed guides the next day, Bones going with Doctor Evans; Indian Johnnie with Mr. Snyder, and Indian Paddie with me. Billy Slimpert had expressed a desire to hunt sheep that day and accompanied us. Traveling up a small valley we saw rams on the mountain side, some distance ahead of us and to our left. There was no way of approach except in plain view of them. I thought this would be impossible but the Indian said it could be done. We hitched our horses in a small clump of willows and started up the creek bed in their direction. We hoped to reach the foot of the bluff on which they were located without being detected. Never have I seen such skill in stalking game as the Indian displayed. We followed the bed of the little creek, which was then dry, stooping low and keeping behind the banks. But soon they became so low we were obliged to get down and crawl upon the ground. Farther up the creek bed ran out altogether, and having no protection whatever, we lay

At timber line in the foothills of Mt. Nazahat. Holmes Creek in the foreground; the White River, six to eight miles in the background.

flat. Using our elbows, we "wormed" our way forward for several hundred yards. The Indian, with his keen sight, watched the rams on sentinel duty. He could tell when they were looking in our direction. When they turned their heads toward us, the Indian would instantly stop. We were fully an hour reaching the foot of the bluff—where we were out of sight of the sheep—and it was a relief to stand erect again after the strain we had endured.

Leaving Billy at the foot of the mountain, the Indian and I started climbing, taking advantage of a draw where we were concealed from the view of the sheep. Reaching the head of the draw we crawled upward with great caution. The Indian was in the lead, with his hat off, and when we were almost on the crest of the ridge, he motioned for me to remain quiet while he stealthily made his way forward and peeped over at the sheep. After watching them a few moments to ascertain which had the best head, he returned as cautiously as he had gone forward, and in a whisper, told me of the location of the best ram. Approaching the crest as he had done, I looked over and saw the sheep were quite restless; so I quickly raised to my knees and was about to take aim at the largest ram, when I fell sideways and rolled over a time or two before I could regain my balance. I had not noticed I was directly over a gopher hole, which caved in under my right knee, causing me to fall when I raised to shoot. After getting up I fired twice at what appeared to be the largest of the fleeing rams, before they disappeared in a

CAUGHT IN A STORM

gully. We hurried in the direction they had gone and a few minutes later, seeing them topping the mountain far above us, concluded it was not worth while to follow them. I was thoroughly disgusted with my unfortunate experience, more so after the Indian had led us in such a difficult but successful stalk.

On returning to camp that evening we found that Mr. Snyder had killed a ram having a very good head. Bones and Doctor had seen several sheep during the day but had not succeeded in getting within shooting distance. It was evident the large rams of that locality had become disturbed by our several days' hunting and had moved farther back into the still larger and more inaccessible mountains. Bones decided the next morning to return at once to the White River. I was very glad of this as I was quite stiff from several days of hard climbing, and preferred less strenuous hunting for a time.

Taking the Indians, Mr. Snyder, Doctor and I started in advance of the pack train. Crossing over a high hill we stopped in a low gap for a few minutes, when Mr. Snyder caught sight of two large bull moose feeding close to the shore of a small lake below us. Drawing his gun from the scabbard he started in their direction, and Doctor concluded to accompany him. I watched these monster animals with much interest, first with my naked eyes, then through my glasses. One of them had an unusually large spread of horns and the other one was fairly good. Scrubby timber covered the hillside to within a short distance of where they stood, and I hoped it would enable my companions to get within shooting distance before they were alarmed; but was doubtful, as they appeared restless. Presently the bulls walked to the edge of the lake and stopped for a moment. I heard two shots from below and saw the moose plunge into the water, apparently unharmed. It was a wonderful sight to see those animals swim the lake, which at that point was about four hundred yards wide. When they reached the farther side they disappeared in a clump of timber. On their way back, Mr. Snyder and Doctor saw a moose with a still larger head, but were unable to get a shot at him before he reached the timber.

Reaching the bar of the White River that evening we were surprised to find so great a change in the foliage during our nine days' absence. The frost had done its work; the leaves had taken on a different color and the entire landscape had been transformed. The willows growing along the bar were now a pale yellow, while the clumps of cottonwood were a beautiful golden shade. It was August twenty-ninth and we realized from the chill in the atmosphere and the appearance of the foliage, that it would not be long until the short autumn season of that country would pass and cold weather would be upon us. We had made our plans to reach White Horse by October first. Allowing one week in which to make the trip, from the point where we would end our hunt, we had only three and a half weeks left for hunting and we wanted to make good use of the time.

We camped that night on what is known as North Fork Island, and arose the next morning to find the mountains and hillsides as far down as timber line, covered with fresh snow. Down in the valley it was raining so hard that we spent the day in camp.

All of us started moose hunting the next morning—Bones with Doctor and the Indians with Mr. Snyder and me. After traveling up the timbered slopes for several miles we separated, Johnnie going with Mr. Snyder. It started snowing about noon and continued the rest of the day. Reaching a point a short distance above timber line, Paddie and I stopped a little while, and saw two cow moose below us. After watching them a short time, we discovered a bull farther down the mountain and about two hundred and fifty yards away. The Indian insisted that I shoot immediately, exclaiming excitedly, "Him big moose! him get way soon!" But I hesitated until I could examine his horns. Looking at them through my glasses, I concluded he had a spread of about forty-five inches and that his horns were not entirely free of the velvet, which hung from them in loose strips. The bull walked from one tree to another, rubbing his horns and hooking the bushes, in a frantic effort to rid them of the strips of velvet which seemed to annoy him.

I was undecided what to do. I disliked killing a moose having a spread smaller than fifty inches, yet realized that I might not be able to get larger heads and perhaps I had better try for this one. The Indian was very much excited and still insisted that I should shoot. I took into consideration that we were fully ten miles from camp, and as it was snowing very hard, it would be a disagreeable task to take the head in with us that night. To return for it the next day meant a long hard

CAUGHT IN A STORM

trip for a comparatively small head, so I concluded to pass him up. The Indian then made a peculiar guttural noise and none of the moose lost any time in getting out of sight. Paddie surmised the bull would make a large circle around the spur on which we stood, and being interested in the Indian's prediction,

Loading sheep meat on saddle horses.

I went to the top of the hill and watched. In about fifteen minutes I saw him traveling at a good rate of speed in about the direction the Indian had said. Our disagreeable ride back to camp, which was reached long after dark, had been compensated for by the interesting experience of watching the moose.

Crossing to the south side of the White River the next morning, Paddie and I rode for miles through the timber into the tundra above timber line. With my glasses Paddie located caribou tracks in the snow some two or three miles farther up in the foothills; and we traveled in that direction, leading our horses, as it was too steep to ride. When only a short distance from the point where we had seen the tracks, Paddie caught sight of a grizzly bear feeding at the edge of timber line far below us. We each took a turn looking at him through the glasses, and saw that he was very large. After making our plans, we hitched our horses to some scrubby alders and moved around the mountain to a point where the wind was more favorable and where we could descend without being in plain sight of the bear.

I still felt the effect of my several days' strenuous mountain climbing and my right knee was so stiff it was with great difficulty and much pain that I traveled down the steep grade. The surface was covered with low birch and blueberry bushes and because of my inability to raise my right foot, I was forced to drag it through them, thereby making considerable noise as we hurried on. The Indian stopped and told me I should lift my feet high and not make so much noise. When I tried to comply with his request the pain was so great I could not keep up with him. I then insisted that we take more time and travel quietly, under the circumstances, which we did during the remainder of the distance. We had taken careful note of the place where the bear had been seen and nearing the spot, we advanced cautiously around a little knoll—my gun to my shoulder ready to fire. But a great disappointment awaited me. When we came in sight of the place—which was about fifty yards away—no bear was to be seen. We went to the edge of the timber, where we found from his tracks that he had heard or "winded" us, and had gone down the mountain and through the timber at a good rate of speed. The Indian was of the opinion that the bear had heard me dragging my lame leg through the low bushes, and in this he was probably correct. It was useless to follow him, and there nothing to do but to make another long tiresome climb to our horses. When we reached them we decided it was too late to follow the caribou tracks.

That morning Bones had directed Gene and Billy to pack up and travel down the river to the mouth of Holmes Creek; then up that creek for five or six miles to a designated point, where camp should be made. The Indian was not familiar with the territory; therefore, had little idea of the direction of the camp. Feeling we would have difficulty in finding it, he decided to go directly to the White River, find the tracks of the pack horses and follow them to camp, notwithstanding the distance would be much greater. When we arrived at the river we rode down the bar several miles and before reaching the mouth of Holmes Creek found their tracks.

CAUGHT IN A STORM

The width of the creek bar from the edge of timber on one side, to the edge on the other, was almost a mile. The area between was a bed of rock over which travel was difficult. This bar is entirely covered by the glacial floods of spring and summer, although the creek at its normal stage, averages only twenty feet in width. Numerous tree trunks and large boulders were scattered about the bar, as a result of the tremendous force of the floods.

We walked and led our horses the last two or three miles as it was becoming too cold to ride. Just as it was getting dark we heard several shots close by, and looking across the bar, saw a bull moose coming toward us. I raised my gun to fire but the bull was already staggering. Another shot rang out and the moose fell. On going over we discovered Mr. Snyder had the honor of killing the first moose on the trip. We found we were in sight of our camp, and that Johnnie had stepped out to wash his hands, when he saw the moose crossing the bar only a short distance above. Hurrying into the tent where the others were eating supper, he told them to bring their guns quickly, whereupon Mr. Snyder ran out and started firing. The Indians removed the moose's entrails but postponed skinning him until morning.

Bones assigned Indian Johnnie to me the next day, and this was to be our first hunting experience together. Paddie told him about the caribou tracks we had seen the day before and we decided to return to that locality. We did not take our horses but went afoot through the forest. Soon after starting, the Indian discovered an unusually large moose track which we followed for two hours before we finally gave up and decided to try for the caribou. The snow that had fallen two days before had melted in the lowlands and timber but was plentiful above timber line, so that the caribou tracks were easily located. After following the tracks for two or three miles we caught sight of the caribou, eleven in number, well up against the mountain side and across a deep gorge from where we stood. There appeared to be only one way of reaching them; that was to climb to the head of the gorge, cross a small glacier and descend to within shooting distance on the other side.

After much slipping and sliding we reached the glacier, which was crossed with difficulty, and approached to within shooting range of the caribou. I was somewhat winded and requested the Indian to wait a few moments until I could recover. We then got down on our hands and knees and crept forward in the snow. The animals were herded close together, pawing the snow for the caribou moss that lay underneath. The great array of horns presented an attractive sight—not unlike small, dead tree tops—and I could not refrain from watching them for a few moments. Selecting the only large bull among them, I rose to my feet and fired. As they ran down into a ravine, then up the steep slope beyond, I saw that he was hit. I fired two or three more shots, using care not to wound any of the others. Presently the large bull dropped back and I was able to make a good shot, whereupon he fell, sliding down the surface of the snow in toboggan fashion, until he reached the gully some two or three hundred feet below. He had a fairly good head, having about forty-inch beams and thirty-two points.

We removed the entrails from the caribou and started for camp, as it was getting late. I noticed that when walking the Indians always wanted to reach camp by dark. In fact, they seemed to have a horror of being caught out after night, evidently for fear of meeting a grizzly. We were walking around the mountain above timber line at a good rate of speed, when the Indian suddenly stopped and pointed below. I turned my head quickly and saw a caribou with a fair set of horns, standing at the edge of timber not more than seventy-five yards away. I quickly fired and the caribou fell. It could not have been ten seconds from the time the Indian stopped so abruptly until I fired and the caribou was down. His horns were not as large as those of the first bull, but were a nice size for a trophy to be used in my home. We removed his entrails also and left him until the following day. When we reached camp I was rather tired after my long day's tramp, but felt well repaid for my efforts.

Billy Slimpert went with Indian Johnnie and me the next day to get the caribou heads and such portions of the meat as we might want to bring in. We rode horseback, and took two pack horses. Gene had said he would keep us supplied with doughnuts if we would maintain at camp a store of fat from the animals killed. We were, therefore, careful to take in all the fat from the two caribou. Reaching camp, the remainder of the day was spent in skinning the heads and removing the flesh.

CAUGHT IN A STORM

There is much work in connection with the proper preparation of game heads, and as we were securing trophies almost every day, there were few idle moments to be spent. The skin from the shoulders forward—the cape—is removed in one piece, great care being taken in skinning the ears and around the eyes and nose. The head, with cape attached, was then brought to camp, where one could work to better advantage. It is highly important that the brains be removed and all flesh scraped from the skin.

On this expedition, the skulls of the moose and caribou were split lengthwise with a meat saw, leaving one-half of each skull attached to an antler. This method enabled the men to load the trophies to better advantage when packing the horses. Skulls so split would later be wired together by the taxidermists. We had supplied ourselves with triplicate-numbered tags, made from scraps of leather and bearing our initials. These we attached, one to each skull, or in the case of moose and caribou, to the half-skull, and the other to the cape, so the items could be matched when they reached the taxidermist.

One of the first things to do after reaching a camping-place is to stretch lines on which to dry the scalps. The trophies of many a big game hunt have been spoiled by lack of knowledge, or lack of attention, in properly caring for them. Bones and his men took great interest in looking after our trophies, not even asking us to assist them unless we cared to do so; but as the trophies increased in number we were glad to help, in order to expedite the work.

Doctor Evans had wounded a large brown grizzly the day before and taking the malamute dog, Jumbo, he and Bones had spent some time that day trying to locate it. These dogs are used almost exclusively as a means of transportation, and are of little or no value in hunting; therefore, they were unsuccessful in running down the bear.

Mr. Snyder reported a good day's sport, having killed a large bull moose early in the morning. A cow moose was first seen and while watching her a medium-sized bull appeared. Mr. Snyder was about to fire, when to his surprise a large bull stepped in sight, whereupon he quickly killed him. He had a spread of fifty-one inches and very wide palms. They spent the remainder of the day skinning the moose and bringing in the head, fat, and such meat as was needed. This completed Mr.

ALASKAN-YUKON TROPHIES

A herd of caribou bulls swimming the Yukon River. Courtesy of U. S. Dept. of the Interior.

Snyder's limit for moose on the Alaskan side, and he was ready to continue to the International Boundary Line; thence into the Yukon Territory. I disliked leaving there, as a number of large moose tracks had been seen, but Bones thought it advisable to move on as horse feed was very scarce in that section. Furthermore, the nights were becoming much colder and as we were camped at a high elevation, the horses traveled some distance down the creek each night, to where they were sheltered from the winds and where feed was more abundant. Bones decided we would move two days' travel ahead to Little Boundary Creek, so named because the International Boundary Line between Alaska and the Yukon Territory is located close by. We reached Travis Creek the first day. The hunters preceded the pack train, hunting as we went, in different routes, but no game was seen.

Chapter XII

ON BRITISH SOIL

*"It's the great, big, broad land 'way up yonder,
It's the forests where silence has lease;
It's the beauty that thrills me with wonder,
It's the stillness that fills me with peace."*

ON expeditions such as we were making, the horses are loaded to their capacity with food and supplies when starting out. But this load is gradually diminished, as the food is consumed. Later, as the hunters secure game, the load is increased because of the heads, hides and meat that are taken. By this time our load had become quite heavy and Gene and Billy had experienced much difficulty in moving the outfit from Holmes Creek to Travis Creek. Therefore, the next morning Bones suggested that Paddie and I walk to the location of the next camp, as this would allow them the use of our saddle horses to help carry the load, and it would give us a splendid opportunity to hunt moose. Notwithstanding, my knee was still bothering me greatly, I was willing to walk,—especially as it afforded a better opportunity for seeing moose.

About noon we reached Klutsan Creek and stopped to eat our lunch. We found close by a crudely constructed cabin where a trapper had spent several winters. We opened the door and went in. Several moose skins hung against the wall and strips of moose-hide covered the cracks. There was a bunk in one corner, a cook stove in another, and cooking utensils suspended from pegs in the log walls. The cabin had no floor. A few old books, including a Spanish Dictionary, were found in the cracks between the logs, which evidently comprised the trapper's library. I was impressed with the loneliness of the cabin and its surroundings, and thought of the long winters this man had spent there alone; but such is the life of trappers and prospectors. Many of them are educated men, but who for various reasons, have left friends and the comforts of civilization far behind and have adopted a life in these solitudes.

During the afternoon we crossed the International Boundary Line—which divides the possessions of the United States from those of Great Britain—into territory belonging to the Crown. Seven years were spent in surveying and establishing this line. The engineers and their helpers, employed by the United States, were in charge of the Honorable Thomas R. Riggs, later Governor of Alaska. With the exception of a short distance after it leaves the Pacific Ocean, the line runs due north, without variation, to the Arctic Ocean. Bronze posts, about three feet high and perhaps ten inches in diameter at their base, are set in concrete foundations on the more prominent and accessible points of the mountains. Some of these posts, as well as the concrete, had to be carried many miles on the backs of strong men, to points where pack horses could not go. Through wooded country all timber was cut for a uniform distance of thirty feet on each side of the line, making a strip sixty feet wide. My eyes followed the line down the mountain through the many miles of dark green spruce, across the wide bars of the White River, through the timber on the opposite side, then up the mountains above timber line and over the top. With my binoculars I distinguished through the clear atmosphere a bronze post on another mountain top, perhaps twenty miles away. Farther on a still higher mountain loomed up, and sighting across I could see the exact spot where the line crossed it. As I gazed down at the line running through the timber below, it looked like a great swathe cut through a meadow. Gradually this swathe narrowed in perspective until in the distance it looked like a straight black streak. I stood for some time as if riveted to the spot—while the Indian feasted on the large ripe blueberries that were so abundant. I thought of the barren and little known land lying to the north, into which this line penetrated.

All day we had traveled in a circuitous route, looking carefully for game, but had seen nothing until toward evening when we suddenly sighted a cow moose and her calf standing in some scrubby timber. The wind being in our favor, they did not scent us, but watched us curiously as we approached; then slowly walked away. It was late in the evening when we located a white speck in the distance close to Little Boundary Creek; and with our glasses we could see that Gene and Billy had arrived and had the dining tent up. It was far up in the tundra, in a plateau country, with a few scattered, scrubby spruce trees close by. We reached camp about dark and I was very tired and in low spirits. The Indian and I had walked fully twenty miles, and all day I had suffered because of my knee. Mr. Snyder and Doctor had killed two fine caribou each, on the Alaskan side of the boundary line. In contrast to myself they were in high spirits.

The weather was ideal, the sun coming out warm during the day, but the nights had been gradually getting colder. That night it was five degrees or more below zero, but we did not know how cold it was at the time. After reaching White Horse and consulting the official temperature records, for the time we had been in the interior, we found it had been five degrees below zero on the night of September fifth — which was our first night on Little Boundary Creek. As we were at a higher elevation than White Horse and in a glacial country, it was probably somewhat colder where we were.

A handshake across the International Boundary Line. Dr. Evans stands in Yukon Territory, the author in Alaska.

Again provided with our saddle horses, Indian Paddie and I started out on the morning of the sixth. He sighted thirteen caribou standing in a small patch of snow on the mountain side about two and a half miles away. We circled around the mountain so as to take advantage of the wind and keep out of their sight, hitching our horses to a rock perhaps a half-mile from the caribou, and proceeding cautiously to a point above them. Getting down on all-fours we crawled to within seventy-five yards of them when we raised up slowly and saw that two of the bulls in the lot had horns larger than either of those secured by me on the Alaskan side. Picking out the larger of the two, I fired two shots, making a hit each time; then directed my attention to the other bull which had longer beams but fewer points. By this time the entire herd was running down the slope and I was obliged to use care not to hit any of the others. I fired three times at the bull as the opportunity presented itself and at

Left: Mt. Nazahat; elevation, 16,000 feet. Right: A section of the great spruce forest which extends five to ten miles back from the White River.

the third shot he fell dead. We then hurried toward the first bull and saw he was still alive. As we approached he succeeded in gaining his feet and appeared to be in the act of charging me when I placed another shot at the base of his neck. I have often marveled at the great vitality of wild animals and the force that is necessary to kill them, in contrast to domestic animals. I found this to be especially true of caribou, and this one in particular. Two shots from the .280 Ross rifle had been placed in his shoulder, but a third one, at the base of the neck was necessary. Going to the other caribou I found that two shots had taken effect, one of these also in the shoulder and the other directly behind.

The next day being Sunday, we remained in camp, with the exception of Paddie, who took two pack horses and brought in the heads of the caribou and the fat and such meat as was wanted. We devoted the greater portion of the day to mending, sewing on

Many-channeled bar of the White River.

ON BRITISH SOIL

buttons, and shaving. The guides spent most of the time working on the heads of our game, while Gene "worked" on our heads, cutting a seven weeks' growth of hair.

Grayling fish were abundant in the little creek, and having lines and flies with us, Mr. Snyder and I succeeded in getting quite a number on different occasions. These fish are gray in color and about the size of brook trout. We relished them, as a change in diet for the first meal, but cared little for them thereafter, especially since one craves meat containing much fat when in a cold country. Our manner of fishing amused the Indians as they were not accustomed to seeing fish caught with a hook and line. Johnnie remarked to me one day, "All time you and Mr. Snyder tryin' to catch fish with little hook and string. All same you want 'em fish, me catch 'em all you want maybe; me get Paddie, we build little dam 'cross creek with rocks; me get club, Paddie, him go up creek and run 'em down; all same me club hell out of 'em, maybe so." They do not view the killing of game or the catching of fish from the sportsman's standpoint. Their object is to get the meat, in the easiest and quickest manner possible.

The following day was spent by all of us in hunting moose, but we saw none. I had noticed on several occasions that the Indians sought a high knoll when we stopped to eat our lunch; and that it was often their custom, where wood was available, to build a fire. On this day when a high point was reached and a small fire was started, I observed that Paddie placed an abundance of dry leaves and sticks on the fire—his purpose evidently being to make as much smoke as possible. It was not long until his face brightened and he pointed many miles away, where another smoke could be seen. The smoke from our fire was a signal to the other Indian, and he had returned it in the same manner. This had not been possible in the country where we had hunted sheep and where wood was unobtainable, but whenever they could secure anything to burn, and when there was a chance of their signals being seen, a fire was started at the time of eating.

Some kinds of food were becoming quite scarce. The supplies that we had used thus far were those purchased and brought from McCarthy. One more day's travel with our outfit would bring us to the Generc River where Bones had cached the food brought from White Horse, on his way to McCarthy. As our load was now too heavy to be moved in one trip, it was decided that Gene and Billy should take some of the pack horses, loaded with trophies, and go to the Generc River, where they would cache the trophies, and return the next day with such food as was most needed.

I have already mentioned that I left Holmes Creek quite reluctantly, it being a matter of much disappointment to both Doctor and me that we had not secured any moose on the Alaskan side. We felt that Bones had made a mistake in crossing into the Yukon Territory so abruptly. We thought we should have remained at Holmes Creek longer, even though it had been necessary to move our camp to lower ground. Moose appeared quite scarce in the section where we were hunting, and it was decided that Doctor and I should return to Holmes Creek, with the two Indians, taking a small tent, and such food as would be required.

Billy had the horses rounded up and in the corral ready for an early start next morning. Little Pinto and another horse called Peavine, were packed lightly with a four days' supply of food and a few cooking utensils and blankets. Two days had been required in traveling from Holmes Creek to Little Boundary Creek, with the entire outfit, but we planned to make it back in one long day of continuous travel. We reached our destination about dark, strapped bells to the horses' necks, and turned them out on the creek bar to find food. After eating supper, which the Indians had prepared, Doctor and I retired to the small tent and the Indians lay down in the open beside the fire. The large glacier extending from Mt. Nazahat was quite active that night and we were frequently awakened by sharp reports and the weird sounds as the ice gave way and thundered down the mountain side. During our stay there the water of Holmes Creek, which is a glacial stream, was really unfit for use on account of the silt, sand and volcanic ash that it carried. There being no other water close by, we were obliged to use it; and not having our filter with us, we would dip a bucketful and allow it to settle; then decant the clearer portion from the top. In fact, we suffered from thirst while there, as we found it impossible to drink the water except in tea or coffee.

We were desirous of making good use of our time while at Holmes Creek; and after an early breakfast we started our hunt, Paddie with Doctor, and Johnnie with me. The Indian and I rode all forenoon through the scrubby timber; and reaching a small area of open country about noon, we tied our horses and ascended a high knoll to eat our lunch. While eating, the Indian constantly cast his eyes about in every direction—always on the alert for any signs of game. With the advantage of their wonderful eyesight, they are almost certain to detect anything that appears within their limits of vision. Johnnie was particularly alert in this respect.

Suddenly the Indian stopped eating and in an excited manner pointed to a hillside about a half-mile away, where I immediately saw a large bull moose, his horns showing plainly in contrast to the dark green color about him. Just after they shed the velvet, their horns appear almost white in the sunlight; and in contrast to the green color of the spruce, can be seen for a considerable distance. We hurriedly looked at him through the glasses and saw that he had a large spread of horns entirely free of velvet. Just then we discovered a cow moose close by—as the mating season had started. This season begins after their horns shed the velvet —which is soon after September first. (Our Indians claimed that it was with the first full moon after September first.) During this period, which is of about one month's duration, the bulls lose much of their fear and often approach danger instead of running from it. In fact at such times they are often ferocious, and on rare occasions in the North Country men have been obliged to find safety in trees to escape the fury of these monster animals.

We quickly planned our attack and circled to the right to take advantage of the wind. On stopping for a few moments, to make certain of the location of the animals, we saw them start down the slope to more level ground, quartering to our right. The Indians always made use of moccasins when hunting moose, wearing out a pair every few days. I had worn hob-nailed shoes while hunting sheep on the high mountains and rubber shoe-pacs with leather uppers when still-hunting in the forests or lowlands. On this day, for some unaccountable reason, I happened to be wearing my high laced boots. I preferred them when riding horseback, but found them a decided disadvantage when still-hunting. The Indian told me I must remove them when we approached closer, and proceed wearing only my heavy woolen socks. Of these, I always wore from two to four pairs, depending on the weather. I whispered to him to signal when he wanted me to take them off.

Stealthily we went forward, like a cat slipping up on its prey. There was no wind—and everything was quiet. My nerves were at their highest tension. When the Indian stopped to listen, I did not move a muscle; when he stole forward, stooping low as he went, I did likewise. The ground was easy to get over, being almost level at that place, with no stone and little underbrush, and as we made no noise whatever, it was not necessary for me to remove my boots. Suddenly the Indian dropped to his knees! I did the same. He beckoned me to him and I crawled forward until I was by his side, and saw the cow about a hundred yards away, with her head turned from us. The Indian whispered, "All same bull, him close; you crawl past trees to open place; you see him maybe; he see you maybe, then he go fast like hell. You shoot him quick." Cautiously I went forward step by step, my gun off safety and ready to shoot instantly. Passing a little clump of trees, I came into full view of the bull, about a hundred and twenty-five yards away, his head up in the air and quartering toward me. I had approached in a crouched position and instead of rising to my feet to shoot I dropped, and resting my elbow on my left knee, aimed just back of his shoulder, and fired. I saw I had hit him. The cow started running to my left, while the bull quickly disappeared from sight behind some trees to my right. I was unable to get a second shot as the ejector of the Newton rifle failed to throw out the empty cartridge, and I was obliged to extract it with my fingers.

I started after the bull as fast as I could run, ejecting the cartridge and throwing a load into the chamber as I went. I ran for fully one-third of a mile, only occasionally getting a glimpse of him. The Indian afterwards expressed surprise at my speed, saying he could hardly keep up with me. Had it not been for the excitement, I could not have maintained such speed over the distance. The moose was badly wounded, otherwise I would have been outdistanced at the beginning of the race. Suddenly I caught sight of him as he swerved to the left and ran up a little bank. I fired quickly and thought he was going to fall, as he was hit again. He hesitated for a moment only, then disappeared from sight. I ran up the bank and saw him attempt to jump a fallen tree, but he failed in his effort and fell beside its trunk.

So anxious was I to see his horns at close range that I was approaching the fallen animal, when the Indian arrived and called for me to get back and behind a tree. I had no fear, however, as my gun was in readiness should the moose succeed in reaching his feet. I approached close enough to see from

Moose killed by the author on Holmes Creek. This was a freak head, because of the unusually large points at the base of the palms.

his eyes that he was not dead, and as I moved a little closer, he made two or three lunges and reached his feet, but another shot brought him down for good. All three of the shots had struck within an area that could be covered by the palms of my two hands. He had been hit just back of the shoulder but a little too high to produce instant death.

While the Indian was gone for the horses, I took some measurements and found the spread of the horns to be only forty-nine inches. There were twelve points on one palm and thirteen on the other, and the points were exceptionally long and of unusual formation. His head was twenty-nine inches from its base halfway between the horns, to the nose, half way between the center of his nostrils. His girth was eighty-six inches. After arranging his front legs in the position they would have been when standing, his height was six feet and seven inches. The bell under his throat was thirteen inches long. He was a large moose but not unusually large. I give these measurements in order that my readers who are not familiar with moose may have some idea regarding their size. When the Indian returned, we took some pictures, and then gralloched the animal. On leaving I took note that the Indian left no blazes, made no marks, and apparently took no mental notice whatever of the general surroundings or the particular place where the moose had fallen. I wondered if he could find the exact location when we would return the next day, but made no comment.

Reaching camp we found that Doctor had had an unsuccessful day's hunt; his guide had located a moose, but when they were almost within shooting distance, the animal had winded them and escaped.

Chapter XIII

ARRIVAL AT GENERC RIVER

*"So gaunt against the gibbous moon,
Piercing the silence velvet-piled,
A lone wolf howls his ancient tune—
The fell arch-spirit of the Wild."*

JOHNNIE and I returned to our moose the next morning, taking with us Pinto and Peavine for the purpose of bringing in the head and hide. The distance was about seven miles from camp and through a vast forest of spruce timber. No attempt was made to retrace our tracks of the evening before—in fact, we varied our course and followed a fresh moose track for awhile. The Indian apparently took no notice of direction as he led the way through the forest mile after mile. He rode to within forty yards of where the moose lay; dismounted, hitched his horse, and walked up to the carcass. It was done with as much ease as a farmer would travel seven miles along a public road to his accustomed trading place; tie his horse to a hitching post, and go into the store. It should be remembered that prior to our trip, the Indians were never in this country.

Knowing it would take some time for the Indian to skin the moose head, I concluded to visit the carcasses of the two caribou killed by me a week before—as I thought they could not be more than two or three miles away—and hoped to find a grizzly feeding there. Locating them without difficulty, I approached cautiously but neither of the carcasses, which lay about a mile apart, had been disturbed. I then circled about on my return trip thinking I might run on to another moose but had no success. When I returned to the Indian we ate our lunch, loaded the head and horns on Pinto, and the skin on Peavine and went back to camp. I skinned the legs of the moose from a point above the knee down, leaving the hoofs attached, intending to use them for the four legs of a table for my den. The hoofs of a moose are as black as ebony and take a very high polish. We took little of the meat and none of the fat, as the distance to our main camp was too great and the cook was already well supplied.

I disliked very much leaving all of that fine meat. It was equal in weight to a large steer, and when I thought of the price of prime beef back home, I was impressed with the value of the fine tender moose meat we were leaving. However, there was some satisfaction in the fact that the meat would likely be devoured by wolves or other carnivorous animals, and while doing so they would not be preying on live moose or caribou. In conversation with many hunters and trappers throughout the North Country, I have found them unanimously of the opinion that the amount of game taken by sportsmen and trappers is small in comparison to that taken by wolves.

Doctor and Paddie reported another unsuccessful day. A moose had been seen, but only the top of his back was visible to the hunters. On firing, Doctor missed him and the moose disappeared in the dense timber before he could shoot again. He was somewhat discouraged and downhearted that evening. I offered to remain for another day—even though we had only a limited supply of food—but it was decided to return to the main camp on Little Boundary Creek the next day. Getting an early start Doctor and Paddie hunted in the general direction of the main camp, while Johnnie and I took the two pack horses in a direct route. Reaching a clear stream of water about noon we quenched our thirst, made tea and ate our lunch. We remained there for some time giving the horses an opportunity to graze, as we were traveling in the tundra above timber line. The Indian expressed the hope that Doctor and Paddie would see our smoke and join us before we emptied the tea pail. It was a beautiful day and there was not a cloud to be seen. As we sat there smoking I tried to draw the Indian into conversation, but he appeared to be uncommunicative. He spent the time gazing far off in the distance as if in deep thought. At last, after finishing his smoke and knocking the ashes from his pipe, he pointed far away to our rear and said, "Back that way we come from McCarthy over glacier ice. Over that way we hunt sheep all same one week; this way we got camp on Little Boundary Creek; we go there tonight. All same we go to Generc River and build boat." Then pointing in the direction the White River ran he said, "All same down that way Morley Bones him take you all in boat; him no young man; all same him don't see good. Morley Bones, him good man, all same him can't see good to run boat in White River, maybe so. Paddie and me say goodby to you and Doctor and Mr. Snyder; we go with Gene and horses to Kluane Lake. Me get my squaw; me get my little boy; me go trap all winter. You come back sometime maybe; me and Paddie want to hunt with you. All same we like Mr. Snyder and Doctor and you. All same you never come back maybe so."

He said this in a rather pathetic voice; indicating first, that he had some apprehension about our running the White River successfully; and second, that he disliked the idea of parting company with us. I tried to engage him in further conversation by asking some questions concerning our chances of making the river trip successfully, but he would say nothing more and during the afternoon was as quiet as he had been all forenoon. Soon after finishing his remarks he arose and said, "Now we go," but about this time we saw Doctor and Paddie approaching—Paddie having located us from the smoke of our fire. We waited until they had their lunch, after which we traveled together during the afternoon to Little Boundary Creek.

We found Mr. Snyder in high spirits. He had killed a large ram that day, the head of which, according to Bones and the others, was one of the finest they had ever seen. Mr. Snyder considered this his most exciting hunting experience of our trip. On leaving camp that morning he and Bones rode up the creek and after traveling for about three hours, saw a ram coming down the mountain side about a mile ahead of them. They watched him cross the creek and go up into an old moraine. Bones then brought his telescope into use and announced that the ram had exceptionally large horns. They moved on until they found a place to leave the horses, then started walking toward the ram, but did not go far until he started running. Bones thought their only chance of getting him was to shoot from where they were, whereupon Mr. Snyder fired five shots— but the ram disappeared around the mountain side—apparently unhurt. Returning to their horses and eating their lunch they started down the creek along the same route they had come up. After traveling an hour they noticed a ram coming down the mountain side a half-mile away. Looking at him through his telescope, Bones announced it was the large ram they had seen on the moraine and that he had been wounded, as a large red spot could be seen on his hip.

There was no way of approaching him except in plain view, so Bones told Mr. Snyder to mount his horse quickly and they would try to run him down. In relating their experience, Mr. Snyder said it was the wildest ride of his life. The ram saw them coming and started around the mountain as fast as he could run. Mr. Snyder was riding Spot, as we had exchanged saddle horses for a few days. Presently he fell, but the rider stayed in the saddle and the horse was soon on his feet and in the race again. They forced the horses over the rough ground to the limit of their speed, and after keeping this up for some time, saw they were almost exhausted and could not keep up the race much longer. In the meantime they noticed the ram was losing speed also. Finally they could force the horses no farther, and jumping off, they started running after the ram on foot. Gradually gaining on him they got close enough to try a long shot and Mr. Snyder succeeded in hitting him the first time. Several more shots were fired, before a final one brought him down. His horns measured forty-two and one-fourth inches; had a large base circumference and were perfect in every respect. Gene and Billy had returned and we were once more a united family, with an abundance of food.

On the following morning we were just finishing breakfast when Indian Johnnie ran into camp and told us a band of twelve or fifteen caribou were passing on the barrens close by. We rushed out of the tent and saw them going in a trot, about a quarter of a mile away. Mr. Snyder and I grabbed our guns, and running toward them, saw that only the leader had large horns. Mr. Snyder waited until he could get a shot at him, without danger of striking the others, and fired—just as they were starting down into a little valley. I did not think the shot was successful at that great distance, but we concluded to investigate, as Mr. Snyder was of the opinion the large bull had been hit. We went to the place where they disappeared, and found him lying dead. I considered it one of the best shots I ever saw, taking into consideration the great distance and the fact that the caribou was running. Mr. Snyder had been quite fortunate. He had killed a moose on Holmes Creek as he was about to sit down to the supper table, and a caribou as he had arisen from the breakfast table, only a few days later—both of them having been sighted by Johnnie. However, I do not mean to leave the impression that game can ordinarily be secured so easily. Even in that country where it is fairly plentiful, much hard work is required to be successful. In both instances the animals had been traveling from one section of the

ARRIVAL AT GENERC RIVER

country to another and it was only a matter of luck that the Indian was outside the tent as they were passing.

Throughout our trip the wonderful eyesight of our two Indians and their ability to quickly detect game, or any living object that came within their long-range limits of vision, was a matter of never ceasing wonder to me. Bones stated that almost all healthy Indians, of both sexes and not too far advanced in years, were equally capable in this respect. He told me it was almost impossible to locate sheep in the mountains, after the winter snow has fallen, as there is little contrast between their almost white fleece and the pure white snow. He said there had been times when he found it necessary to employ an Indian to locate them for him. On one occasion he hunted for several days without success, and visiting a small tribe of Indians, camped not far from his place, found all the men away on their trap lines. Two of the children—a girl of about twelve and a boy of ten—volunteered their services. Going to a point which enabled them to command a good view of a nearby mountain range, where sheep could usually be found, the children almost instantly pointed to a group far up the mountain side. Not until their exact location was pointed out and his binoculars brought into use was Bones able to detect them, after which the children returned to their camp while Bones climbed the mountain and secured his meat. He said it was the most outstanding demonstration of unusual eyesight that he had ever seen.

Of equal interest was the ability of the Indians to detect evidence of any living thing having passed or crossed their course of travel, whether a track, an occasional upturned leaf or stone, or a broken twig. They were able not only to quickly observe tracks or any object which was out of its accustomed place, but they could tell with a fair degree of certainty how recently such signs had been made.

Bones remarked that when he was a young man he considered himself an expert in identifying the tracks of all kinds of wild life, and whether or not they were fresh, as he was regularly engaged in trapping. As he grew older, and had come in more frequent contact with Indians, he concluded that his knowledge in this respect was quite limited and he thought this to be true of all white men—as compared with Indians. When some of us called Bones' attention, or the attention of some of the other white men of our party, to what appeared to be a fresh track—fre-

ALASKAN-YUKON TROPHIES

A carpet of volcanic ash distinguishes this section of high plateau country.

quently that of a grizzly bear—they would usually summon one of the Indians. Carefully placing his hand in the track, or several tracks, we were usually able to judge how fresh they were by the expression on the Indian's face. If his countenance was illuminated his remark was usually, "Him go just before we come"; if only slightly illuminated, it would probably be "Him go just before daylight." If his face indicated no signs of enthusiasm his expression might be, "Him go night before last."

I was interested in an experience related by Gene. He and his brother, Louie, had brought a well-bred stallion to Kluane Lake for the purpose of improving their stock of horses. In fact, some of the horses used on our expedition were bred from this stallion and were larger, of better disposition and less treacherous than the full bred cayuses that were used. The stallion was kept in their stable, but one morning they found him missing. Eugene and Louie tracked him all the way to the Donjeck River, where the tracks were lost on the gravel bar. They remained there several days looking for the missing horse, but finally gave up and returned to their home. Later they employed an Indian and going with him they again tracked the horse to the Donjeck. Arriving there the Indian did not hesitate but continued on the horse's track, apparently with as much ease as he had tracked him to the Donjeck. Mile after mile he led the way, in a circuitous route,

ARRIVAL AT GENERC RIVER

first on one side of the rocky gravel bar, then on the other, following a trail that was not visible to the eyes of white men, and finally located the horse.

The section of country drained by Little Boundary Creek and its tributaries is a high rolling plateau. From our camp one had to ride only a few miles to the north in order to look down into the wide valley of the White River; or only a few miles to the east to look down into the valley of the Generc; or to the northeast to see the intersection of these valleys and the rivers which drain them. To the south the highest range of mountains in that section of country extends east and west paralleling the White River. Mt. Nazahat the highest peak of the range, estimated to be over 16,000 feet in height, towered above us. We had hunted in various localities for the past two weeks, but always under the shadow of this high peak; and it appeared that our position, in the course of an entire day's travel, varied but little in relation to the top of it.

I have already stated that much of the White River country is covered with volcanic ash, and I observed that perhaps half of the entire area comprising this high tableland was so covered. In the distance it is difficult to distinguish it from snow — so white is the fine sand and ash. At places it extended far up the mountain side, and often it required close observation to be able to tell where the white areas of ash ended and the lower lines of perpetual snow began. This plateau was so high that one could see far away to the north, east and west. In all, it was a very interesting country and I spent many hours gazing on it, with the view of fixing its general contour permanently in my mind. It was an ideal country for caribou, and a number of small bands were seen at various times, but most of them had small heads. Farther up in the foothills of the great mountain range, sheep were numerous, but they were usually in places impossible of ascent. It was high up in the foothills of Mt. Nazahat that Mr. Snyder secured his splendid sheep head.

Preparations were being made that morning to move to our permanent camping place on the Generc River, and the killing of the caribou delayed us somewhat. Doctor, Mr. Snyder and I, with our guides, started off in different courses, hunting on the way, while Gene and Billy remained behind to bring the outfit. The wind blew with terrific force that day and Johnnie and I did not go far until we were obliged to dismount and take shelter behind our horses. On looking back, we could see that the dining tent had blown down and that Gene and Billy were having much difficulty in keeping the outfit together. When we came in sight of the Valley of the Generc, some five or six miles below, we saw a great sand storm raging there in full blast. The sand and white ash were being swept down the valley in such quantity and with such force that it looked like a blinding snow blizzard. High up on the tableland we found it almost impossible to proceed, and at times dismounted and stood for a while, protected by our restless cayuses. To the north we could see the sand storm raging with equal force in the valley of the White River—some ten or twelve miles away. Later we often heard the crash of a large spruce, as we were approaching a section of country where the timber was of considerable size.

In traveling through the valleys one frequently sees large areas close to the base of the mountains, which have been gradually undermined by the force of the wind. These are called "cut sand-banks," and are sometimes several hundred feet high. More and more was I impressed with the great forces of Nature which are constantly at work in this strange country,—especially when I saw the many trees which had been undermined by the wind's force that day.

In descending the mountain to the Generc River we had the roughest traveling that we had yet encountered, having to walk and lead our horses much of the distance. Had I not seen it accomplished, I would have declared that no horse could make such a descent. My saddle horse, Spot, was very stiff from his hard run of the day before when Mr. Snyder was after the large ram, and fell with me seven times during the day. Twice I went entirely over his head, and at one time landed fifteen feet below him —but fortunately on a soft spot of ground. In fact, the soft spots were partly responsible for the horse's falling. They consisted of small patches of loose volcanic ash, covered with moss and vegetation, and were obscured from view. Most of the horses of our outfit had large hoofs, but not so with Spot, which accounted for his miring more easily and falling more often. One of the prerequisites of a desirable horse for a trip of this kind is large feet—"hoofs like snow shoes," as the men termed it. It may be of interest to note that because of their small feet mules are seldom if ever used in Alaska or the Yukon Territory.

ARRIVAL AT GENERC RIVER

A cut sandbank along the Generc River; Mt. Nazahat in the distance.

When about half-way down the mountain we came to one of the most beautiful small lakes it has been my pleasure to see. It had an area of three or four acres and was located on a bench in the mountain, surrounded with spruce trees, extending to and overhanging the water's edge. Wild ducks of different varieties were swimming about on the emerald green surface. As we descended the steep slope, leading our horses—which were walking and sliding together—a cow moose suddenly sprang from the edge of the water on the opposite side and trotted off into the timber. I stopped long enough to take a picture of the lake, although no picture can do justice to so beautiful a spot.

Most of the timber we had traveled and hunted through during the past two weeks had been like large groves, with little underbrush, but the forest sloping toward the Generc River was altogether different. As we neared the valley the trees were found to be large and the underbrush thicker. The forest became so dense that it was difficult to proceed; and in doing so, my clothing was badly torn. Reaching the valley we crossed the gravel bar, which was about two miles wide, and down which the river coursed its way in several treacherous channels. These had to be crossed with caution, as their bottoms, in many places, consisted of sand. The wind had subsided by this time and the entire valley was suggestive of peace and contentment. Tall spruce timber, larger than any we had encountered, extended back from the river bar and across the valley for a distance of several miles. With the Indian in the lead, we rode through the dense forest of the valley and I wondered if he would be able to find the cache without difficulty. He had been in that country but once before and that was during July, when they had camped and cached the supplies, while on the way to McCarthy. They had arrived at the location of the cache and departed in different directions from the course we were traveling, yet the Indian never looked to the right or left. He proceeded onward, making no comments, and rode to the cache as straight as he had ridden to the carcass of the moose in the Holmes Creek country, a few days earlier.

When within two or three hundred yards of the cache, my horse almost jumped from under me. I looked and saw a large gray timber wolf coming diagonally toward me,—not over twenty-five feet away. Seeing me he appeared to be as surprised as I was, and turning abruptly, disappeared in the forest. The wolf no doubt had been attracted to that locality by the scent of the heads and scalps that had been cached there by Gene and Billy a few days before, and had almost run into me before seeing us. I had frequently heard wolves howling in the evening and during the night in different parts of Canada, but this was the first wild one I had ever seen alive. They prowl about in a sneaking way, and while they are often heard, are seldom seen.

I examined our cache in the fading daylight with much interest. It had been erected in accordance with the general custom of the country. Three trees sufficiently large to sustain the weight, yet not large enough to permit a bear to climb them, had been selected. They stood in triangular position, about ten feet apart, and were cut off some twelve or fifteen feet above the ground. Cross sections were lashed from one to the other at their tops, on which had been laid a crude platform consisting of poles. On these poles the food and supplies were placed and covered with canvas, the edges of which were weighted down with stones.

Food caches are common among the trappers and prospectors and a winter's supply of food is stored in this manner. Even though it might be found by another, it would not be molested, except in case of dire necessity, in which event the owners would afterwards be advised and perhaps the food replaced. These stern men of the North have their own code of ethics or unwritten laws, which were established in the early days of that country and which are rigidly adhered to. Perhaps the first and most important law of that land is that no man shall rob or molest another's cache. Second, that no man shall steal or harm another's dog—for upon these dogs much depends, as they transport food into the interior during the winter. A violation of these laws might result in the loss of some lonely prospector's or trapper's life by starvation.

Gene and Billy arrived with the heavily laden horses; each carrying a pack ranging in weight from two hundred and fifty to three hundred pounds. Doctor Evans arrived shortly afterwards wearing a broad smile. He had killed his first moose that afternoon—a very good head, with a spread of fifty-one inches.

The day after we arrived at the Generc River I remained in camp mending my clothing, which had been torn almost beyond repair in traveling down the mountain to the Generc. I had additional clothing, but was holding it in reserve until we would start back to the coast. Paddie and Billy Slimpert went with Doctor after the head, hide and meat of the moose that he had killed the day before. Towards the end of the hunt Bones had all the choice meat brought to camp and suspended and dried on a framework of poles. This was to be taken out on the pack horses at the conclusion of our hunt, to be used as fox food, as he was engaged in raising foxes as a side line.

Mr. Snyder returned in high glee that evening. He had killed a fine moose with a fifty-one inch spread. Having a few choice cigars left, he passed them around in honor of the occasion.

Five or six miles from camp there was a moraine which covered an old icefield. It had an area of several square miles and a very rough and hilly surface. The thickness of earth and gravel over the ice varied from a few inches to several feet. Scrubby willows, alders, and birches, with an occasional dwarf spruce, grew in patches over the surface; and in all it was a barren, desolate place. It was on this moraine that Mr. Snyder killed the moose, and as it looked to him like favorable moose country, we decided to hunt there next day. The following morning we all went together to the moraine where we soon located the moose; and Bones, Billy, and Snyder went to work skinning it. Doctor and Paddie chose to hunt the west side of the moraine, while Johnnie and I took the east side. The surface from there on was so rough that we left our horses with Bones, to be taken back to camp.

Perhaps an hour after leaving the others we came to a little knoll where we commanded a good view, when the Indian suddenly dropped low—gazing in the distance. After looking intently for a few moments his face brightened, and he said that he could

Snyder's excellent caribou heads; above, the early-morning trophy.

see two moose lying down, and that one of them had horns. I looked for some time in the direction of his gaze, but could see nothing whatever that resembled a moose. He described their exact location clearly, but not until I brought the glasses into use could I see them. In fact, it was at first with some difficulty that I saw them through the glasses, as they were in a low place and their color blended perfectly with that of the barren surroundings. Several times I removed the glasses and tried to make them out with my naked eye, but was unable to do so. It was the most wonderful demonstration of good eyesight I have ever seen, as the distance was fully three-quarters of a mile.

We saw that if proper precautions were taken, we could likely approach to within shooting distance. An unfavorable breeze made a direct approach impossible, so taking advantage of the small knolls and rough ground to keep out of their sight, we circled far to the right, with the view of reaching a certain small knoll close by the moose. As we approached, all of the knolls looked alike, with no trees or other means of marking them, and I did not think the Indian would be able to identify the particular one we had decided on. Presently he led the way to a certain knoll, which proved to be the one selected, and with his hat in hand crawled, cat-like, to the top. After looking over, he motioned for me to creep up beside him. Reaching the top, instead of seeing two moose, I saw five—a large bull, three cows, and a calf almost as large as the cows—none of them over one hundred yards away. I wished for a camera more than at any time on the trip. The bull, one cow and the calf were standing, while the others were lying down. Quickly I arose and aiming at the base of the bull's neck, fired. He took a step or two forward as though about to fall, but regained his balance and stood motionless. Instantly the cows arose, and not getting our wind or the direction of the sound, ran wildly about for a few moments; then started off in the opposite direction from us, but stopped about fifty yards beyond the bull. Although the Indian and I were standing in full view and talking audibly, the cows walked back toward the bull. The setting was ideal for an unusual picture, as the great monarch of the northern forests stood in the foreground, with the cows and calf a short distance in the rear. The bull stood bracing himself to keep from falling and tried to walk, but he was unable to move out of his tracks. The shocking power of the 280 Ross was so great that his entire body quivered, and he would have soon fallen from the one shot, but I did not want him to suffer unnecessarily; therefore, placed another bullet just back of his shoulder, and he fell instantly. The cow moose appeared reluctant to desert their fallen lord and master, and turned every few steps to look back, as they finally went away.

We found the bull to be about the same size as the other one I had killed—his gross weight afterwards estimated at 1300 pounds. His horns were larger and more perfectly palmated than my first specimen, having a spread of fifty-one inches. Bones said it would be useless to save the skins of all of our trophies, as it would be impossible to take them down the river in the boat, but he thought we would have room for the skin of one moose and one caribou for each hunter. Notwithstanding the fact that I had saved the skin of the first moose I had killed, I saved this one also, thinking there might possibly be room in the boat for an extra one. After removing the skin from this animal and gralloching him, we ate our lunch and started on our long walk to camp.

ALASKAN-YUKON TROPHIES

Upon arriving we found Doctor Evans had also killed a large moose on the old moraine that day. It had a spread slightly in excess of any we had secured—about fifty-two inches. Old hunters claim the horns of these animals vary in size from year to year. This is probably true as it is quite natural to conclude that a moose would be in better condition when the seasons are early and food abundant, resulting in a larger growth of horns. The heads of those killed by our party ranged almost uniformly from forty-nine to fifty-two inches in spread, which is not especially large. But Alaskan moose usually have horns with wider palms and a greater number of points than those of the same spread found in the eastern provinces of Canada. We afterwards learned the moose heads secured throughout Alaska and the Yukon that fall were below the average size for that part of the country—due no doubt to the backward season. We had killed seven moose. Our limit was two each in Alaska, and two each in the Yukon, making four moose for each hunter, or a total of twelve. We did not care to take advantage of our legal rights in this respect as we thought seven was a liberal number to be taken by one hunting party. Therefore, this ended our moose hunting. The following day was spent bringing in the heads, hides and meat of the two moose.

None of us had killed any sheep on the Yukon side, nor had we secured our limit of caribou. As already stated, six caribou could be killed on each license, but only three could be exported. However, we had no desire to kill game in excess of the number that could be taken out.

By this time we realized we must begin making preparations for our return trip. The weather was now perfect, but there was danger of cold weather setting in and the rivers freezing over. Every moment was enjoyed and we regretted to see the time approaching for our departure.

Gene and Billy had cut five spruce trees a mile below camp, from which an equal number of twenty-two foot logs had been sawed. This was the first step in constructing our boat. On the morning of September seventeenth all of us decided to take a hand in getting the logs together preparatory to whipsawing them. Few people in this generation are familiar with this process of making lumber. A log framework is built sufficiently high to enable a man to stand under it without stooping. Skid-ways are laid against this framework and on them a log is rolled to the

Indians whipsawing lumber to be used in building the scow.

top. A strip of bark is removed from the entire length of the log to be sawed, after which a guide line is run the length of the exposed surface. This guide line is placed underneath a slab sawed off by the use of a rip-saw—about equal in length to a cross-cut saw. In operation one man takes his position on top of the framework and directly over the log, while another man operates the other end of the saw from beneath the framework. The downward stroke does most of the cutting; therefore, the man underneath must be somewhat of an expert to follow the guide line and make the lumber true. When the first slab is cut off the log is turned with the flat side down and again lined, after which a second slab is cut, and this operation repeated until the log is squared. The ends and underside are then lined according to the thickness of the lumber desired, and the boards sawed—one at a time. It is a slow, laborious task, and I know of no other work that requires so much physical exertion and patience as whipsawing lumber.

The old saddle horse Bob—used by Doctor Evans—and little Pinto were taken for the purpose of hauling the logs to the sawpit. The ends of two strong ropes were tied to a log and the other ends to the horns of the saddles. Billy mounted Pinto and Bones mounted Old Bob. We watched with much interest as this manner of logging was new to us. All in readiness, Bones dug his heels into the sides of his horse; whereupon he pulled as though he were in harness, but Pinto would not move. Billy tried coaxing, then whipping, but this manner of pulling was as new to Pinto, as it was to the onlookers, and he refused to be taught. The refusal of this splendid little horse to pull a heavy load in this manner, in my opinion was another demonstration of his unusual intelligence. Removing Pinto's rope from the log, Bones tried it with old Bob alone and after several efforts succeeded in pulling it to the pit. In this manner the five, twenty-two foot green spruce logs—which squared from six to eight inches—were hauled over level ground to the saw-pit, a distance of about one hundred yards. It really seemed cruel to pull Old Bob so hard and I think Bones regretted doing so, as the horse showed the effect of it for several days. A log was then rolled on the framework and lined, a chalk line having been taken for the purpose, while some charred coals were used in place of chalk.

There had been much speculation in camp when Bones was not present, as to who would be called on to do the whipsawing—

ARRIVAL AT GENERC RIVER

all of them hoping to get out of the job. This was settled the following morning, when Bones announced we would make a side trip of several days to the northeast of Harris Creek, and during our absence Gene and Billy should put in their time whipsawing the lumber.

Chapter XIV

UNUSUAL EXPERIENCES

*"I rose at dawn; I wandered on. 'Tis somewhat
    fine and grand
To be alone and hold your own in God's vast
    awesome land;
Come woe or weal, 'tis fine to feel a hundred
    miles between
The trails you dare and pathways where the feet
    of men have been."*

TAKING as few supplies as possible we crossed Harris Creek near its mouth at the Generc River, climbed the mountain to above timber line, then traveled around the mountain side over the caribou barrens, camping that night about fifteen or twenty miles from our main camp. It was an undesirable location, especially after we had spent several days in the valley of the Generc where water and wood were plentiful, and where we were protected from the cold wind.

On removing the packs from the horses we found that by some oversight the tent had been left behind, and that Doctor Evans had also overlooked his sleeping bag. We camped on a bed of rocks beside a small creek that flowed down a deep ravine in the mountain—the only place available. A canvas that had been used to cover one of the horses' packs was thrown over some scrubby willow stakes, as a shelter from the wind. Fortunately, I had with me my twenty-seven by forty-eight inch air mattress, which I shared with Doctor Evans. We placed it under our hips, and as I was using blankets instead of a sleeping bag, I was able to share them with him. We spent a disagreeable night because it was very cold, and our bed of rock made it impossible to find a comfortable position. Horse feed was scarce in that locality and the Indians were obliged to get up two or three times in the night, heading the horses off when they attempted to leave the gulch. Accustomed to the sound of the bells, the men were quick to detect the absence of the horses when they wandered away during the night. However, in compensation for our beds of stone, we

UNUSUAL EXPERIENCES

witnessed that night a most magnificent display of the Aurora Borealis.

The Northern Lights are seen quite frequently in the interior of Alaska and the Yukon Territory. They are likely to appear almost any time in the fall and winter months, when the nights are still and clear, and there is little or no moon. I have seen these lights throughout different parts of Canada—at about the fifty-second parallel of latitude—and my observations have been that they were far more brilliant and gorgeous than any display I ever witnessed in the states. But the Northern Lights seen at that latitude in Canada do not compare in brilliancy with those of Alaska and the Yukon. In the latter countries they are of such frequent occurrence during the long nights of the winter months, that one soon becomes accustomed to them and they are little noticed, except when on a grand scale.

> "Oh, it was wild and weird and wan, and ever in camp o' nights
> We would watch and watch the silver dance of the mystic Northern Lights.
> And soft they danced from the Polar sky and swept in primrose haze;
> And swift they pranced with their silver feet, and pierced with a blinding blaze.
> They danced a cotillion in the sky; they were rose and silver shod;
> It was not good for the eyes of man—'twas a sight for the eyes of God."

The Auroral display on this night was by far the most beautiful I have ever seen, and the guides stated they had never seen the lights more brilliant, or more variegated—perhaps freakish would be a better word. From out of the north, apparently from the high mountain top, streamers of light shot across the heavens, and the entire mountain side lighted up. Remaining motionless for a short time, they gradually receded and disappeared, leaving the sky in darkness. Several times these streamers reappeared, as before, but they were only forerunners of what was to follow. As they blazed forth, one after another, they appeared to be signaling each other to prepare for a night of frolic. Presently they radiated in fan-shaped streaks and the heavens became brighter and brighter. Then they receded and reappeared in all kinds of fantastic forms and colors; some were a pale green, others a crimson color, while some took on a variation more nearly resembling the colors of a rainbow. They danced toward the east, then toward the west, and finally spread out over the entire heavens. Again they receded, only to appear as great waves rolling across the skies—but how useless to attempt to describe such a magnificent phenomenon. On an occasion of this kind one may receive impressions that will linger for a lifetime.

Leaving our horses to graze, Paddie and I started out at 6:30 the next morning on foot. This day stands out in my memory as the most eventful and interesting day's hunting experience of my life. Traveling up and around the mountain for about two miles we saw a band of eleven caribou—one of them having large horns —but they got our scent before we were able to plan a successful stalk, and made a hasty retreat. We followed them for about three miles, but the topography of the mountain side was such that we could not get around them to take advantage of the wind, so we finally gave up and continued on our course up the barrens. We saw a red fox at one time walking slowly across a small draw about two hundred yards away. The Indian asked if he could try a shot at it, but after obtaining my consent he decided not to do so, as the fox's coat was not prime and would command but a small price.

Presently we changed our course in the direction of the small creek to our right, which was the same one that ran down the ravine where we had camped. On the opposite side of the creek was a high mountain which looked favorable for sheep. With our glasses we made a survey of the mountain, about three miles above camp, and soon located five sheep in an amphitheatre which extended back into the mountain for at least a mile, and in which a branch of the little creek had its source. At first there seemed to be no means of approach without their seeing us, but studying the situation for a time we noticed a small bluff located a short distance up the side of the amphitheatre and not far from the sheep. We planned to try to reach them by keeping well up against the side of the mountain instead of going along the creek bed, hoping to take advantage of the bluff to keep out of their sight. Drawing near we found it was necessary to cross a slide of loose flat rock, perhaps two hundred yards in width, and that it was going to be difficult to do so without alarming the sheep. I

Mountain sheep in their Alaskan setting of rock and snow. Courtesy of U. S. Dept. of the Interior.

removed my hobnailed shoes, but it was unnecessary for the Indian to remove his footwear as he was wearing moosehide moccasins.

In crossing the slide we were often obliged to remove a loose stone, before taking a step, to avoid making any noise. Cautiously we approached the bluff and made our way to a boulder. Peering around I selected the ram having the largest head and killed him with one shot. The others were bewildered and for a few moments appeared undecided which way to run. I was in no hurry about firing a second time as we had them in a pocket and there was no way they could escape, without giving me ample opportunity for a number of shots, if necessary. Soon they started running up the slope, and selecting the next best head, I fired again and missed; but the ram fell at my third shot, rolling to the small stream forty yards below. The others had only fair heads, and were not molested as they hurriedly made their way up the steep walls of the amphitheatre, disappearing from sight a half-hour later. The first ram killed had large, perfect horns with a thirty-nine inch curl; the horns of the other were "broomed" on their ends for two or three inches, otherwise being equal to those of the first one killed. Paddie dressed one of the sheep and I dressed the other, although I confess that I was only half-through when his task was completed. We wanted to save all the mutton secured as we relished it more than any other meat, and were afraid the entire country might soon be covered with snow, making it more difficult to locate the white fleeced animals.

For some time I had sought an opportunity and favorable conditions to hunt by myself. I wished to roam about at will in an effort to locate and secure game without the assistance of a guide. I hoped to take advantage of a clear day and climb some of the high mountains alone. Much of my hunting throughout various sections of the north country—sometimes for an entire trip,—has been without, and independent of guides. Among the most pleasant days I remember have been those spent in the forests or mountains, or on lakes or streams, entirely alone. I considered this a splendid opportunity to carry out my plans, as it was a perfect day, and then only the middle of the forenoon. I told the Indian of my intentions and suggested that he return to camp about four miles away, get two pack horses, and come back for the sheep heads and meat. He objected, saying Bones would not like it if he left me to hunt alone, and added I might lose my way and not be able to return to camp in the evening. I tried to reassure him in this respect, but not until I commanded him to carry out my orders, with the promise I would take all responsibility so far as Bones was concerned, was he willing to leave me.

I then started the long climb up the mountain. The several weeks of outdoor exercise had hardened me, and it did not require much exertion to make the ascent in an hour and a half, as we had already gained some elevation by stalking the sheep. There was the usual fascination as I approached the top—anxious to get a view of what lay beyond. On numerous occasions when climbing mountains, I have caught myself unconsciously making all possible haste over the last few rods—intent in my eagerness to view the scenes which awaited me on the other side. As I reached the summit on this occasion, I beheld a beautiful sight. Down the several gorges and valleys small creeks coursed their way, all of them converging into one stream, which I afterwards

UNUSUAL EXPERIENCES

learned was the Caldern. Far down the main valley this creek wound its way, disappearing from view through a rugged gorge ahead. A great forest of dark green spruce covered the valley and extended some distance up the mountain side. There was no wind; everything was as quiet as death, and in the clear atmosphere my vision extended to the horizon of mountain peaks far beyond. The stream and occasional waterfalls below glistened in varying tints in the bright sunlight, while here and there small lakes were seen, not only in the lowlands, but well up on the benches of the mountains, where they appeared to be suspended from the mountain's side. I realized it would probably be my last climb to the summit of a high mountain during the trip, so I gazed for a long time on this bewildering sea of summits, the more distant ones gradually fading from sight and suggesting the mysterious unknown. Finally awakening myself from this daydream and the enjoyment of the loneliness, I proceeded along the knife-like edge of the mountain. Ascending a high peak, I made a complete survey of the country in the direction of our camp, as well as that in which I was traveling, so that I might not experience any difficulty in returning, by whatever course I might take in the evening.

Several small bands of sheep were observed some distance down the mountain to the right, but seeing that their heads were small, I continued for some time and finally located two rams standing on the crest of the mountain about a mile ahead of me. My eyesight had grown stronger and I was able to recognize animals or objects at greater distances than had been possible at the beginning of our hunt. I have observed that one accustomed to indoor or office work can find no better rest for the eyes—and nerves—than to get out on high mountains, where he has the advantage of long distances of vision in the clear atmosphere. Since a young man I had been accustomed to wearing glasses, yet so strengthened did my vision become on this trip, that I was able to discard them until I returned to my regular duties.

Rounding the comb of the mountain peak, I varied my course so as to keep out of sight of the rams, until I reached a point where the ridge sloped downward, forming a large saddle between me and the sheep. I could not proceed farther without coming into plain view of them, so I watched for a while with my glasses. One had a very good head, while the other had one which was only fair. I noticed the sheep appeared quite restless and cast their heads about nervously—a fact which I could not account for, as I did not think they had detected me. To the right of them the mountain broke away in a perpendicular cliff, making escape on that side impossible. Beyond, on the crest of the mountain, was a cliff so straight up that they could not ascend it. It looked as though their only means of escape was around the more gradual slope of the mountain to the left. In this direction they continued to turn their heads in a nervous manner. My sole hope of killing one of them was to shoot from where I stood, but the distance appeared to be too great. However, I had wished for an opportunity to try a long shot, under favorable conditions, when I was not short of breath from the exertion of a hard climb. This appeared to be my chance, so kneeling down, I looked through the sights of the Newton rifle and found my aim to be quite steady. I tried this two or three times, estimating carefully the distance, then fired at the larger ram and saw the bullet strike just over his shoulder, but to my surprise the sheep did not move. Taking just a little finer aim I fired a second shot and the ram pitched forward dead. Again I was surprised to note that the other ram did not run. Instead he walked up to his fallen companion and stood there without taking any notice of the direction from which the shot had come, although he continued to watch around the slope to the left. This was the third ram I had killed on the Yukon side, and all of them had been taken that day. I was entitled to one more, but hesitated to shoot at this one as I hoped to secure a larger head.

I was pleased with the shot and decided to step off the distance to the fallen ram. Going forward, approximately one yard to the step, until I had stepped off five hundred yards, I stopped and sat down on a rock to watch the other ram. He still held his position, notwithstanding that I had approached in plain view. Occasionally he glanced toward me, but with little interest, and continued to look around the mountain to the left. I could not understand why he did not retreat. I arose to my feet and bleated like a sheep; whereupon he again looked at his dead comrade as if for the last time, and then moved slowly away—but for a few yards only. I felt sorry for the lonely animal and wondered if his reluctance to leave was because of his attachment to the other ram. I then considered the matter of taking him also, but it appeared somewhat greedy to kill my limit of rams in one day. I thought of the many days I had spent on

UNUSUAL EXPERIENCES

the mountains of Beaver Creek, Alaska, without meeting any success, and of the comparative ease with which I had already killed three fine rams that day. I took into consideration the fact that I would not likely have another opportunity to get my fourth ram, as our time was almost up, and most of it would be spent in hunting caribou. I, therefore, decided to end my sheep hunting by killing this one.

Leisurely taking aim, I fired—killing the ram instantly—when to my surprise, a large wolverine jumped from behind some rocks, perhaps thirty yards from where the ram stood. I fired at him as he ran, but missed; and he disappeared around a cliff before I could get a second shot. The uneasiness on the part of the sheep was now accounted for. They were evidently aware of the approach of the wolverine from the only direction in which they could make their escape without running toward me. It had been a fascinating experience—but another one equally interesting awaited me that day. I continued stepping off the distance to the first ram killed and found it to be an additional hundred and eighty steps, or a total of six hundred and eighty steps in walking to the ram. I estimated the distance to be about five hundred yards on a direct line, and considered it the best shot I had ever made.

In spite of its being a very inaccessible place and far from camp, I concluded to dress the sheep—thinking that Bones might send after them. Sharpening my hunting knife on a pocket whetstone, I went about my task somewhat hurriedly, as it was growing late. I found that the first ram had been shot through the heart, and the second one through the shoulders. Presently a shadow shot over the summit, and looking westward, I saw a large golden eagle circling about. Watching it for a few moments I then proceeded with my work, while the eagle continued to soar above me, gradually coming lower. I had no fear of the large bird, of course, and thought he was attracted by the fresh meat; but his close presence annoyed me. Ammunition was becoming quite scarce and I did not want to waste a shot in scaring him away. Furthermore, I had only a half-dozen cartridges with me and wished to conserve them for a possible shot at a bear before reaching camp. I picked up some stones and when the eagle came closer I threw at him several times, but he paid no attention to this. Suddenly he swooped down to within a few feet of my head; in fact, so close that I felt the wind from his great wings.

I shouted at him in a loud tone of voice, whereupon he quickly flew away, and I watched him until he disappeared beyond some distant high peaks. I have often thought of the incident and wondered if anyone else ever had an experience of this kind. The bird took no notice of me, or the stones I threw at him, but upon hearing my voice—a sound which was so strange to him—he took fright and departed immediately. These large birds prey upon young lambs and kids, and sometimes sheep of considerable size, taking quite a number every year. They attack with their beaks, claws and wings until their prey becomes exhausted and an easy victim.

Completing my task I placed the unskinned carcasses on stones sufficiently high from the ground to permit circulation of air; and after smoking my pipe, and enjoying the solitude for a few minutes, picked up the heads and started. The heads, horns and capes of two rams—skinned back to the shoulders—is by no means a light or convenient load. The weight of the skin does not counterbalance the weight of the head and horns. To attempt to carry them by grasping the tapering horns, requiring a firm grip, which soon becomes very tiresome. I did not go far until I found I could not carry them in this manner, as the two green heads weighed easily sixty-five pounds. Removing my belt, I strapped it around the largest head, thereby giving me a good hold. I then strapped the gun to my back, and taking the smaller sheep head in the other hand, I was able to make better progress.

I decided not to return along the crest of the mountain as I had come, but instead, to continue until I could find a place to descend to a creek that could be seen in the narrow valley below. Upon reaching the creek, I intended following it to its source; then crossing the divide and going down the other creek to camp. By taking this course I knew that it would not be difficult to find my way back, even though it would be dark before I could get there.

After walking along the mountain for quite a distance, I found a place where I thought I could get down, so decided on my course while on the crest, from which I had a full view. Cautiously I descended—step by step—sometimes over shale, sometimes over loose rock and at times down ledges and over cliffs. Presently my arms became very tired from the weight and inconvenience of my awkward load, and I watched for a place to deposit the heads while I rested. Not finding a spot, I kicked aside

UNUSUAL EXPERIENCES

some loose shale and placed the heads in such a manner that I thought they would not roll. Soon I saw a band of eight caribou, feeding on a small grass-covered bench, well down toward the bottom of the mountain. Quickly looking through my glasses, I saw that their leader was a large bull, having good horns. I began estimating the distance for a long shot, when some shale loosened under the larger sheep head and it started rolling down the steep slope in the direction of the caribou. Alarmed by the approaching object which was gaining speed all the time, the caribou started running around the mountain in a downward course. I unstrapped my gun and fired at the largest animal. He dropped to his front knees but quickly regained his feet. I fired two more shots at him and missed. Off to the west the sun was about to disappear behind the summit of a snow-clad mountain; from its fading rays there was sufficient light for me to see only a portion of the way down the mountain on which I stood, the valley below appearing almost dark. The last two shots were fired after the caribou reached this shaded area and with that disadvantage, together with the great distance that intervened, my chance of hitting him was poor, so I wasted no more ammunition. With one exception this was the only animal on the entire trip that I wounded without killing, but fortunately neither of them was seriously wounded—a fact which was very gratifying to me.

Taking up the small head, I continued down the steep incline until I reached a small gorge where the other head had lodged. Finding it was not damaged, I decided to let both heads roll the rest of the way down, which I did successfully. The surface of the mountain, during the remainder of the distance, was composed of loose shale with no slide rock, which made footholds easy and permitted me to travel without loss of time. I made the descent from the top in one hour and fifty minutes, after deducting the time spent in resting and watching the caribou. I thought it best to leave the heads and send one of the Indians for them the next day; therefore, I cached them on a large rock, a short distance from the creek, where the Indian might find them without difficulty.

I was in high glee over my unusual experiences of the day. I had discovered and followed a herd of caribou in the early morning; seen a red fox; stalked and killed two rams from a band of sheep; observed a number of other sheep; killed the two rams on

177

the high mountain, and had shot at the wolverine. Then, too, there was the encounter with the eagle, and later to my regret, I saw a herd of caribou and wounded one. I was reviewing these experiences in my mind, when, on reaching the creek bed, I found the largest bear tracks that I had seen! Examining them, I saw

Snyder's moose—killed on an old moraine, and his large ram.

that they were fresh, and concluded they had been made only a short time before—perhaps during the time of the shooting. With the three remaining cartridges in my gun I followed them for several hundred yards, but with increasing difficulty as it was getting dark. Concluding it was useless to follow a large grizzly so late in the evening, with only three cartridges in my gun and in the opposite direction from camp, I retraced my steps.

Reaching the head of the creek, I crossed the divide, and in the darkness was making my way down the other creek, when I thought I heard a noise below me. I stopped and listened. Soon I heard the noise again, and listening for some time, it sounded like the footsteps of a large animal. Presently the sounds became more distinct. I took the gun from my shoulder and held it in readiness, although it was then too dark to take aim at any object. I realized that the animal was approaching me and was of the

UNUSUAL EXPERIENCES

opinion that it was a grizzly. Suddenly I saw a ghost-like white object on the opposite side of the creek, but approaching in my direction. What could it be? It was far too large to be a sheep—or goat. I realized no other large animals on this continent are white, except Polar Bears, which are found in the Arctic Ocean. I was not scared, but I must confess I felt somewhat uncomfortable, as I was unable to understand what the animal could be. On it came! Presently I thought of the horses and wondered if my white saddle horse, Spot, might have wandered from the others. As it approached I called the horse by name and was answered by Indian Paddie! Mr. Snyder, on returning to camp, had found the Indian there and learning of my plans, had become uneasy when I did not return at nightfall. After waiting a while he had told the Indian to take Spot and go to meet me. Although not in need of help, I appreciated Mr. Snyder's kindness very much and also the opportunity to ride the rest of the way.

On arrival I found Doctor Evans had not yet returned and that Johnnie had gone in search of him. Bones had hunted with Doctor that day, and locating rams in the afternoon, directed Doctor to take his time and try to get up to them, while he took the horses back to camp to graze. Doctor did so and succeeded in killing two rams having good heads. Leaving them to be brought in later, he located another band and started for them, going some distance from where Bones had left him. In the course of time Bones returned, but it was not until after dark that he found Doctor, who was in high spirits, as he had that afternoon killed his legal limit of sheep, and had given no thought to the approaching darkness. On the way back to camp Doctor became exhausted and Bones had to return without him.

Describing the place where he had left Doctor, Bones sent Johnnie back for him with a horse. In the meantime Doctor had attempted to come on alone, and had missed his course. Johnnie had much difficulty in finding him and it was late bedtime when they arrived. We gave him a cup of hot coffee, which revived him somewhat, but he immediately retired—too exhausted to take any food. Mr. Snyder had also met with success that day, having killed a ram with a very good head. After a late supper we lay down on our bed of rocks where we again spent an uncomfortable night.

Mr. Snyder hunted sheep the next day, as he was entitled to one more ram on the Yukon side, but he had no success. Paddie brought in the heads of the two rams which I had left at the foot of the mountain, while Bones and I spent the forenoon skinning and fleshing the heads of the two I had killed the morning before. Bones thought it too far to send to the high mountain for the meat of the rams I had killed and so carefully dressed the day before. In the days to come and before reaching civilization, I thought often of that excellent meat left on the mountain top, and longed for a morsel of it.

Chapter XV

OUR CAMP MENU

*"I'm sick to death of your well-groomed gods, your
  make-believe and your show;
I long for a whiff of bacon and beans, a snug
  shakedown in the snow;
A trail to break, and a life at stake, and another
  bout with the foe."*

NOT wishing to spend another night on our bed of rocks, we moved a mile and a half farther that afternoon to the next gulch, where a limited supply of horse feed was found and where we had a better camping place. Taking a bucket, Bones and I picked a gallon of low bush cranberries, growing in abundance throughout that section and which, after the heavy frosts, were well ripened. We were all very fond of these berries when cooked with at least an equal portion of sugar. Large blueberries, such as I have never seen any place else, were also to be found in almost every section above timber line; and we often feasted on them, as well as on the wild currants which grew in some places. Many other berries were found, some of which the Indians liked very much. Soap berries—so called from the fact that they appeared to lather in the mouth, and with a taste slightly resembling soap —were also found. Bear berries were abundant. They had a bitter although rather pleasant taste, and when mixed with the blueberries were very palatable.

About dark it started snowing and continued all night. We spread our canvas over a clump of low willow bushes and after supper which Bones prepared, the other members of the party immediately crawled under the canvas and retired. The Indians had cut for fuel a lone dry spruce on the barrens above us, and had brought it to camp. As I sat on one end of this burning log until almost midnight watching the falling snow, my thoughts strayed toward home and I compared that Saturday night with the usual Saturday night within the bounds of civilization.

We intended to break camp by noon next day and return to the Generc River by way of Harris Creek, which we expected to reach by night. Mr. Snyder was entitled to one more sheep, so he decided to spend the day hunting with Johnnie, then join us at Harris Creek. Bones and Paddie spent the forenoon bringing in the heads of the rams Doctor had killed, and as much of the meat as he cared to take along, while Doctor and I remained in camp. The two of us had our lunch, and in order to get an early start when Bones and the Indian returned, I prepared a meal for them, frying a large pan of mutton and making what I thought was an abundance of tea. Bones was out of sorts that day, however, and on returning, he stated that I had fried only enough meat to make a good bite for Paddie, and that there was hardly enough tea prepared for one man—that if I would fry just twice as much meat and make double that amount of tea, with "double the strength 'into' it" that perhaps they could make out a meal! He also discovered I had allowed the dishcloth to partially burn from flying sparks, and that we would be obliged to get along during the remainder of the side trip with a dishcloth much abbreviated in size.

When we packed up it was necessary to load two of the saddle horses, as the heads of the nine sheep and the meat that we were taking added very much to our load. One of the horses packed was Spot, and as a result I was asked again to walk—perhaps as a penalty for burning the dishcloth! On our way down the mountain to Harris Creek we saw a band of thirteen caribou feeding on the tundra above timber line. The curiosity of these animals usually exceeds their keenness of vision, and when they do not get the scent, they often allow one to approach within plain view, or sometimes they even approach the object of their curiosity. In this instance they started toward us, circling first to our right, then to our left, but always keeping in front. Their actions were most interesting and I regretted that it was then too late in the day to try for a photograph. Since none of them had very large horns they were not disturbed. For perhaps two miles they jumped and played like young lambs and continued to circle about, ahead of our horses. Finally they moved a little farther to the right, and getting our scent, departed at break-neck speed.

We did not reach Harris Creek until nine o'clock, where we found Mr. Snyder and Johnnie waiting for us. Mr. Snyder had killed two caribou that day, both of them having good heads. A band of forty or fifty Indians was camped close by. There were Indian bucks, squaws and children, and as many dogs as Indians,

OUR CAMP MENU

all of them on their way to the Generc River for a fall moose hunt. It was a clear, frosty night, and as there was no snow on the ground at that elevation, we did not put the canvas up, but slept in the open.

Next morning we found that Mr. Snyder's and Johnnie's horses had returned to the main camp on the Generc during the night. Bones said Doctor, Mr. Snyder and I need not remain with the pack outfit, but that Mr. Snyder could take one of the other horses, and the three of us should go to the Generc River, twelve miles distant. On arriving there we were to tell Billy Slimpert to return with two saddle horses; and also two additional pack horses to help carry the load. Our course was over country which we had not traveled, but we experienced no difficulty in finding our way. We found Billy and Gene hard at work, whipsawing lumber. After rounding up the horses Billy started back as directed, and returned with Bones and the Indians about midnight. Mr. Snyder and I were unable to retire until they arrived, as our blankets had been left with the outfit.

During our absence the San Francisco party had arrived at the Generc, where they camped for two days. While there, they related to Gene and Billy an exciting experience that occurred the day after we left them at the Nazina Glacier — where we hunted goats early in August. They said that as they traveled up the glacier they saw where Bones had left his horses when we hunted there two days before. Seeing crevasses and rough ice ahead they concluded to leave their horses there also. Traveling up the glacier in single file, they had gone about a quarter of a mile when Mr. Lyons—who was in the rear—saw Mr. Crouch just in front of him, suddenly disappear as if the earth had swallowed him. In fact such was the case, and all he could see was the hole in the ice through which he had gone. Mr. Lyons gave the alarm to those ahead and they quickly ran back. Baxter called and received an answer from Mr. Crouch, who had landed on a shelf in the crevasse some distance below. On being asked if he was hurt, he stated he was but that he did not know how seriously. Baxter told him to remain quiet while he dispatched one of the men back to the horses for lariat ropes. Mr. Crouch called to them that he was getting very wet from dripping ice water, whereupon Baxter took off his hunting coat and dropped it to him. The men who went for the lariat ropes soon returned, and two of the ropes were tied together and a loop made on one end. The rope was let down through the hole into the crevasse, and Mr. Crouch adjusted it around his body. He was then carefully drawn up, but could not be pulled through the small opening at the surface, so they were obliged to let him down. Close by was a narrow opening to the crevasse, and through this a second rope was lowered. Mr. Crouch tied this to his body also. He was then drawn up to the surface as before and pulled out through the slanted opening with the other rope. He was badly bruised and bleeding from several cuts. The experience had been a dreadful shock to him, the horrors of which will forever be stamped on his memory.

The crevasse, where they crossed it, was bridged over with snow which had crusted and, therefore, was not visible at that point. It had sustained the weight of the members of our party, as well as the balance of Baxter's party, but had broken through with Mr. Crouch, who weighed about two hundred and twenty-five pounds. The walls where he went down were not perpendicular but slanting, which checked his descent; and had it not been for the small bench, he no doubt would have gone to the bottom. Mr. Crouch said he could hear the sound of running water far below. By measuring the ropes they found the distance from the shelf where he landed, to the surface of the glacier to be fifty-five feet, and it was fifty-five minutes from the time he disappeared until he was rescued. Mr. Crouch felt the effects of this shock for several days and the experience cast a gloom over the party. In an article contributed by Mr. Baxter to *Outdoor Life* he gave an account of this experience and pictures showing the scene—including one of Mr. Crouch, which showed his horrible condition when drawn to the surface.

Billy Slimpert told about an experience of three men on the Nazina Glacier several years before. With fourteen dogs, they started with a load of supplies from McCarthy to the Chisana Gold Fields. Going up the glacier one of their number suddenly disappeared in a crevasse and it was some time before they received answers to their calls. Even then the replies were quite faint, indicating that he was some distance below. Presently all became quiet and they were unable to get any further response. Soon darkness came and they prepared to camp on the ice—using their sled as a protection from the piercing wind of the cold winter night. Frequently during the night they called, but without an answer, and when morning came they were at a loss to know what to do. Presently a voice was heard, and looking down the glacier

OUR CAMP MENU

With the breast band of his pack harness used as a collar, and a cinch rope as traces, old 'Fox-feed' hauled the several loads of whipsawn lumber to the river, a mile distant.

they were surprised to see their missing companion, staggering about. They went to his assistance and he collapsed in their arms —unconscious. Unloading their freight, except such food and blankets as would be required, they placed the unfortunate man on the sled and started back to McCarthy. It was not long until he regained consciousness and started to tell them about his experience finding a way out of the crevasse, during the night, but his story was never finished, as he again lapsed into unconsciousness, from which he never recovered. Such are the dangers of these hardy men, who choose a life of this kind.

Mr. Snyder wished to try his hand at whipsawing lumber, and assisted at the task all afternoon and the following day, until it was thought that sufficient lumber had been cut to build the boat. In the outfit was an old pack horse which Bones intended killing for fox feed when he returned to his home. Learning of his intentions we had named this horse "Fox-feed"; he was used in pulling the lumber to the river, about a mile from where it was sawed. His pack saddle and breast straps were put on him, with cinch ropes for traces, and by evening he had hauled all the lumber to the bar of the Generc. Paddie, being quite handy at almost any kind of work and having some reputation among the Indians as a boat builder, was assigned the task of building our boat, with Billy Slimpert as helper.

Baxter and his men built their boat during their stay at the Generc River—from the lumber which he had cut and stacked there during the early summer. For about twenty-five miles below the mouth of the Generc the White River is very rough and for nine or ten miles runs through a dangerous gorge. Baxter had two of his men take the boat through this rough water to a point about thirty-five miles down the river, where it was to be held until he arrived there with the outfit. He planned to leave some of his horses at the Generc where pea vine was plentiful, and take only a portion of his outfit down the river to the boat. Since he thought it would be very difficult, if not impossible to take even a small pack horse outfit down the river, he was to guide his hunting party around the high mountains that paralleled the White River, hunting and camping on the way, until they would arrive at the location where the boat was being held. The party was fortunate in having with them an experienced river man, Roy Lozier, who was to help Baxter run the river, while the horse wrangler and cook were to return with the horses to White Horse. They had shown good judgment in getting the boat finished and through the rough water before it turned so extremely cold.

I have said little about our food or how we passed the time in camp. Breakfast was usually over by six in the morning,—and what breakfasts! Cereals of some kind were first served—rolled oats, cream-of-wheat or Pettijohn's breakfast food—with sugar, and condensed milk diluted to the consistency of ordinary milk. We usually had three kinds of meat: moose or caribou steak, lamb chops and breakfast bacon; fried mush, great plates of buttered toast, Wagstaff's orange marmalade or Cross and Blackwell's imported jams, both of which are well known throughout the North as the best obtainable. We always had stewed prunes, apricots or peaches. Then came the griddle cakes with maple syrup, and what cakes they were! Each person consumed anywhere from five to eight. Often we had pie for breakfast but the meal was always finished with doughnuts. Most of the time we took

OUR CAMP MENU

lunch with us, which consisted of a sandwich of roast lamb, caribou, or moose, and sometimes cold moose tongue; another sandwich of bread, butter and marmalade and often a piece of fruit cake, but always three or four doughnuts.

The evening meals were the most elaborate. First, a rich, heavy-bodied soup, frequently of barley. Then roast moose meat with brown gravy, caribou steak with mushrooms, roast lamb with mint sauce, canned sweet potatoes, baked beans, hot rolls, jams and evaporated fruit of some kind. We frequently had French pastry, consisting of chocolate éclairs or cream puffs; lemon, raisin or fresh blueberry pie; and plum pudding with "temperance sauce," as Gene termed it. In fact, Gene, our French cook, often prepared dishes that were altogether new to us and which were designated by various French names. We were served with coffee, cocoa or tea as we preferred, but we always finished with doughnuts. We had an abundance of meat sauces such as Worcester, H. P., and Snyder's tomato catsup, with various kinds of pickles, relishes and olives. Our butter was packed in one-pound, sealed cans and remained in perfect condition.

All of us consumed much meat and preferred it with a great deal of fat on it. However, each Indian ate perhaps as much meat at one meal as Doctor, Mr. Snyder and I ate in two meals combined. Doctor often remarked that he would not like to undertake to feed those Indians at the price of meat back in the States, but it was no object there, as we were unable to consume one-tenth of the excellent meat we secured. Caring little about knick-knacks of any kind, their meal consisted principally of fat meat—although they too were fond of doughnuts. All of us preferred wild mutton to any other meat and never grew tired of it, as we considered it by far the most delicious meat we had ever tasted. We were told that the men of that country often eat it three times daily, the entire year, without tiring of it.

One also requires a greater amount of sugar in a cold country. Outfitters, prospectors and trappers purchase about half as much sugar as flour when laying in their winter's food supply. Since one craves both fat and sugar, it was no wonder that we relished doughnuts. I declared that upon returning home I intended to have them served on my table three times a day. Gene fried a bushel box full every three or four days—a supply of powdered eggs having been taken for use in making them. Bones told of an Englishman who had come to the Yukon Territory for the purpose of prospecting. In custom with the men of the North, he soon acquired an appetite for doughnuts, and not knowing how to make them, he visited Bones to find out. "I told him," said Bones, "there isn't much to it; all that you have to do is to make a little sweetened dough, wrap it around a hole and fry it in grease."

I was amused at Bones one evening when pie was passed to him. For some reason it had been cut in six pieces instead of four as usual. When handed to Bones, he refused, saying, "When pie is cut into two pieces, I always eat pie; when cut into four pieces, I sometimes eat pie, but when cut into six pieces, I never eat pie."

We could readily understand why Gene had gained such a reputation as a cook. No better meals could have been obtained in the finest hotels or restaurants of our larger cities. No expense had been spared by Bones in securing an abundance of food of the very best quality. In fact, throughout that country, only the best foods are used. There is perhaps no country in the world whose people are more discriminating in this respect than the residents of Alaska and the Yukon Territory.

The days were rapidly growing shorter and by five-thirty or six o'clock it was dark. We usually had supper soon after dark and instead of going to our sleeping tent, we preferred remaining in the dining tent for a smoke and a chat. We were usually very much in Gene's way, but he was at all times good-natured and never objected. Doctor and Mr. Snyder were in the habit of retiring about an hour after eating, while it was my custom to remain an hour or two longer in conversation with Billy Slimpert. He was well informed on almost any subject pertaining to that country and its people, and I found him very interesting and secured much information from him.

As we sat in the dining tent smoking one evening I suggested to Bones that he try some of my tobacco. After he had smoked a pipe full, I asked him how he liked it and he replied, "Now I don't want to hurt your feelings by running down the tobacco you smoke, but it ain't got a d----d bit of strength 'into it' and I don't think much of it." I had with me three or four twists of genuine Perique tobacco, which was as black as coal and so strong I could not use it, even when a very small portion was mixed with ordinary tobacco. Getting a twist, I asked Bones to try it, but warned him he should not smoke it without diluting with other tobacco. He filled the large bowl of his pipe with the pure Perique and after

OUR CAMP MENU

smoking it said, "That is the best tobacco I have ever used." It is needless to say that I was no longer burdened with my stock of Perique.

On another occasion, Bones declared with an oath, that his pipe had not been smoking properly for several days and asked if he could borrow my .22 Remington rifle. I wondered what connection there could be between his complaint about the pipe and the request to borrow my rifle, but asked no questions. In about fifteen minutes he returned carrying a nice cock ptarmigan. Handing me the rifle, he pulled the tail feathers from the bird, placed them in the pocket of his hunting coat, with the remark that he should have no further trouble with his pipe. I told him I had plenty of pipe cleaners and could have supplied him, but he said he preferred the ptarmigan feathers.

The small heating stove in our tent was seldom used, except when some of us took a bath; although on a few cold mornings Gene very kindly came to our tent before we got up, built a fire and closed the fly. During the entire trip, regardless of the temperature, we always slept with the fly of the tent wide open. Doctor and Mr. Snyder had sleeping bags but I had not brought mine. The one I had used for a number of years was very heavy and due to my inability to secure a genuine Arctic sleeping bag of eiderdown, I decided to use blankets on this trip. I regretted this decision, however, as much time was required in rolling and strapping my blankets together each morning, as well as in making my bed in the evening. When spruce or balsam boughs were unobtainable, our beds were made directly on the ground. At such times I would have been at a great disadvantage had I not been provided with a small air mattress.

On the morning of September twenty-fourth Bones announced we would make a side trip of three or four days, to the head of Count Creek, for the purpose of hunting caribou; and that this would be our last hunt. It was a section of country where Bones and the guides had never been. We were highly pleased when he told Gene to accompany us, because this meant that we would have plenty of well cooked food. By this time we were growing uneasy on account of remaining in the interior so long. We had planned to be at White Horse by October first, and to do so, we should have been on our way before now. In fact, Doctor, Mr. Snyder and I were willing to end the hunt at once, but as we had not secured any unusually large caribou heads Bones disliked starting until we had done so, even though every day we remained meant additional expense to him, to say nothing of the danger of being overtaken by extremely cold weather. Another matter of considerable importance was the necessity of turning their horses out before the weather became too cold. The ability of the horses to withstand the long winters, depends largely on their condition when winter begins; and if worked until late in the fall, with no opportunity to take on flesh, their chances of wintering are greatly reduced.

Of late, our conversation frequently turned to the danger of the rivers freezing over, and of not being able to go down the White River in our boat. The small creeks were already frozen and Mr. Snyder was somewhat skeptical concerning this undertaking. He expressed the thought that we had better abandon this project and return overland with the horses. Bones admitted we would be taking chances; that the river might freeze up any night as it was already getting much colder—or that it might freeze up after starting. On the other hand, he said, it was impossible to take all of our trophies out on the horses at one load; and if we were to leave some of them, it would necessitate a special trip back there during the winter with dog teams, or in the spring with the horses. In either event, he pointed out, they would likely be attacked by woods mice and ruined. He, therefore, thought it best to take the chances of carrying out our plans, so we reconciled ourselves to the caribou hunt, while Paddie and Billy were building the boat.

Chapter XVI

CARIBOU ON COUNT CREEK

*"O'er soundless lakes where the grayling makes a
  rush at the clumsy fly;
By bluffs so steep that the hard-hit sheep falls
  sheer from out the sky;
By lilied pools where the bull moose cools and wallows
  in huge content;
By rocky lairs where the pig-eyed bears peered at
  our tiny tent."*

GETTING an early start we traveled some five or six miles to the old moraine above, but could not find a passage across it with the horses. We retraced our steps about half the distance, crossed St. Clair Creek, and traveled up the opposite side. In the course of time we found ourselves in a canyon, the walls of which extended to the banks of the creek along which we were forced to travel the greater portion of the afternoon. We found it the roughest traveling we had encountered, and made slow progress. Gene led the way, along the rocky banks where possible; at other times in the water, crossing and recrossing every few hundred yards, and some places every few yards. On numerous occasions we had traveled over country that appeared impossible for horses, but we had found nothing that compared with that afternoon's travel. The creek bed was filled with large boulders, and at times it looked as though we would have to give up the trip and return. I fully expected to see a horse crippled or perhaps killed.

Late in the afternoon the snow began falling so fast that we could see only a short distance ahead. Fortunately, however, we covered the roughest portion of the distance before darkness overtook us, by which time we were above timber line. It turned very cold and we were obliged to walk in an effort to keep warm. Knowing nothing whatever about that section of the country, the men had no knowledge of where horse feed might be found. We moved on until nine o'clock, when we reached a point that looked favorable for horse feed, so we stopped for the night. The horses were hobbled before being turned out, something that was done only as a last resort. We were at a high altitude and as it was

Our caribou camp on Count Creek.

a very cold night, we were afraid if they were not hobbled, they would undertake to return to the Generc River—which would certainly have resulted in some of them being crippled. The packs, saddles and luggage were piled together and covered with canvas, as it continued to snow very hard. We were far above timber line but a scrubby spruce tree was found and cut; and with the dry branches that grew close to the ground, a fire was started. The small tent was erected, and after a bountiful supper quickly prepared by Gene, we spread the saddle blankets on the six or eight inches of snow and spent a very comfortable night.

Bones was an expert in judging caribou horns, and I was pleased when he told me, the next morning he would hunt with me that day. After riding two miles up the mountain, we sighted the largest band of caribou seen on the trip, there being fifty-five in the herd. Tying our horses to a small willow bush, we started stalking them, but found it difficult to climb the steep slope in the snow. I was wearing rubber shoepacs, with leather uppers, and the soles were worn so smooth it was almost impossible to get footholds. Before we were within shooting distance of the animals I was somewhat out of breath, so we rested for a few minutes and watched them. It is easy to determine the boss of a caribou herd, especially during the mating season. The boss of this herd was engaged in fighting another bull, almost equal in size, which had evidently contested his supremacy. Several times they clashed horns with great force, and each time the smaller bull was forced down the mountain by the "boss." While these two were engaged in fighting, the smaller bulls gradually worked their way into the herd consisting mostly of females. After running his antagonist away, the large bull set about running the smaller bulls out of the herd, and in this task the other large bull assisted. It was an interesting sight to watch the two largest bulls running among them, charging with all their force, until all of the small bulls had retreated some distance down the mountain. The "boss" would then return to the herd, and after grazing for a while, the next largest bull would gradually work his way among them; but no sooner did he arrive than he was attacked by the "boss" and a fight again ensued. We witnessed the largest bull conquer his contestant three different times. Each time the small bulls worked their way into the herd, only to be routed by the "boss" with the assistance of his antagonist. The females appeared to take no notice of the contest, but continued to paw the snow for the choice bits of lichens underneath, of which they are so fond.

With our glasses we found that each of the big bulls had an unusually large spread of horns. There was no way to approach the herd except in plain view, and the wind was somewhat unfavorable, but we succeeded in getting to within three hundred yards of them when Bones asked if I thought I could make a hit from there. I felt somewhat doubtful, as it was uphill and a long shot, but was willing to try. Watching for an opportunity, I fired at the largest caribou and saw he had been hit. I then fired at the other one, hitting him also. They started running in opposite directions around the mountain side, while the remainder of the herd started up the mountain spur. I continued firing at the bulls as they ran, first at one then at the other, until I had fired twelve shots.

By this time both of them had disappeared from sight, but I felt certain they were too badly wounded to get away. We lost no time in climbing to the point where they had stood when I first shot at them. From here, in one direction, the largest bull could be seen standing some three or four hundred yards distant around the mountain. In the opposite direction we could see the other bull standing about an equal distance away. I was using the Newton rifle and had only three cartridges left. I had purposely used the ammunition for that gun first, so that it might be taken down and rolled up with my bedding, when we would start down the White

River. I planned to carry the Ross rifle on our way down the river —as it is not of the take-down style—and had reserved fourteen cartridges for the trip. I realized that I must now make good use of the three Newton cartridges that were left. I fired at the largest bull and missed. This left two cartridges for the two bulls and I knew that I must do better shooting. The large bull again moved a short distance around the mountain and I followed cautiously, giving him a fatal shot when he stopped. I returned in the direction the other bull had last been seen, having one cartridge left. We found him down and breathing his last, so the remaining cartridge was carried home as a souvenir, since our hunting was practically ended. We returned to the largest caribou and found his head exceeded in size any that I had killed. In fact, taken as a whole, it was the best caribou head secured by any of our party. The beams were fifty-three inches in length and eight and a half inches in circumference at their base. There were twenty-nine points, and the palms were unusually large. The head of the next largest was an exceptionally fine one, having a greater number of points than those of the "boss," but the horns were without palmation, and the beams were not quite so heavy, nor of such great length. I was delighted with my success, notwithstanding I had done poor shooting that day. Having Doctor's camera with me, I made pictures of each of the fallen animals; and regretted I had not taken time, after wounding the two bulls, to get a picture of the fifty-three caribou ascending the mountain spur, as they should have shown plainly in contrast with the background of snow. I wanted to take the skins of these animals, but Bones said he would be compelled to limit us to the restrictions that had been placed upon us in this respect.

We arrived at our camp about the middle of the afternoon and it was not long until Doctor and Johnnie returned with two fine caribou heads. One of them had beams fifty-six inches long, although they were smaller in circumference and had smaller palms with fewer points than the largest one I had killed. Mr. Snyder and Gene had hunted together that day without having any success. They saw two or three small bands of caribou but none of them had large horns.

We returned to the main camp the following day, selecting a route which was much longer but less difficult. Soon after starting, Slim, one of our most active pack horses, mired in the quicksand. After removing his pack several efforts were made

CARIBOU ON COUNT CREEK

The mountainous country drained by the Generc River. (1) Where the two fighting bull caribou were killed. (2) Our Count Creek camp, two miles below.

to get him up, but without success. Again Doctor's saddle horse, "Old Bob," was brought into use, and with one end of a lariat rope tied to the strong leather halter of the mired horse, and the other end to the horn of Bob's saddle, and with all of us helping Bob to pull, the horse was hauled out. After a long day's travel, we reached our camp near the Generc River late that night.

The following morning we went to the bank of the Generc River a mile distant to inspect the boat which Paddie and Billy were building, as we were very anxious to see it. We found it almost completed and we were surprised at the skill the Indian had shown in its construction. It was twenty-two feet long at the top, and eight feet wide, the lumber from which it was made being one and one-eighth inches thick; but as an extra precaution, many strong braces were placed on the inside in such a manner that it looked as if it could not collapse with any reasonable amount of hard usage.

The weather until the last five or six days had been unusually fine, with clear skies and sunshine—although the nights had been very cold. However, by this time the days were becoming much colder and ice was forming each night, even on the swiftly running creeks, but it was broken up and carried out during the day. Much concern was being shown by the entire party regarding our river trip—and especially by Mr. Snyder, who felt we should abandon it, even though it would be necessary to leave some of our trophies. I thought frequently of the remarks made by Indian Johnnie while we were eating lunch on our return from Holmes Creek. We fully expected Bones would take one of the men down the river for the purpose of assisting in running the boat and doing the cooking, and there was much conjecture as to who would be selected. We knew it would not be Billy Slimpert as he intended going direct to McCarthy, hoping to overtake "Cap" Hubric's outfit and return with them. From a culinary standpoint we hoped it would be Gene, but we were of the opinion one of the Indians would be chosen—although Bones had said nothing concerning his intentions.

We spent the day following our return from the caribou hunt in shaving, bathing and getting everything in readiness for the start. The big task that remained was to gather pitch from the spruce trees for the purpose of calking the boat. With a pail in one hand and a stick in the other we went from tree to tree, knocking the loose pitch from the trunks. A good portion of two days was spent in collecting a sufficient amount, after which the pitch was mixed with caribou fat—two parts of pitch to one of fat—melted together and strained. Just before using it was remelted on a fire built close by the boat, carefully poured into the cracks and allowed to harden. It was a slow process, and we became very impatient and more and more uneasy because of our delay in getting started; therefore, assisted at every opportunity in an effort to keep the work going faster. In the meantime clouds had been gathering for several days and it was becoming much colder. Each morning the ice extended farther out from the shores of the river, while the entire country, even in the lowlands, was covered with snow.

We did not know the distance we would have to travel before reaching the Yukon River, but Baxter had estimated it to be two hundred miles. He had made the trip down with Mr. Corcoran in five days, but they had started about thirty-five miles below our starting point. We hoped by getting an early start each morning, and by traveling as late in the evening as possible, to make the trip in five days. We knew there was great danger of

Dr. Evans' largest Count Creek caribou; fifty-six-inch beams.

The author's largest caribou.

our awakening some morning while enroute, to find the river frozen over—a fact which Bones freely admitted; but he said the ice sometimes broke after the first freeze, although he had known the rivers to remain frozen solid from the first freeze-up of the winter until the following May.

Doctor had with him a large trap which had been set at the carcass of the moose killed by Mr. Snyder on the old moraine. Mr. Snyder and I had gone with Doctor, a week before, to watch Bones set the trap. A scrubby spruce tree about eight or ten inches in diameter and sixteen feet long was secured, and after the branches were removed the iron ring of the chain on the trap was slipped on the small end. This end was then split and a wooden wedge driven in to keep the ring from coming off. The trap was then set by opening the wide jaws, placing around it some stakes and logs, thus making it necessary for a bear to cross the trap in reaching the moose carcass which lay in a small narrow gulch.

While the men were working on the boat, Doctor, Mr. Snyder and I visited the moraine to ascertain whether or not a bear had been caught, and to bring the trap in. At Doctor's request I took his camera, as he had frequently stated if he were so fortunate as to catch a bear in the trap, he would want a picture of it before it was killed. We had not gone far until we were overtaken by a blinding snow storm. On reaching the moraine our horses began shying and snorting so we knew a bear must be somewhere in the vicinity. In fact, during our entire trip, and sometimes several times a day, we were able to detect the nearby presence of a grizzly by the actions of the horses. At times they would throw their heads up and wheel around so suddenly that their riders were caught unawares and almost dislodged from their saddles before they could grab a tight rein and get them under control. On numerous occasions some of us were awakened at night by the sound of the bells as the horses ran wildly from the location where they were feeding, and we knew a grizzly was close by. Almost invariably the Indians found bear tracks the next morning in the vicinity where the horses had been.*

---

*Anyone familiar with sections of country where coal stripping operations have been carried on and where large areas of upturned earth and stone have left the surface barren, unsightly and with a general appearance of desolation, can visualize the appearance of an old moraine such as this one. Judging from the size of the occasional clumps of small cottonwoods—with here and there a dwarfed spruce—the glacier which had once covered this great expanse of desolation, must have become extinct perhaps forty or fifty years before. There had been a great upheaval of earth and stone forming hundreds, yes thousands of small knolls—as far as one could see—with deep hollows or depressions between, some of them containing pools of water, making it impossible for one to see very much of the surrounding surface.

ALASKAN-YUKON TROPHIES

We forced our horses over the almost impassable surface of the moraine; and as we neared the place where the trap was set, we could scarcely manage them. I was riding a young sorrel mare —the same one I had mounted and ridden when Bones arrived in McCarthy with the pack train. She reared, bucked and plunged until it was with difficulty that I remained in the saddle. Finding it impossible to force her any farther, I got off and tied her to a bush, after which Doctor and Mr. Snyder did likewise with their horses. When we started toward the gulch where the bear trap had been set, I looked back and saw that all of the horses, and especially the sorrel, were so frightened they continued to plunge about and try to get loose. Fearing they would succeed and go back to camp, I returned to them, while Doctor and Mr. Snyder proceeded to the location of the bear trap. We felt certain there must be a bear in the trap or near, because of the unusual fright of the horses.

As I stood near them I took note of a small cottonwood tree standing close by with a diameter of about six inches, and observing that its surface had been torn to shreds for a distance of about eight feet up its trunk, I felt positive it had been done by a bear. Shortly Mr. Snyder returned to the top of the knoll and called to tell me the trap was gone and that the bear must be close by. He hurried from knoll to knoll looking carefully in the low places between for the bear. It was only a few minutes until he called to Doctor,—"Here he is. Come quick with your gun." It was probably not more than ten minutes from the time he had left the horses until he was looking down on the bear. Taking chances on the horses getting loose, I hurried over to Mr. Snyder and saw the bear standing in a small basin, the jaws of the heavy steel trap clinched on one of his hind feet, and with the body of the spruce tree still attached to the chain of the trap.

The bear let out some growls that made the hair stand straight on our heads and sent the chills down our backs. He lunged forward in a ferocious manner, but was unable to free himself. Mr. Snyder called to Doctor to hurry, as he was afraid the bear would get loose from the trap. In the meantime Snyder was standing with his gun in readiness, pointing directly toward the grizzly, when Doctor approached with his gun raised, ready to fire. I asked them to wait until I could run to the horses for the camera, but they objected, saying it was dangerous as the bear might free himself and attack us. I insisted on getting the

CARIBOU ON COUNT CREEK

The author and his second-largest caribou, one of the two bulls killed while they were fighting.

camera, while the bear continued to lunge forward and give vent to those blood-curdling roars. It was only a few seconds from the time Doctor arrived at the top of the knoll until he started firing directly at the bear's head. He fired the first shot when the bear had made a desperate lunge forward. The enraged animal—with eyes fiery red—roared in a manner that made our blood run cold. A second, third and fourth shot were fired—all of them at the bear's head—but not until he had received the fifth shot from Doctor's 30-40 Winchester did he fall dead, rolling the length of the chain into a little pool of water at the bottom of the basin.

In the meantime I had glanced back at the horses, which were badly frightened and making every possible effort to get loose. I then returned for the camera, and after we pulled the bear out on the bank, made two or three exposures.

Going to the moose carcass we traced the course of the bear. When cutting the spruce, Bones had trimmed it so as to leave the branches protruding four or five inches from the trunk. He said this would make it impossible for a bear to drag the tree trunk very far, as the chain was attached to the small end and the branches would catch in the ground. However, the bear had dragged the trap, with the tree trunk attached, over an area of two or three acres, plowing up the earth as he did so. He had gone to the cottonwood tree referred to and in his frenzy had torn it almost to shreds for eight to ten feet up. When he reached the small basin, where he was found, the log caught between some

ALASKAN-YUKON TROPHIES

Indian Johnnie with the doctor's second-largest caribou head. This horn formation is known as a 'peach-basket.'

rocks, and as his foot was evidently becoming sore and tender, he no doubt gave up and had perhaps been there for several days. I cannot refrain from saying that after this experience I felt this bear had been secured in an unfair and unsportsmanlike manner. We took the bear's measurements, but as I did not record them, I am unable to state what they were; but it was a large female grizzly, having a splendid coat of brown. We found that all five of the shots had entered the bear's head. Doctor and Mr. Snyder returned to camp to have the guides come for the purpose of skinning and bringing in the hide.

I decided to visit the carcass of the moose killed by me about two weeks before, thinking I might find a bear feeding on it. Leading the sorrel mare I started in the direction of the carcass, but after going a half-mile, I found it impossible to force her any farther. Because of the horse's actions, I thought another bear must be close by. I tied her to a small cottonwood and continued afoot. Going about one-fourth mile I stopped on a high knoll and looking back saw that the horse was making every possible effort to get loose. With my binoculars I could see she had circled the

CARIBOU ON COUNT CREEK

cottonwood until the halter strap was wrapped completely around its trunk. Realizing she was likely to cripple herself on the rough ground, I quickly returned and released her. There was only one thing to do if I were to go to the moose carcass and that was to turn the mare loose and let her return to camp alone. By this time it was again snowing so hard that I thought it dangerous to venture farther on the rough moraine during such a storm, and so late in the evening. Furthermore, I disliked walking the five or six miles back to camp; therefore, decided to give up the bear hunt.

Chapter XVII

A DAY ON WHITE RIVER

*"The river writhed beneath the ice; it groaned like one
   in pain,
And yawning chasms opened wide, and closed and yawned
   again;
And sheets of silver heaved on high until they split
   in twain."*

IT snowed so hard on September twenty-eighth that it was impossible to make any headway in calking the boat. We were becoming quite impatient over our delay in getting started; and quite uneasy, as the river carried an increasing amount of running ice each day. Bones had not made any comment concerning whom he intended taking down the river as a helper, but we asked no questions.

On the twenty-ninth day of September our fine collection of trophies which we prized so highly, was taken from its cache, properly grouped, and some pictures made of them. This was done at the suggestion of Mr. Snyder, who said that should we meet with disaster of any kind and lose any or all of our trophies we would at least have a picture of them. The seven bear skins secured by Doctor on his spring hunt were not included, as they had been taken out by Baxter, to be delivered at White Horse in accordance with their agreement. Not counting these skins, the three of us had a total of fifty-one trophies or seventeen each. It was a matter of interest and much satisfaction that each of us had exactly the same number. Doctor Evans had killed two moose, five caribou, six rams, three billy goats and the grizzly caught in the trap. Mr. Snyder had killed three moose, five caribou, six rams, two billy goats and one grizzly. I had killed two moose, six caribou, six rams and three billy goats. In addition to this I had killed a small goat and a small ram, at the direction of Bones, when we were in need of meat at the beginning of the hunt.

On the morning of September thirtieth about half our trophies were taken to the river a mile below, and placed in the boat, which was then completed. Bones said there was not suf-

Our fifty-one trophies, photographed before their removal to the scow.

ficient water in some of the channels of the Generc to enable us to embark from there with our heavy load, and that he and Paddie would run the boat, lightly loaded, to the mouth of the river; that the rest of us should take as many horses as necessary and with the remainder of our trophies and our supplies, join them. We now felt confident Paddie would be selected to accompany us down the river.

After seeing Bones and Paddie off we returned to camp and made preparations to start. The horses that were not needed were left there to graze. We were unable to get everything in readiness and start until soon after noon, and on leaving we took a farewell look at the camp and surroundings.

Slow progress was made in crossing the channels of the river so it was after dark when we reached Bones and Paddie, who were waiting near the mouth of the river. It was too late for the men to return to the main camp that night, so they stayed there with us. We afterwards regretted they had done so, as supper and breakfast for these four men resulted in quite a depletion of the food that had been brought for our estimated five days' trip. We put up the small sleeping tent and all of us, except the Indians, crowded into it. The latter slept outside by the fire.

We arose early and had breakfast long before daylight. The eventful day had at last arrived—Wednesday, October first—a day I shall never forget! The night had been bitter cold and the ponds and still channels of the river were frozen over. Ice extended far out from the banks of the swiftly running river, against which running ice was grinding.

We finished loading the boat soon after daylight and at last Bones announced his plans. He said he had intended taking a helper down the river, but had changed his mind because the boat was already overloaded, having about a ton and a half on it. He told the men to return to the main camp, load the camp outfit and dried meat on the pack horses, and take them to his home at Kluane Lake. On reaching Kluane Lake, Gene was to take four of the horses and start to White Horse, where Bones would be waiting for him to take back his winter supplies. The command was given in very few words and we knew it was final. His decision not to provide a helper, simply because the boat was overloaded, seemed to me poor logic. This appeared to be all the more reason why a helper should be taken,

A DAY ON WHITE RIVER

as additional weight would no doubt require additional manpower in running this dangerous river. Furthermore, the weight of an extra man could not make any considerable difference. My first thought was to protest against his decision. I reasoned that perhaps the necessity of his having to pay an additional fare on the Yukon River steamer, from the mouth of the White River to White Horse, might have had some bearing on his decision. I knew Mr. Snyder and I would have to assist in running the boat, and also do much of the cooking and camp work.

However, I further considered that we should be liberal in this respect, because Bones had shown a great interest in seeing that we secured our limit of trophies, and had remained for a longer period than our contract called for, regardless of the extra expense. We, therefore, offered no objections as we felt we should be willing to assist Bones and save him the expense of an extra steamboat fare.

On seeing the running ice and the swift waters of the river, Mr. Snyder again questioned the advisability of the undertaking and rather insisted we should yet abandon the trip and go with the horses. Doctor and I were of the opinion that we should undertake to carry out our original plans, notwithstanding we realized that it was going to be a hazardous trip. In fact, I was surprised at the courage displayed by a man of Doctor's age. Bones had little to say, but it was evident that he was very reluctant about the undertaking. Finally he said, "It has taken much work to saw the lumber and build the boat; only a small number of the trophies could be taken out on the horses and there would be great chances of losing those that we would leave. This cold spell may break up, and we may again have some good weather, and I believe we had better go ahead with our plans."

Until this time I had not asked Bones a single question concerning the river trip. However, after giving the matter some thought, I asked him how he expected to "read" the current of the river from the rear of the scow, from which place he was going to operate the long sweep. I pointed out that the trophies and skins were piled so high he could not see over them. With an oath he replied, "I'm not any afraid but what I can 'read' the water and make out our course, even if the load is high."

The morning was clear, and as the first golden rays of sunlight cast their beams across the snow-clad range, I lined the men up in a row and secured a photograph of them, together with Jumbo, the large malamute dog. Bidding the men good-bye—not forgetting a farewell caress for little Pinto—and with one more look at the high peaks of Mt. Nazahat, which loomed up so cold and forbidding, I took my seat at the front of the scow beside Mr. Snyder. A warm nest of skins had been provided for Doctor in the center, and with Bones at the sweep in the rear, we were ready to start. The ropes which held us fast were loosened by the Indians and thrown on board. The scow was quickly caught by the current, and as we waved a final farewell we passed out of the Generc and into the swift water of the White River.

All went well and as we drifted with the current, which then ran at perhaps six miles an hour, we soon became reconciled to our new mode of travel. Four long cottonwood poles had been cut, peeled and dried for use as pike poles. Mr. Snyder and I were provided with one each, while two lay in reserve on the load. Approaching an island where the river divided and which Bones had not noticed, we called back and asked which channel to follow, and he directed us.

At first Mr. Snyder and I did not assume the responsibility for selecting our course, but called to Bones to direct us. He did so for a while, but often by the time we had received his

Eugene Jacquot drying moose-meat at our Generc River camp.

A DAY ON WHITE RIVER

Loading the scow in the early morning.

orders, the boat was caught in the current of a different channel from the one selected, and we were obliged to let it go.

It was evident that Bones' remark of that morning was in error, as he finally admitted that from the rear of the scow, and with his view obstructed it was impossible for him to always select a course.

He told us to use our judgment and to pick channels into which most of the ice appeared to be flowing. Ordinarily the boat could be steered from the rear but this was not always possible in bends of the river, or in swift water. It was necessary for one of us to stand when approaching islands or sand bars; and with our pike poles, reach forward and push with all our might to direct the boat into the channel selected. It was not long until we saw we had a difficult task, and one which required quick thought and action. We soon discovered that the channels through which the greater amount of ice flowed were not always the main ones. The river often divided and sub-divided into many channels, and in some of these the water was quite shallow.

Presently our boat was stranded on a sandbar and we could not push it off with our poles. Bones got out in the water and tried to push it off, but was unable to do so. I then climbed out and assisted him, and after much lifting and pushing it cleared the bar. Quick action was necessary to board the boat before it was caught by the current and carried into deep water below. Time and again we found ourselves in shallow channels, and as my boots were already full of water, I got out and assisted Bones as often as necessary.

It was interesting to look ahead and judge the course of the river by the contour of the mountains. We could see that

Paddie guarding the heavily laden scow.

the valley was narrowing ahead, and that the high mountains on either side appeared to come almost together. We thought we were approaching the long canyon Baxter had warned us about. The channels of the river began converging, later coming together in one stream. This was a relief, indeed, and all went well for a little while. I took Doctor's camera from our packs first making a picture of the running ice, and later as we approached a sharp bend in the river, I endeavored to secure a picture of the opening through the mountains, to our right, which we concluded must be the beginning of the so-called Nine Mile Canyon. However, as the mountains appeared to close in on us, we experienced a feeling of uneasiness. We could see the river but a short distance ahead, as there were numerous bends, and we could not tell one minute what awaited us the next.

Suddenly we heard the roar of water and soon we could see the rapids, with large boulders protruding above the surface. We called to Bones, who quickly rose to his feet and took the situation in at a glance. We proposed going to the shore, with the view of "lining" the scow over the white water, but by this time it was too late and we were caught in the current and carried downward.

Bones called loudly to us to try to keep the bow of the boat from striking the protruding rocks in the river, or the walls of the canyon which we were then entering. Frantically we worked, Mr. Snyder on the left and I on the right, and Bones at the sweep. The horns of our trophies were crowded about us giving little room for freedom of action; so I arose to my feet that I might work to better advantage, but Mr. Snyder called to me to sit down, saying I would be thrown from the bow of the boat. As we approached protruding boulders we tried to ram our pike poles against them, and when able to do so, we pushed with all our might to keep the scow from striking. Our strength amounted to little, however, compared to the great force of the water, but we succeeded in diverting the course of the boat so as to miss most of the boulders. Presently the water became more swift, and suddenly the scow struck a submerged rock reaching nearly to the water's surface, and we almost capsized. The stern was caught in the current and whirled about. We lost all control of the boat for a time and it was tossed like a chip in the dangerous waters. No sooner had we righted it than the bow struck a protruding rock—head on. The water splashed over me and into my face—momentarily blinding me. Bones lost control at the sweep, and as the current caught the stern, we were whirled about like a top.

At times it looked as though the scow would go to pieces, in which event we knew we would drown or possibly be killed outright by being dashed against the protruding rocks. Most of the current appeared to flow against the right hand, perpendicular walls of the canyon. Therefore, I stood on the right-hand side of the scow, and as we were swept toward the canyon walls, I rammed the pike pole against them or otherwise, against the rocky shoreline, in an effort to keep the bow from striking. Quite frequently I succeeded, but at other times the current was so swift that I was unable to get holds with my pike pole; whereupon, the current caught the rear, whirled it about, and we drifted for some distance, rear end forward, before Bones could right the boat about with the long sweep. In the meantime the scow was so strained by the head-on impact with the rock that it sprang a leak, and Mr. Snyder bailed out the water as fast as he could. Had the Indian not braced the boat unusually well, it would certainly have gone to pieces under the strain. At times when the bow struck the canyon walls we lost all control, and were whirled around and around in the current. I considered

Running-ice in the White River, from the front of the scow.

it by far the most exciting experience of my life and probably one of the most dangerous.

In the course of time the water became somewhat smoother and we experienced little difficulty. Later we passed out of the canyon and the river broadened out and was not so swift. We hoped the worst of it was over.

Spruce timber larger than had been seen farther up the river extended to the shores. In many places the banks had been

A DAY ON WHITE RIVER

undermined causing the trees to be uprooted and to fall into the water. It was not long until more trouble began. Time and again we were forced into these treetops and almost capsized. Frequently the current swept us under the fallen tree trunks and we were obliged to crouch low in the scow in order to clear them. We soon realized we were now having greater difficulties than we had while running the canyon. The banks of the mainland were often composed of loose moss-covered earth, making it impossible to get firm holds with the end of the pike pole. There were times when we lost all control of the boat, and once my pike pole broke and I pitched forward—almost into the water, before I could recover myself. I grabbed the pole Mr. Snyder had been using, and it was soon broken in like manner. The third one was made use of, and later it, too, broke. With the remaining pole I stood in the bow of the boat, hurriedly poling to the right and to the left, sometimes against banks or boulders, at other times against sandbars or fallen trees, while Bones worked at the sweep and Mr. Snyder bailed out the water.

At two o'clock in the afternoon we ran into some fallen trees, where we lodged. Finding it impossible to push off, and realizing we were in great danger of being upset, we quickly made fast to the scow a long rope; then jumped to the tree trunks, taking the other end of the rope with us. After reaching the shore we succeeded in towing the boat upstream a short distance; then with the pike pole we pushed it far out into the current and let it go. It cleared the tree trunks as it floated down, after which we hauled in on the rope and snubbed it to a tree. Securing our tea pail, we built a fire and made some tea, after which our meagre lunch was eaten in silence. We realized we had undertaken a hazardous trip, and that we should have returned with the horses as Mr. Snyder insisted upon doing. I thought often of those nineteen trusty cayuses, which were no doubt starting on their long journey to Kluane Lake. Our tea finished, we again took our places in the boat and pushed off.

Dark clouds had been gathering during the day, and by this time it was snowing and becoming much colder. The valley widened and the river divided and sub-divided into numerous channels. Mr. Snyder and I were constantly on the lookout to select the ones carrying the greatest amount of water and appearing to have the least obstruction. I was very tired from the unusual exertion of the day, and already had visions of a

As the rapids were approached, the mountains on either side appeared to come together.

cheerful camp fire, a warm supper, and a good night's rest. My clothing in front was frozen stiff from the water that had splashed over me when we entered the canyon.

About four o'clock we approached a wedge-shaped bar which divided the channel in which we were drifting. We looked ahead to determine our course and saw that the ice was running in a

A DAY ON WHITE RIVER

narrow channel to the left; but as we neared the bar, we could see that the right channel carried the greatest amount of water. Bones worked the sweep and I poled the sandy bottom, trying to steer the boat into the right, but it was too late, as the current of the left hand channel caught the scow and carried us down with the running ice. Presently we saw a sharp bend to the left, with tree trunks and driftwood lodged against the right hand shore, in the bend. Above the water was very swift and we called to Bones to be on the lookout at the sweep. Rising to his feet he saw the danger, and told me to keep the bow of the boat far out in the current so that it would pass the drift pile. I jammed the pike pole against the cut bank on the right and pushed with all my strength, but it amounted to little as compared with the force of the water and the weight of the heavily loaded boat. Mr. Snyder was powerless to do anything as he had only a piece of one of the poles that had been broken.

Each time I pulled my pike pole in order to get a new hold against the bank ahead, I lost all that I had gained and it was evident we were going to strike the driftwood. As we rounded the bend with the current, we were forced down sideways until the scow struck the logs. Immediately the running ice jammed against the upper side, tilting it down until it started to dip water. Bones called for everybody to get off quickly, so we hurriedly scrambled out on to the tree trunks. The scow continued to dip water on the upstream side and we saw it would soon go down. There was no time to be lost! Quick action was necessary if we were to keep it from sinking; but what could we do? The swift current rocked the upstream side of the scow as one would rock a cradle, and each time that it was tilted, it dipped an increasing amount of water.

There was only one thing to do, and that was to save what we could, so Bones and I jumped back onto the scow. When loading it, Bones had taken note of the exact location of the food, blankets and more essential luggage, and he tried to get at them first, but could not do so until some of the skins and capes which had been placed on top, could be removed. Seizing these he threw them to me, and I in turn threw them to the shore, where Doctor pulled them back from the water's edge. We worked with all our might and finally reached some of the heavier and more important baggage, which was thrown on the drift logs, where Mr. Snyder placed it in a safe position. By that time the boat was dipping lower from the weight of the accumulated water inside, and the force of the current and ice above. Suddenly Bones called for me to jump as the boat was sinking, and springing to the driftlogs, we turned just in time to watch it capsize and go down. All that could be seen of it was the right-hand corner of the stern, next to the driftwood, protruding about two feet out of the water. It was not more than four or five minutes from the time we struck the driftwood until the boat sank; but, like carrying goods from a burning building, one can do much in that time with concerted effort. However, we had to stand helpless and watch the capes and lighter articles being washed from the boat by the swift current.

Chapter XVIII

STRANDED ON AN ISLAND

*"This is the Law of the Yukon, that only the
    Strong shall thrive;
That surely the Weak shall perish, and only the
    Fit survive,
Dissolute, damned and despairful, crippled and
    palsied and slain,
This is the Will of the Yukon,—Lo, how she makes
    it plain!"*

AS WE stood in silence, looking at the sunken scow, we thought only of the loss of our trophies, not yet realizing our perilous situation or the hardships that were to follow. Taking account of the articles recovered we found we had lost not only the greater number of our trophies, but our camp stove and frying pans, Mr. Snyder's new Newton rifle, Doctor Evans' 35 Automatic Remington, my hat and gloves, and many of our personal belongings. We had saved seventeen of our trophies, our limited amount of food, blankets, duffel bags, small tent, the ax, and four guns. Seven of Doctor's trophies were saved, consisting of the large bearskin, four rams and two caribou. Seven of Mr. Snyder's were saved also—his bearskin, four rams and two caribou. It was a coincidence that an exact number of the same kind of trophies had been rescued for each of them. I did not fare so well, as only three of my trophies were saved. One was the head of the second largest caribou—killed on Count Creek; the other, my fourth best caribou killed on Little Boundary Creek; and the third, my smallest sheephead, from the one which had been watching the wolverine. No effort had been made to rescue any special trophies, other than Doctor's bearskin. It had been a matter of throwing off anything we could lay our hands on, in an effort to get down to the food, blankets and guns. I was much depressed because only three of my trophies had been rescued, but was determined not to complain, and felt we should consider ourselves fortunate in having saved as much as we had, especially our food, blankets, and ax.

We now looked about and saw that we were on a long narrow island or sandbar, with an area of perhaps three or four acres. It was getting dark by this time, and we hurriedly pitched the small tent on the snow. There was no means of producing heat inside the tent, since our stove was gone, so we built a fire on the outside; but the water-soaked driftwood was of such poor quality that it made little heat. Furthermore, our tent was of the mosquito style, with only a small hole for an entrance, so that no heat was radiated inside.

After making tea and eating a small amount of food, we spread our beds on the snow inside the tent, and sat down on them to discuss our deplorable situation, and to attempt to decide on some means of reaching civilization. There were four large channels of the river, with some smaller ones, at this point. We were camped at about the center of the bar, with three channels on the left, and the main one on the right. We had no assurance that a crossing could be made to the mainland. Our first thought was to try to recover the sunken boat, but this idea was soon dismissed as impossible. We next considered building a raft, since we had our ax, but decided such a craft could not be built to hold together in this river. Furthermore, this would mean a delay, and we knew the river might freeze over solid any night, which would necessitate our walking all the way to its mouth. If the White River froze, we knew the Yukon would freeze also, and there would be no steamers running. In this event we would be stranded nearly four hundred miles from White Horse. We were, therefore, obliged to give up all thought of continuing down the river and to consider only some means of getting back up this stream to the Generc, with the view of following the trail of the horses. How to get there we did not know. The first thing was to get off the island. Bones was of the opinion we could find places sufficiently shallow to cross to the mainland. However, assuming we could cross and start up the river, there were the steep walls of the long canyon that had to be reckoned with. If this were undertaken, it would be necessary to travel high up against the mountain side above the rim—a task that only the strongest and most active men should attempt. In any event, should we succeed in reaching the Generc River, the horses would be far along on their journey; and to walk to Kluane Lake was out of all question. We thought of Baxter's outfit, but they were no doubt well along on their return trip also. The few trophies recovered were now of second consideration, as we thought only of saving our lives. We were about three hundred and fifty miles from White Horse, with sufficient food to last us only four or five days, on limited rations.

In discussing different plans to reach civilization, the most serious obstacle was constantly in our minds—Doctor Evans' inability to walk any distance. He appeared strong and able to withstand many hardships, as evidenced by his long trip, yet we noticed he was never able to walk more than a mile or two without becoming fatigued. We had favored him in every possible way, and Bones had always placed him in the most accessible hunting territory, where it would not be necessary to do any climbing, or even any worthwhile walking. For him to undertake the trip afoot, even back to the Generc, was not to be considered, except as a last resort. It seemed there was but one thing to do, therefore, and that was for Bones to attempt it alone, with the hope of securing assistance. However, the Indians who had hunted moose on the Generc had started for their winter trapping grounds before we left, so there appeared to be little chance of securing help closer than Kluane Lake. With this plan in mind we lay down in our blankets, very tired from the hard work and strenuous experiences of the day.

Mr. Snyder awakened us at four o'clock the next morning, telling us he had not slept, but had spent the night worrying over our plight. Being much fatigued, I had slept soundly, and had risen ready for action, but powerless to do anything. Bones told us he had lain awake most of the night considering various plans, and that he had decided to undertake the trip to the Generc River. After arriving there, he intended to follow the course taken by the horses, with the hope of seeing signs of Indians on the way. If he succeeded in finding Indians, he would employ one of them to go to Kluane Lake, with a message to Gene to bring horses and food. In the meantime he would try to secure some food from the Indians and return, bringing one of them with him if possible.

He directed us to remain there for five days. This was Thursday morning, and he told us to stay there until the following Tuesday morning. If he was not back by that time we would know he had failed to find Indians, and was obliged to continue on foot to Kluane Lake, or that he had met with disaster in crossing some of the glacier streams. In this event we should start out on our own initiative. The night before he had mentioned another danger. He had said that when the rivers were filled with running ice, it was not uncommon for large ice jams to form against the rocks or against the drift-piles of the channels, backing the water up until the force would cause the jam to give way sweeping everything in its path. We were advised to watch the river closely, and if the water started falling, it indicated an ice jam was forming above. He said we should lose no time in getting to the mainland where firewood was abundant and where we would be safe.

Mr. Snyder insisted we should not wait there five days for Bones to return; that we had but little food, and that we should be on our way, even though we made only a few miles a day. Bones thought we should not attempt this as he might have difficulty in finding us should he return. Taking an opportunity when we were on the outside of the tent, Bones told me that the situation was very serious—much worse than he had cared to admit in the presence of Doctor Evans and Mr. Snyder, who already seemed to have little hope of getting out. He admitted Mr. Snyder's argument was a logical one, if Doctor could walk any distance, but since that was impossible, there was nothing for us to do but try to cross to the mainland and remain there for the present. If he failed to return there was little hope of our being rescued, or getting out—unless we deserted the Doctor, and this, he knew, we would not do.

Starting a driftwood fire outside the tent, we prepared a little breakfast for Bones, after which he made preparation for his departure. He disliked taking any of the food, but knew it would be absolutely necessary to have something to eat, as he intended traveling early and late; so he took a piece of cold mutton, a slice or two of bread and three or four doughnuts. The bottom of one of his rubber shoepacs was worn until his foot was in contact with the ground and we knew this would add very much to the hardship of his journey.

As soon as it was light enough to see, Bones bade Doctor Evans goodbye, telling him to keep his spirits up and all would be well. Mr. Snyder and I accompanied him up the bar, looking for a shallow place in the river where he might cross. We soon saw it was impossible to cross to the left—on which side Bones preferred to travel—so we went to the upper point of the island, where the water divided, at which place Bones decided to attempt a crossing to the right. Before he left us, I told him that we would like additional information on one point. We had been instructed to move off the island to the mainland on our right, as we faced

STRANDED ON AN ISLAND

upstream— provided we could do so—and at the expiration of five days, if he had not returned we were to take our blankets and a gun and start up the river. We wished to know what should be done in the event we succeeded in reaching the Generc. We did not know the country from there on, and the trail of the horses would be already snowed over. He replied, "I cannot tell you what to do, nor where to go. I am going to travel day and night, never stopping so long as I am able to go. If there is any man in the Yukon who can get you out of here it is me, and if God is willing I will come back. If not you will have to make the best of it. That is all I can say; goodbye, Mr. Snyder. Goodbye, Mr. Young." As he grasped our hands tightly I saw tears come to his eyes; and as if embarrassed by his emotion, he turned quickly and picked up a pole that he had provided; then going a short distance, he stepped off the bank into the icy current. This was the swift channel in which our scow was caught the evening before and which carried the running ice. It was narrow and deep, except at this point, and here it was shallow and swift, being spread out over a wide gravel bar. The water was only waist deep, and although we could see that it was all Bones could do to stay on his feet, he made it over safely.*

Crossing some narrow, shallow channels, then a larger one, he continued across the bar to the last channel, which was about a half-mile away. He walked up the river a little ways, then stopped and stood for some time as if undecided; but soon disappeared from sight below the river bank. Presently Mr. Snyder expressed doubts concerning Bones' ability to make the crossing,

---

*On a recent visit with Mr. Snyder, an argument arose as to Bones' course after leaving us. This was the only incident of our entire trip on which we disagreed and our recollections were so directly in conflict that we wrote Bones and requested him to inform us on this point. I will quote from his letter received several months later, using his exact language. "Mr. Snyder and you went with me a short distance up the main stream to a place where it were divided in two parts; there I told you goodby and promised to be back with you in three or four days. I tried to make a crossing but the water was too deep so I worked up the stream on the left limit, (bank) or right side (of the island), looking up stream, and crossed the first channel. Then I went for a distance of a quarter to three quarters of a mile; crossing channel after channel until I crossed them all except one narrow, deep, swift channel and it were there that it took courage to tackle. I had confidents in making the ford, as I have had quite a lot of experience in swift water and I will say without any intention of braging on myself that I have not met up with anyone who can beat me. The sistem is to go with the water and not try to hold yourself or fight against it; go quick with long strides; try to go faster than the water if possible and pick a place where the channel runs towards the side you want to make.

"Well, this channel was probibly about fifty feet wide. I took a pole and sounded it and found it to be a little less than up to my arms. The side I were on was running against drift timber, but the other one were clear, so with due consideration of what would happen to you all in case I failed to make it safe ashore, I took my watch and put it in my cap and pulled my cap on tight and eased myself off the drift-log I were standing on, holding on to it till I had my footing good, and I can almost now feel that cold water as it soaked through my clothes and chilled my whole body. Well, with long strides, I soon landed safe on the south side of the river but I were afraid to build a fire for fear you folks would see the smoke and think something rong, so I run about half mile in my water soaked clothes, then I built up a fire and took my clothes off and rung the water out of them and warmed up and started off fast in order to keep them warm."

as he had had more than ample time to do so, provided he had not met with trouble. We stood for awhile, watching the opposite shore, until I shared Mr. Snyder's fears. But finally, in the gray dawn of the cold winter morning, we could see him climbing the bank on the opposite side, and it was not long until he disappeared in the green timber on the mainland. This relieved our anxiety very much and we immediately returned to the tent.

Bones' hasty farewell and his plunge into the cold water had impressed Mr. Snyder and me very much. The picture of him struggling in the swift current was constantly on our minds, and we thought of the many rivers that would have to be crossed before help would likely be found. Now that we were left alone to shift for ourselves, we realized more than ever the seriousness of our situation. Mr. Snyder insisted we should not wait until Bones returned, but should try to get off the island and travel such distance each day as Doctor would be able to make—even though it be only four or five miles. I agreed that we should get off the island, if possible, but insisted that we should remain on the mainland. Mr. Snyder finally declared that if Doctor would undertake it, they would start to the Generc River together. I replied that in that event I would not insist further, but would try to get across the river and remain there until the expiration of five days, as Bones had directed. In taking this stand I explained that it had always been my policy, when in the hands of a reliable guide, to follow his instructions without variation; notwithstanding, I then realized we should have followed Mr. Snyder's advice when he had insisted that the trip down the White River be abandoned altogether.

We made coffee and ate a small amount of food after which Mr. Snyder and I began looking about for some means of getting off the island. We found several tree trunks that had lodged on the barren island, and selecting the longest one we could find, we trimmed it and cut off the butt; then with the use of hand spikes, rolled it to the narrowest stretch of the channel, a hundred yards below the sunken scow, hoping it would reach across. Holding on to one end, we pushed the upstream end out into the water, where it was caught by the current and swung around; but it lacked several feet of reaching to the opposite bank and was swept away by the swift water.

We decided to try it again, and after much hard work succeeded in getting two tree trunks down to the bank, where we

STRANDED ON AN ISLAND

spliced the ends together as best we could with a lariat rope. The end which lay upstream was rolled into the water as before, while we held firmly to the downstream end, and after the upper trunk had swung around in the current, it lodged securely against the opposite shore, the two trunks reaching from bank to bank. Using a long pole for a support, I walked out on our improvised foot log, but it would not support me. We then secured another tree trunk which we rolled from the opposite side of the island. Placing it in the river as before, it swung around and lodged parallel against the two spliced trunks. We thought the three trunks would sustain a man's weight if it was divided among them. Securing two long poles as supports I tried crossing again, but found it was a dangerous undertaking, as the logs sank with my weight, and I found it difficult to shift poles in the deep swift water. So, after getting about one-third of the distance over, I was obliged to give it up and return. We had spent the entire forenoon, without any prospects of getting off the island, so I told Mr. Snyder I did not intend spending any more time trying to cross in this manner, but intended fording the river as Bones had done. To this he objected very emphatically, saying it was too dangerous an undertaking. Notwithstanding this objection, I was determined to get off the island and find a camping place, so I went inside the tent and changed to lighter clothing.

Securing a pole and going to the place where Bones had crossed, some two or three hundred yards above the sunken boat, I waded in. The water struck me just below the waistline, my height being somewhat greater than that of Bones. I had heard him describe his manner of fording swift waters—as stated in his letter just quoted—and I endeavored to use his method. It required courage to wade into the cold water, and caution to prevent being swept off my feet into the deep water directly below. Like Bones, I can now almost feel that cold water as it penetrated my clothing and chilled my whole body. Making it over safely I crossed the small channels and the next large one without difficulty; then looked for a place to cross the last one, which was deep and swift. Finally I decided on the spot where Bones had crossed. The water was about midway between my waist and arms, and so swift I could not have crossed had I not followed Bones' plan, but I made it over safely. After looking around a little while I found a camping place in the edge of the green timber. Although the ground was rough and uninviting, there was an abundance of wood for fuel. I recrossed all of the channels with the idea of bringing over the supplies, and found Mr. Snyder standing on the bank where I had left him an hour before, and where he had stood in the cold watching me, fearing I might be unable to make the fords.

I advised moving our camp that evening and suggested carrying everything down to the shore immediately, after which I would undertake to carry it across the channels as my clothing was already wet. But Mr. Snyder disliked undertaking the icy fords and thought it dangerous for Doctor to attempt to cross them, so they decided to remain there another night. I then hurriedly removed my clothing, which by that time was freezing to my body. Mr. Snyder declared that he did not expect to sleep that night, but intended going to the river frequently to ascertain if it was falling.

Chapter XIX

THE RESCUE

*"O outcast land! O leper land!
   Let the lone wolf-cry all express
The hate insensate of thy hand,
   Thy heart's abysmal loneliness."*

IT was growing late in the afternoon of the day after our wreck and we were becoming hungry, as we had had little to eat since breakfast the morning before, but realizing we must conserve our food, we limited ourselves to hot tea. I was well aware of the danger in remaining there and feared the approach of nightfall. Likewise, I dreaded the thought of trying to get off the island the following day, knowing many trips in the icy water would be necessary, to carry our supplies over. Mr. Snyder and I sat on a driftlog by the smouldering fire, while Doctor lay inside the tent, covered with blankets. As we sat there gazing up the river, Mr. Snyder remarked that he would gladly pay five hundred dollars in cash for the poorest kind of an old horse, provided he was strong enough to carry us off "Blue Island"—a name which he had given this desolate bit of ground.

Suddenly we noticed a moving object far up the river on the mainland to the left. "What is that!" we exclaimed simultaneously. A moose was our first thought. Then we noticed a second object. We immediately arose and gazing into the distance Mr. Snyder said, excitedly, "They look to me like horses" and called to Doctor Evans, who had remained inside the tent all day, trying to keep warm. I quickly got my binoculars and by the time I had returned, several additional horses had come in sight and we could see that some of them had riders. Looking through my glasses I immediately recognized Bones, leaning forward in the saddle in his accustomed style, his horse's head almost to the ground. One by one the horses came into view until we counted thirteen and three men, including Bones. We recognized them as Baxter's horses, and the men as Bones, Frank Sketch, and Mike Knowles. Mr. Snyder threw his arms around Doctor and then around me, embracing us tightly, and Doctor did likewise. I do not recall what I did in that moment of joy. Slowly the men approached until they were opposite us, but being unable to ford the river there, they returned upstream a ways, where they crossed and soon drew up at the tent. Bones appeared as delighted at the turn of events as ourselves.

It will be remembered that two of Baxter's men had run their boat from the Generc River to a point some distance below the canyon, not far from where we wrecked. Baxter had taken his party in a round-about way as planned, hunting as they went, their hunt finally ending at the boat. They had started down the river September twenty-seventh, before the weather turned so cold and before much ice was running. Sketch, Voss and Knowles started back with the horses, but fortunately for us, two of their best horses had wandered away. Three or four days were spent in searching for them, during which time the men were camped five or six miles above us. Upon finding the horses, they were almost ready to start up the river to the Generc and thence to White Horse, when Bones walked into their camp with the information concerning our wreck.

Notwithstanding our great joy upon being rescued we realized, after Bones had given a brief account of his good fortune in finding these men, that we must waste no time but make all possible haste in getting off the island that night.

With the aid of the additional men we tried to raise the sunken scow, in the hope of recovering the guns and some of the heavier trophies. A hole was cut in the bottom of the corner that protruded above the water and large poles were used as levers. Mike Knowles, the big Irishman who had as much strength as he had wit and humor, took the lead. As the boat was lifted, other holes were cut and additional leverage secured, until it was raised about half way out of the water. Bones crept out on the boat and leaning over the edge, tried to secure any articles that might still be in the lower corner. The men raised the scow as high as possible; while standing on a driftlog I held to Bones' feet as he let himself down head foremost. Reaching into the water at arm's length, he caught hold of a caribou horn and began drawing himself upward, bringing with him a number of horns which were tangled together in one mass. His position was a difficult one but he brought the horns to the surface, when suddenly the force of the water wrenched them

THE RESCUE

from his hands and he was powerless to get another hold. They were carried past the end of the boat and on the surface of the swift water for perhaps fifty yards—then they disappeared from sight. We gave up all hope of recovering any more of the trophies. However, we made certain there was nothing else in the submerged corner of the scow before it was abandoned.

Bones said it might be possible for him to return there in the winter after the ice had frozen solid. He thought that by sinking holes he might recover the guns, camp stove, sheep horns and heavier trophies which probably had gone directly to the bottom where the boat had sunk; but later the river and island would be glaciered over and some kind of a mark would be necessary to enable him to identify the spot. So, he took the long sweep of the boat and stuck it in the driftwood with the blade end upward. The extra capes recovered were useless to us without the skulls and horns, so we placed them in a pile, weighted them down with stones and left an oar protruding upwards as a marker. We then made preparations to depart as it was almost sundown. Before starting, I secured Doctor's camera and took a picture of the sunken scow. We had very few cinch ropes for use in packing the horses, so we used two of our moose skins, cutting them into strips about an inch and a half wide.

Before starting I told Bones that since my moose skin had been cut into strips for packing, I would like to take along the four skinned moose legs with hoofs attached. He thought I should not attempt to do so, as they would add somewhat to the weight of our load. I was as much interested in saving these, for the purpose intended, as I was some of my other trophies, and regretted I had not loaded them on the horses without saying anything to Bones.

Mike Knowles was not going to return to White Horse with Sketch and Voss, but was going with them only to the Generc River. From there Mike planned to walk through to McCarthy. We did not have enough saddle horses for all to ride, as nine of Baxter's horses had been left at the Generc River. Therefore, instead of returning to the Generc with us, he decided to take a westward course, traveling directly over the mountains to the Chisana gold fields where he hoped to obtain food, then to McCarthy, which he expected to reach in ten days. While looking for the lost horses, Baxter's men had used most of their food; so Mike took just enough of ours to enable him to reach the Chisana gold fields. Thinking he would reach McCarthy long before we could get to White Horse, we prepared telegrams to be sent to our homes by him, wording them exactly alike, saying we were safe, but detained in the interior, and would not reach White Horse until about the middle of October. However, the stalwart Irishman no doubt experienced many hardships before arriving at his destination, as the telegrams received at our homes were dated October 21st, nineteen days from the time he left us.

Doctor Evans was assigned "Old Bill" the same horse he had ridden on his spring bear hunt. A splendid roan saddle horse was given to Mr. Snyder. I was told to ride Baxter's saddle horse, Pup, but with the admonition that I must be constantly on guard, otherwise I would find myself going over his head. Sketch cautioned me not to strap anything to the horse's saddle, not even a coat, and that I must use care in placing my gun in its scabbard. In fact, I had heard quite a lot about this cayuse, even before we left McCarthy, and was told no one other than Baxter ever attempted to ride him. Before starting Sketch took Mike Knowles across to the mainland, where I had gone that afternoon, and where he expected to spend the night. It was dark when we got off the island, on the opposite side from where Sketch was camped, and as we traveled up the river, we could look back and see the blaze from Mike's fire. We were much impressed at his quick decision to start to McCarthy from this point. The small blaze in the distance caused me to think of the many nights he would spend, sitting with his back to a tree trunk, with a fire in front of him, as much at home as one who sits in an easy chair in front of his fireside. It was several hours after dark when we reached the place where Bones had found Baxter's outfit. Al Voss, Baxter's cook, had remained behind, while Knowles and Sketch went with Bones after us. He had a meagre supper prepared and after eating it we retired, feeling very thankful, indeed, that Bones, by the merest chance, had found these men.

It appeared we were now safe, but such was not the case. Our troubles had just begun. The winter had set in unusually early and the weather was growing colder. It was late in the season to have horses out and they were losing flesh daily. Little pea vine had been found in that section and the horses had been obliged to browse on willow brush, which contained but slight nourishment. Some of them had lost their shoes, while others had worn theirs so smooth that it was impossible for them to get footholds on the frozen, snowclad mountain sides.

It sounds unreasonable when I state that by traveling until midnight of the following day we covered only seven or eight miles. An hour was lost in the morning trying to get the pack horses into the river, which had to be crossed immediately after leaving our camping place, as shore ice extended fifteen or twenty feet from the banks. The men cursed and whipped them but without avail. Securing long willow whips we rounded them up time and again, all of us closing in behind them, but invariably some of them broke through the line and ran back. Only by corraling two or three horses at a time, and all of us getting behind them with whips, were we able to force them on the ice and into the river. All over, we traveled up the river bar on the right hand side of its several channels, until we reached the canyon. At that point we were obliged to recross the river to the left side, after which we gradually made our way upward through the timber until we were far above the canyon's rim. We now had trouble in keeping the packs on the horses. The caribou horns could not be placed on the packs with the points down as they would have snagged the horses—something no cayuse would endure. It was necessary that they protrude upward and this resulted in their often catching in overhanging limbs and turning the packs. Over and over this happened. Some of the gentler horses would stand until the turned pack was removed, but others took the situation more seriously and proceeded to remove them themselves by kicking and bucking. The scrubby spruce timber along the steep mountain side became thicker and we made little progress. We hoped to pass by the canyon before night.

Late in the afternoon we arrived at a deep, narrow gorge, which extended down the mountain at right angles to the river's course, and we saw that we could not proceed farther. Bones and I went some distance up the mountain and found it would be impossible to cross, for as far as we could see the walls of this gorge were almost perpendicular. On returning we decided that the only thing to do was to try to make our way down the slope of the main canyon to the river, cross the creek—which ran down the gorge—at the point where it intersected with the river, then climb back up the mountain on the other side of the creek. The descent to the river was not so steep at that point, yet sufficiently so to make it a hazardous undertaking. Looking down again, we could see there was a narrow strip of shoreline, between the foot of the grade and the swiftly running current of the river; otherwise, the descent could not have been undertaken.

Bones went first, leading a horse; I followed leading Pup—the most active saddle horse in the lot. When about half-way down I heard a commotion, and looking up, saw that one of the pack horses which had been started down the mountain, had lost his footing and was rolling. I jumped aside, pulling my horse with me, just in time to escape being struck by the rolling horse. I fully expected him to be killed, but upon striking the narrow shoreline at the bottom, he got to his feet and shook himself, unhurt. Bones and I reached the bottom without accident, followed by Doctor and Mr. Snyder. Sketch and Voss remained at the top, allowing only one horse to come down at a time. One by one they were forced to descend, some of them sliding most of the way, others falling and rolling before they reached the bottom. A roan horse by the name of Strawberry, carrying a heavy pack, lost his footing soon after starting, and in his downward course—sliding and rolling—struck a snag and lodged against it. Sketch and Voss hurried to assist him to his feet, but the horse had gone but a few steps when he fell again, rolling all the way to the bottom, where he landed with a dull thud. We experienced a sickening sensation as we saw him coming. Mr. Snyder turned his head, remarking that it was too much for him and that he positively could not watch another horse come down. When the last of the thirteen horses reached the bottom we examined and repacked them and found that a snag, larger than a man's wrist, had penetrated the roan horse's side and had to be extracted with force. His load was removed and divided among the other horses as we could see that he was badly hurt. In the cold days that followed the wound froze, making drainage impossible, and it was necessary to heat water each morning and night and apply hot cloths, so that it would properly drain. During the remainder of the time he followed in the rear, without saddle or halter, and while he withstood the return trip, he died soon afterwards.

Now that we were all down on the narrow shore, between the foot of the mountain and the water's edge, the next difficulty

The partially-raised scow, as we left it. The corner protruded about six-and-one-half feet above the water.

was to get back up the mountain on the opposite side of the creek. The wall of the main canyon, just above the mouth of the creek, was almost perpendicular, but above the intersection of the creek and the river was a point where we thought we might ascend, although it was as steep as the place we had just come down. We attempted to force Buck, the small buckskin and by far the most active pack horse in the lot, but urging and whipping availed nothing and he refused to even try. I then led Pup up some distance, thinking the loaded horses would be inclined to try it. Some of them did make an attempt, only to lose their footing and roll or slide to the bottom. Others absolutely refused to try, and quickly turned back. The men cursed and whipped the horses in a desperate effort to get them out of the canyon, but we saw we could not get up at that place. The shoes remaining on the pack horses were worn so smooth it was impossible for them to get footholds on the frozen, snow-covered ground. In their fear, at being forced to try the steep ascent, some of the more nervous horses wheeled around and tried to escape by going into the river, and constant watching was necessary to prevent their doing so. There was little or no shoreline on the other side of the river, or immediately below, and had any of them attempted to cross, they probably would have been drowned in the deep, swift water.

The situation was alarming, as it was almost dark and we were confronted with the possibility of having to spend the night on that narrow strip of shoreline—with little more than room enough for the horses. I had never been in a situation that appeared more discouraging. Addressing me, Mr. Snyder gave way to his feelings completely. He said he did not believe we would ever be able to reach civilization. He referred to his wife and two daughters, who were at the coast anxiously awaiting our return, and said he had little hope of ever seeing them again. I felt about the same way, but would not admit it. Bones had asked me, soon after the wreck of our scow, to try to maintain a spirit of cheerfulness for the effect it might have on the others, and I was endeavoring to do so.

Never before had I heard such profanity as on that day, and it increased as our troubles piled up. I have never heard men inject as many oaths into a single sentence as they did that night and the days that followed. Mr. Snyder, Doctor and I felt that we were a burden on them, for had they not been called

THE RESCUE

on to come to our rescue, they could have been far along on their way—lightly loaded. We felt somewhat embarrassed because of the circumstances and it was agreed that when an opportunity presented itself Doctor, as spokesman for us, should speak to them concerning our position. They were employed by Baxter, and Bones expected to pay him for the extra time required in getting us to Kluane Lake. However, we felt something was due these men for the extra work and inconvenience we caused them; therefore, Doctor later told them that on reaching civilization we would reimburse them in addition to their regular pay. They assured us that we were not to feel any embarrassment and that they were glad to be of assistance to us. We found them to be among the best hearted men we ever met, and that their outbursts of profanity were not on account of the extra work we had caused them, but were in common with the custom of the majority of the men of the North, nearly all of whom live alone and away from the environments of civilization.

Bones and I then went up the small canyon, trying to find some place where we might get the horses up, and at last found a location that looked possible, if steps were cut, so we decided to try it. Returning for the ax we worked for some time in the darkness, cutting steps in the frozen shale, while the others looked after the horses. When our task was completed the horses were brought up—Pup in the lead. The steps formed a zigzag trail and Bones stationed himself at the upper corner to turn the horses in the proper course, as they came up, while I remained at the lower corner. After jumping the creek, which was narrow and deep at this point, Pup was started up the steep slope which he made safely. It was surprising the distance some of those cayuses could jump, as witnessed on this and other occasions. Buck, the most intelligent pack horse in the lot, came next and made it up. One by one the others were brought up and by giving the heavily loaded ones their time they all succeeded in making the ascent without accident. It was just eight o'clock, or about three hours after dark, when the last horse reached the top.

We continued up the mountain over the rough steep ground and through scrubby spruce timber. A moon, four days old, showed faintly from behind the clouds, which were rapidly gathering. At times it became so dark it was difficult to keep our course. Time and again the caribou horns on top the horses' packs were caught in the timber and turned. I insisted we abandon the idea of trying to get our trophies out and that we should leave them; but Bones always replied, "No, let's try them a little longer." Some of the tired, half-starved horses could not be kept in line, frequently running up the mountain; and we had to stop until they were rounded up. We spent two hours going a half-mile after getting out of the canyon. Each time a load was turned it had to be removed and repacked. One horse alone was repacked three times in that distance, requiring about twenty minutes each time. At one place I realized something was wrong just in front of me. Running forward I found a horse down and his pack turned—close to the edge of a precipice. Seeing the danger, I ran below him and bracing my shoulder against his breast, and with my feet against a friendly protruding stone, I held on to him with all my strength and called for help. I could feel the weight of the horse getting heavier and called for them to hurry as I knew I could not hold him much longer, and could not have done so thus far had I not been fortunate in getting a good foothold. Mr. Snyder soon came to my assistance, followed by Sketch, who quickly cut the cinch, and relieved of the load, they got the horse on his feet.

At times it became so discouraging that the men halted and stood cursing for several minutes, even though a horse was down. Bones was so outclassed in swearing that he almost stopped for a while, but would occasionally remark, "Well this is just one continuous round of pleasure; if it ain't one d— thing it's another." The clouds became heavier and it began snowing so hard that we made no progress. Al Voss always took the lead, trying to select the best course through the timber, while Sketch brought up the rear, walking, to see that none of the horses turned back. Bones walked also—anywhere along the line that he was needed. We could always tell when a pack was turned or a horse down; for when one of them met with a mishap, those behind always stopped, and the man closest in the rear would call to Voss to stop, telling him something was wrong.

At one time we heard a horse struggling and found that he had attempted to pass between two saplings, wedging his pack so tightly that he could not go forward—nor could he back out. This horse carried my largest caribou horns on top

THE RESCUE

of his load, and when Voss took hold of one of the saplings to bend it away, the horse made a lunge to extricate himself. Bones, who was close by exclaimed, "Look out Voss, that horse will catch your hands between that sapling and them caribou horns!" but it was too late. Voss' right hand had been caught, crushing the thumb and injuring his fingers so badly that he could not use that hand during the remainder of the trip. The pain was so severe that for fully five minutes he gave vent to his feelings by such cursing as I had never heard. My hair seemed to stand straight up on my head, while cold chills ran down my back. The fury of the snow storm increased, and for a few moments the moon peeped forth from behind a black cloud, as if in reproach.

Doctor bandaged the injured hand, while Bones and Sketch removed the load and extricated the pack horse, after which we moved on. Presently Bones, who had gone ahead of the pack train, returned with the advice that there was a small canyon ahead and if we could get down in it we might find horse feed and a place to camp. We descended without accident and selected a camping place. Looking at my watch I found it was just twelve o'clock when we arrived. A few dwarfed willows grew along the small creek and the tired horses were unloaded and driven up the canyon to browse. The men thought they might return along the trail by which we had come, because of the scarcity of feed, so Bones cut some small trees across the trail to act as a barrier. Cutting some poles by the dim light of the camp fire, we erected our tent, after which we ate a small amount from our limited supply of food—the first we had had since the scant breakfast of the morning before. It was just fifteen minutes after two when we spread out blankets on the carpet of snow and lay down, tired, hungry and discouraged.

Mr. Snyder arose at four o'clock and made coffee. After this and until we reached White Horse, he was the first man up in the morning and assembled what little food we had. From then on I washed the plates and cut the wood for the camp stove. Bones and Sketch usually started to look for the horses immediately after arising, while Voss was unable to do much because of his crippled hand. During the night the horses got out of the canyon by going around the fallen trees, and returned along the trail for some distance before Sketch overtook them. They were a wild lot of cayuses and we had to use care in saddling and bridling them each morning. When ready to start I would approach Pup carefully, gun in hand, in an attempt to get it in the scabbard—at times being obliged to blindfold him before I could do so. After succeeding, it required quick action to mount him. The wildest horse, however, was the small buck-skin pack horse, appropriately named Buck and, like the smallest horse in Bones' outfit, he carried one of the heaviest loads, although no one had ever been able to ride him. When the horses were corraled in the morning it usually required the assistance of everyone to corner Buck and get a halter on him, after which he was often blindfolded while being saddled and packed. He was never still for a moment, but threw his head from side to side nervously, like a wild animal in a cage. He never appeared to be tired, even after an unusually hard day's travel. When unloaded at night Sketch always warned us by saying, "Look out, I'm going to let Buck loose!" and no matter what we were doing, we took time to get out of his way. When in line, he gave us the least trouble of any of the pack horses, and except at the first ford each morning, or where there was shore ice to cut their legs, he was always in the lead of the pack train, and was easily the boss of the lot.

The morning was bitter cold and continued so all day. Leaving our camping place early we finally passed the nine-mile canyon and descended to the bar of the White River, where we found the still channels frozen over and ice extending far out into the swifter ones. We cut heavy willow whips, knowing much force would be required to get the horses into the water. The river wound about from one side of the valley to the other, forming sometimes fifteen or twenty channels, and at such places the water was not so deep. Other fords had only two or three channels, and it was there that we experienced trouble, as the horses were often obliged to swim.

Bones and Sketch had walked thus far as we had only four saddle horses. After crossing a series of channels two men would dismount and walk along with the pack train, while one man would ride back, leading their horses, to bring across the two men in the rear. After this the three men would pass the others and cross the next series of fords; then one of them would return with the horses for the men now in the rear. This system of relaying was kept up during the remainder of the day, and as Pup and Mr. Snyder's saddle horse were exceptionally

THE RESCUE

good in the deep water, they were used exclusively. I made many of these return trips and found they were very hard on both horses and riders as each ford was crossed three times. Ice froze solid in the stirrups and had to be knocked out repeatedly with stones. The situation became almost as discouraging as that of the day before. Ice formed on the horses' packs, and on their manes and tails, weighing them down until they could scarcely travel, and by night the tails of some of them were almost as large as a man's body. It was not long until their legs were cut and bleeding from the shore ice, which often broke through with their weight. Doctor and Mr. Snyder wore their slicker overalls and were able to keep dry in the deep water, but not being thus provided, the rest of us were soon wet and our clothing frozen.

Early in the afternoon I was running ahead of the pack train in an effort to keep warm, and, crossing what appeared to be a sand bar, I suddenly found myself in water up to my arms. It was a narrow, deep, "still" channel which had frozen over early in the season. Afterwards sand and volcanic ash had been blown on the surface of the ice, protecting it from further freezing. To say this was a disagreeable experience, is putting it mildly. Quickly I forced my way through the thin ice and emerged on the opposite side, the sandy water dripping from my clothing. Not only was my clothing drenched but also the contents of my pockets, including the tobacco and matches in the breast pockets of my heavy woolen overshirt, and all my currency contained in a money belt. In order to keep my blood circulating rapidly, I ran back and forth ahead of the pack train. I did not ride any more that day, except to cross channels or to take horses back for those in the rear; perhaps traveling twice as far as the horses did during the remainder of the day. In a few minutes after my immersion in the water my outer clothing was frozen solid. Mr. Snyder rapped on my clothing with his knuckles, which produced a sound like that made by rapping on wood.

On two occasions it looked as though we would lose some of our horses, and their loads. At the first crossing Sketch mounted Pup and rode in first; but had no sooner done so than the horse went down in the sandy bottom until his rider was in the water up to his hips. The horse recovered himself and quickly wheeled around and climbed up the bank, after which another crossing was tested and decided on. The usual whipping was necessary in order to drive the pack horses into the water. Three of the weaker ones were unable to withstand the swift current and were swept down the river, whereupon we called to Voss—who had reached the opposite shore—calling them to his attention. He replied with an oath that if the blankety-blank cayuses were not drowned, perhaps they would learn some sense and keep their feet in the next ford, and rode on. When Bones had a horse down or in a dangerous place, he always hurried to his assistance when possible; but not so with Sketch and Voss, as they sometimes filled their pipes and lighted them before acting, and never appeared the least excited. We took this situation seriously, because these horses carried our personal belongings, including our picture films, which fortunately—upon the suggestion of Mr. Snyder—had been sealed in a waterproof can before starting down the river. Reaching the other side, Doctor, Mr. Snyder, and I watched the struggling horses as they were carried down the river. About four hundred yards below the current washed them toward the side we were on, and striking the bottom, they soon reached the shore; but it was quite a while before they caught up with us, as they were almost exhausted.

We had the same experience at the next crossing. "Old Baldy," the stove horse, gave up in the middle of the stream; and on trying to turn, was washed down the river, but he came out on the same side from which he had started. We forced him into the water again and he made it over successfully. The three weaker horses, which had been carried down before, were again swept away. One of them carried my blankets and I knew they must be thoroughly watersoaked by this time. Again the horses landed three or four hundred yards below the crossing, but on the right side of the river, so we did not wait for them; but traveled on and they finally overtook us. Sketch and I ran ahead for some distance and removed our boots for the purpose of emptying the water and wringing out our heavy woolen socks. I was wearing four pairs, and by the time I had them back on, the outer pair was frozen stiff. Since getting a thorough soaking when I had broken through the thin ice, I had not hesitated to ride into the deep water as often as necessary in relaying Sketch and Bones across, as it was impossible to add to my discomfort.

CHAPTER XX

RETURN TO GENERC RIVER

*"Were you ever out in the Great Alone, when the moon was awful clear,
And the icy mountains hemmed you in with a silence you most could hear?"*

IT WAS dark when we passed the mouth of the Generc River, from which point we had started in our boat four days before. Some of the men were kind enough to suggest that we camp there, because of my frozen clothing, but I insisted that we go on as we had planned. It was eight or ten miles to the location where Baxter had camped on the Generc River, and which we hoped to reach that night. After crossing the Generc a number of times we arrived at ten o'clock. We estimated we had forded no less than sixty different channels of the two rivers that afternoon and night.

The horses were immediately unpacked and turned out to feast on the pea vine, which was so plentiful. It was with much difficulty that the cinch ropes and moosehide straps were loosened, as portions of them were as large as a man's arm; while the saddle blankets and canvas covers were solid masses of ice. At midnight we lay down to sleep, all of us suffering from hunger, as we were almost out of food and entirely out of bread. Since making the last deep fords, my underclothing had dried from the warmth of my body, but my outer garments were like a shell. It required force to pull my frozen blankets apart, and it was impossible to dry them as there was little wood. I realized more than ever that I should have provided myself with some kind of a waterproof sleeping bag, as the others had done.

After a short consultation the next morning, we decided it was necessary to remain there that day, which was Sunday, since it was impossible to proceed until our equipment was thawed out. Bones decided to take Mr. Snyder's saddle horse and start early in the direction of Kluane Lake, thinking he might possibly run onto Indians and perhaps be able to secure food, although he had little hope of finding anyone.

ALASKAN-YUKON TROPHIES

My gun scabbard, with the Ross rifle inside, had been filled with water the day before, which soon froze into a solid cake. The capes of the trophies that had been saved, the cinch ropes, saddle blankets and canvas covers, were all masses of ice. All day long the snow fell, and it required our combined efforts to find wood to keep a big fire burning for the purpose of thawing out everything.

Bones returned that evening with good news. He had found a fresh Indian trail, and pushing forward as rapidly as possible, had overtaken a small band, consisting mostly of squaws, who had remained behind for the purpose of tanning some skins. They were packed up and ready to move on when he arrived. He explained that our party was out of food and succeeded in getting twenty pounds of flour and a can of baking powder. Before leaving, Bones employed one of the Indian bucks to go at once to Kluane Lake with a message for Gene.

There had been an argument in the early fall between some of our guides and Baxter's party—when meeting on the Generc River—concerning dates. Members of each party had kept diaries, yet there was a variance of two or three days, and each party was equally positive that they were correct. In speaking of the time thereafter we had referred to dates by specifying "according to Baxter's records," or "according to our records." Bones, therefore, took the precaution in the note written to Gene to state that we would leave the Generc River the following morning which, "according to our records," would be Monday, October 6th; that nothing preventing, we would camp near the head of Harris River that night; on the Wolverine River Tuesday night; on the Donjeck River Wednesday night; and with a long day's travel on Thursday, we hoped to cross the Tundra Barrens of Burwash Mountain and reach the Duke River. He told him we had little food, and that many of our horses were almost worn out and would not be able to travel any farther than the Duke River Thursday night. Gene was requested to bring or send horses and food to that place, and with fresh horses and something to eat, Mr. Snyder, Doctor and I could return with him that night. Bones planned that he, Sketch and Voss would remain with the horses and continue to Kluane Lake next morning. He told the Indian to make all possible haste in getting the message to Gene and insisted he should travel early and late in doing so. We thought Gene would not wait until we reached the Duke River, but would send someone with food at once, or perhaps come himself. So

RETURN TO GENERC RIVER

Breaking camp on the Wolverine. The author's bed had been in the snow, close to where the horses are standing.

we prepared and ate a hearty meal, the first one we had had for a number of days. We preferred to have one square meal, even though we might be without food later on.

The horses were rounded up the following morning, including the nine that had been left there by Baxter two or three weeks before. They had had a good rest and plenty of food, and therefore they were more heavily loaded. The others were backed in a circle close to the campfire so the ice on their legs and tails would melt while they were being loaded. We now had saddle horses for all and more riding saddles than were needed. These were placed upon the weaker horses which were loaded lightly.

Again we said goodbye to the Generc and traveled up the Harris River the remainder of the day, reaching our camping place close to the headwaters, about two hours after dark. It had snowed steadily all that day and the day before, and travel was difficult. Bones and Sketch unpacked the horses, while Mr. Snyder and I erected the tent with such assistance as Voss could give us with one hand. We had a deep carpet of snow, perhaps twelve or fifteen inches, inside the tent; but it was soon tramped down sufficiently to enable us to spread our beds. We spent a very uncomfortable night as we were much crowded and, on arising the next morning, found the tent weighted down with snow that had fallen during the night. The snow next to the roof of the tent had melted before the wood burned out in the stove, and later had frozen to the canvas, so that it was impossible to take the tent down and roll it up. Large fires were made on all sides, until it had thawed out sufficiently to enable us to roll it.

On reaching the head of Harris River we crossed the divide, passed Tepee Lake, where Doctor had killed a bear and two cubs in the spring, then down the Wolverine, reaching our camping place about three hours after dark. It was the coldest day we had experienced, and as night approached we were obliged to walk much of the time in an effort to keep warm. There was great satisfaction in finding an abundant supply of wood, and the first thing we did was to build a good fire and make Doctor Evans as comfortable as possible, since he had suffered from the extreme cold that evening. A treat awaited us here as Mr. Snyder had found a half-dozen beef cubes in his pack, and after heating some water, made a cup of hot beef tea for each of us. The horses were unpacked and turned loose to paw the snow for food, which was quite limited, and we feared they would return to the Generc that night. Sketch said next morning he had been on the alert all night listening for their bells, had they tried to return.

It had been difficult for six of us to sleep in the tent, as the stove took up much room. After my uncomfortable experience of the night before, I had resolved I would sleep outside at the next camping place. Inside the tent it was always warm when we retired as a good fire was kept burning in the stove; but after the wood burned out, it soon became cold; so I thought there would be little difference whether I slept inside or out. It was a clear moonlight night, and taking the ax I went back in the timber and found some dry wood which I dragged in. Part of this was cut for use in the stove and the remainder for building a fire on a nearby level spot not far from the tent. I then cut some spruce boughs and laid them on the snow close to the fire, and spread my caribou skin and blankets on them. Leaving on everything but my shoes, I pulled my toboggan cap (which I had worn since losing my hat in the White River) down over my ears, and crawling under the blankets, I soon fell asleep and was comfortable until the fire burned down, but after that I could not sleep soundly for the intense cold. It was a beautiful winter night and frequently I found myself removing the cover from my face, to gaze at the moon, through the clear atmosphere. The next morning the hair on my forehead was frozen stiff from my breath. I had much difficulty in getting my frozen shoepacs on and thereafter did not remove them at night.*

The smaller streams were now frozen solid and we were obliged to melt snow for making tea and coffee, and for use in camp and washing. Later we washed our hands and faces in snow, without taking the trouble to melt it as we were out of soap anyway. It was impossible to find water for men or horses, except in the larger streams where there were swift places that had not frozen solid.

Again our food supply was almost exhausted. It was limited to a scant amount of dirty rice—taken for dog food—which we cleaned as best we could and fried in caribou fat. One would naturally think game could always be secured, but even in that country, where it is fairly plentiful, it is usually necessary to travel some distance to find it. Sheep are found on the high mountains; caribou in certain sections of high barren lands above timber line; and moose, at this time of year, in the timber. To hunt them would necessitate side trips and require considerable time that could be better spent by continuing on our way. Furthermore, on account of the extreme cold, no game appeared to be moving about. Strange to say, only one time on our eighteen days' trip to White Horse did we see the tracks of any wild animal, other than those of one snow shoe rabbit.

Digestive trouble produced by improper and insufficient food resulted in so-called "fever blisters" forming on my lips, causing them to swell to almost twice their natural size. They had grown worse until eating—or even taking a drink of water—became a painful ordeal, causing blood to trickle down my chin. I was obliged to protect them from the cold by keeping one hand over my mouth almost constantly. This apparently slight affliction was very annoying, and as the weather had become colder, was quite serious.

It required about three hours to corral, halter and pack the horses each morning. The daily task of taking down the stove

---

*On reaching White Horse we consulted the official temperature records and found that on that night it was ten degrees below zero, and for several nights following, it was from ten to fifteen degrees below.

and tent, packing up the outfit, and loading everything on the horses, together with the other work, became very monotonous. The stove horse was always the last one to be loaded because of the weight he carried; so we always left the stove up until the last moment, with a good fire burning for the benefit of Doctor Evans. Mr. Snyder and I always rendered assistance to Bones and Sketch in packing the horses, but we never learned to throw a cinch rope properly or to make either a "diamond" or a "squaw" hitch. It appeared to me that the more often we saw it done, the less we knew about this complicated procedure. After the wreck I had but one glove, and a mitten that was almost worn out. I did not wear them while assisting in packing, as it was necessary to keep them dry for use in traveling, and my bare hands often became so numb with cold I could hardly use them. The bottoms of Mr. Snyder's shoepacs were worn through and his feet were in contact with the ground, except for the heavy socks which he wore and the strips of canvas that he tied around his shoes.

We traveled down the Wolverine River and were obliged to cross it a number of times, but, by selecting swift water where the ice was broken up, we experienced very little difficulty. Late in the afternoon we reached the mouth of the Wolverine and started up the wide bar of the Donjeck River. Here the cold wind almost took our breath as it blew down the valley of the Donjeck. I pulled the toboggan cap over my ears, turned up the high collar of my mackinaw coat and constantly rubbed my face to prevent it from freezing. It was impossible to keep the horses in line, as they refused to face the cutting wind, and frequently turned back, running down the river bar for some distance before they could be headed off. At other times it was difficult to get them to pass clumps of pea vine. I was now having no trouble with my saddle horse, Pup, and was growing fonder of him every day. When an unruly horse ran out of line, Pup almost instantly sprang forward to round him up. A race of several hundred yards was often necessary—sometimes over very rough ground—but he was surefooted and I had little fear of his falling. The hard trip, lack of feed, and the extra work did not affect his energy.

Regardless of the cold weather, I cannot say that I suffered to any great extent, until we traveled up the Donjeck River that evening. We had been out of doors so long that we had become acclimated, but on this evening the cold wind was almost unbearable. I had taken a pair of heavy woolen socks from my pack the night before, and was wearing them over my mitten and glove, as an added protection against the cold. About dark Bones became alarmed and rode along the line saying, "Doctor appears to be almost frozen and in a very bad way; I will take him and ride ahead as fast as possible to our camping place at the mouth of Wade Creek, where I will build a fire and try to get him warm." An hour later we arrived there and found Doctor fairly comfortable by a big fire Bones had built.

Our course the next day lay across Burwash Mountain—one of the most difficult day's travel of the entire trip and one the men had been dreading. Leaving the Donjeck early the next morning, we traveled up Wade Creek a short distance before starting up the long mountain climb. Five or six miles from the river we passed above timber line, and later on to a high, rolling, tundra-covered plateau country. The cold, piercing wind seemed to cut us to the bone, and we suffered with the cold almost as much as we had the evening before on the Donjeck.

A great expanse of high barren country lay before us with hardly a tree in sight. In the distance it appeared to be quite smooth, but in reality it proved to be a great swamp, covered with small bushes and swamp grass, growing in a bed of watery mire. It is unusual to find such a swamp on the top of a mountain, where one would naturally expect good drainage. Doctor had told us of their experience in crossing it when going in on his spring bear hunt, at which time several horses had mired above their knees, causing trouble and delay. The men said that when the snow was off the ground, the skeletons of many horses could be seen along the way. However, we were fortunate in crossing at a time when it was frozen hard.

It seemed that our hungry, tired horses were making no progress against the fierce gale, and as we proceeded, constant urging and frequent use of our long willow whips were necessary to force them on. We had expected to meet Gene, or a messenger sent by him, before this time, as we thought he would certainly come to our assistance with food if he had received word of our plight. The only redeeming feature of the day's travel was the thought that food and fresh horses would certainly be in waiting at the Duke River that night, and later Doctor, Mr. Snyder and I would have shelter and warmth at Jacquot's cabin six miles farther on.

Burwash Creek, famous for the vast amount of gold taken from its bed, was crossed in the afternoon; and shortly before dark we started down the slope from the rolling plateau on which we had traveled since morning. Presently we came in sight of a fire far down in the valley, and at once concluded that Gene had received the message, and that horses and food were waiting for us. With each twinkle of the flame our spirits mounted higher and higher and the very thought of food seemed to revive us. I rode back and forth along the line of tired pack horses and tried to urge them to greater speed, as we were highly elated and anxious to reach the river as soon as possible. An hour later we started down an abrupt descent of several hundred feet and soon thereafter arrived at the river.

We had observed for some time that light from the fire was growing dim, being now scarcely visible, and were at a loss to understand it. On arriving we found only the dying embers, the footprints of Indian moccasins and the tracks of horses. This was a bitter disappointment, as it was evident an Indian had been there with horses and had gone. There was nothing to do, therefore, but to pitch our tent and spend the night at this place as it was useless to try to force the horses farther. Our food was entirely exhausted, and again we lay down, hungry and tired from our long day's ride—the others inside the tent, while I spread my blankets on the snow outside.

I was impressed, as I had been on numerous other occasions since the wreck of our scow, that man's first requirements are food and shelter. We, who at home are surrounded with the many comforts of life, do not stop to consider this fact, as there are few people, within the limits of civilization, who are not supplied with both. The advance of civilization brings numerous comforts and conveniences, many of which are of only secondary or imaginary value. Our comforts and luxuries of the present day cause us to forget to appreciate these two essentials, as they were appreciated by the pioneers in the early days of our country. Today we think it a serious matter if our train fails to make connections; or if something goes wrong with our automobile. We are inclined to complain at many trivial inconveniences in everyday life that really amount to nothing. Let winter overtake one in the Arctic regions, under circumstances which make it necessary for him to continually match his skill against the forces of Nature—sometimes actually fighting for his life, without food or shelter and at times without sufficient fire for warmth—then these facts are impressed upon him as never before. They are impressions for which one pays dearly, and which are not likely to be forgotten. Notwithstanding my hunger and the affliction of my lips, I soon fell asleep on my bed of snow, and slept soundly.

The horses wandered some distance away during the night, necessitating a late start from the Duke River the next morning. We reached Jacquot's place at noon and found Gene anxiously awaiting our arrival. He was eager to hear of our misfortunes, which Bones related briefly.

The Indian messenger had loitered on the way and did not reach Jacquot's place until the afternoon before. On receiving the message, Gene had sent Johnnie to the Duke River with horses and such food as he could quickly prepare, while he busied himself baking bread in anticipation of our arrival. Johnnie had built the fire and waited for us until after dark and had then returned. As mentioned in a previous chapter, we had observed that the Indians did not like to be out in the forest alone after dark, unarmed. Johnnie's failure to wait had delayed us a half-day, to say nothing of the discomfort of being without food and having to camp out another night.

Bones was furious when he learned the Indian had loitered on the way instead of making all possible haste, as he had promised to do. With many oaths interjected, he vowed, "I will tell him in language just as plain as I can make use of that I consider him an unreliable and worthless cur, whose word cannot be depended upon, and that he need never ask any favors from me, while I will pay him a very small sum as compared with what I intended paying him."

There were no doubts in the minds of any of us as to what kind of language Bones would make use of when he saw the Indian.

A band of Indians was camped close by awaiting Gene's brother, Louie, who was daily expected to return from White Horse with large quantities of food and supplies which would be traded to the Indians for furs. Among them were Johnnie and Paddie, who had joined their squaws and children.

It was not long until Gene had a bountiful meal ready, which included cauliflower, grown by his brother Louie. It was our first fresh vegetable in many weeks, and we devoured it like hungry wolves. Gene had very little food on hand, but let Sketch and Voss have some bread, flour, baking powder and tea, after which they bade us goodbye and started around Kluane Lake on their journey to White Horse. I shall never forget the kindness of these strong, big-hearted, stalwart men, and hope sometime to have the pleasure of meeting them again. I had become much attached to my splendid saddle horse, Pup, and regretted giving him up. By this time I could handle him without difficulty, although I was never able to tie a coat or anything else to his saddle.

Jacquot Brothers' trading post at Kluane Lake.

Chapter XXI

CONTINUED HARDSHIPS

*"Colder it grew and colder, till the last heat
    left the earth,
And there in the great stark stillness the bale fires
    glinted and gleamed,
And the Wild all around exulted and shook with a
    devlish mirth,
And life was far and forgotten, the ghost of a joy
    once dreamed."*

THE Jacquot brothers had four very substantial log buildings consisting of their living quarters, which was the first building we had slept in since staying all night in Chittina about August first; a warehouse, or trading post; blacksmith shop and a stable. The latter was not regularly used as such, as their horses were turned out on the river bottoms to graze on pea vine during the long winters.

Kluane Lake is the largest lake wholly within the Yukon Territory, having an area of one hundred and eighty-four square miles. It is almost one hundred miles long and has a width varying from six to twelve miles. It is said to be one of the most magnificently beautiful lakes in the great Northwest. Lofty mountains edge this body of water on both sides, while deeply corrugated cliffs of variegated colors, often rise from the water's edge. On the more gradual slopes great spruce forests extend to timber line, where they give way to the tundra above.

The Jacquot brothers' trading post is located on the west side of Kluane Lake, while Bones lives at the southeastern end, on the opposite side, thirty-five miles distant. I had heard many comments concerning the dangers of this lake, some having been made by Charles Baxter, while we were still in his camp before leaving McCarthy. I had not followed him closely, as we had no thought of returning this way, but I remembered that he had spoken of the high winds which sweep between the funnel-like mountains on each side and over the length of the lake. He stated that it was a body of water he always tried to avoid, as he considered it dangerous for small water craft.

Notwithstanding these remarks, we were looking forward with a certain amount of pleasure to this part of our journey, as we thought it would be an agreeable change from our two and one-half months' experience with horses. We knew the safety of the trip depended altogether on the weather we would encounter.

It was a very cold night and we were awakened frequently by the howling of the many huskies belonging to the Indians. Breakfast over, we started carrying our supplies to the lake before it was daylight. Paddie and another Indian were started around Kluane Lake with Bones' horses. It was a clear, cold morning and the surface of the lake appeared to be as smooth as glass. It looked as though we were going to be favored with ideal weather for our trip across. There were many Indians standing about to see us off, some of whom we had seen on the Generc River. There was "Big Foot Jim," "Moose John," "Little Shorty," "Big Shorty," "Skookem Jim" and Indians of various names. Some of the older ones retained their original Indian names, which I could not even pronounce—much less remember. A young Indian—one among the few who could speak English—remarked, "All same big south wind come; him come soon, maybe; all same you have big waves, maybe so." It was not long until he pointed far up the lake where a ripple could be seen on the quiet water. Bones and Gene took note of it, and as they glanced at each other, I thought I detected a look of uneasiness on their faces.

A dory (a boat built something like a skiff, although considerably larger) was towed behind. It was to be loaded with supplies on Louie Jacquot's arrival at Kluane Lake, and used as a sail boat on the return trip. A large, husky Indian rode in the dory for the purpose of sailing it back. With Mr. Snyder at the steering wheel, Gene buried himself beneath a large canvas—which had been thrown over the engine to protect it from the intense cold, in an effort to keep it going.

All went well for a short time, but soon the ripples became "big waves" and it was not long until we had the predicted trouble. The engine did not have sufficient power for the size of the boat, and two or three times it stopped, during which intervals we were rapidly blown toward the shore. Bones told Snyder to keep the boat out in the middle of the lake, but he

CONTINUED HARDSHIPS

Indians waiting at Kluane Lake to see us off.

hesitated to do so because of the rougher water encountered there. When he finally attempted it, the waves washed over the bow of the boat and he again turned it towards the shore. Bones reemphasized the danger of being too near the shore, in case the engine stopped, and declared we were then too near. The words were hardly out of his mouth when the engine stopped again. Gene worked with all his might, with his head under the canvas, trying to start it. He was in great danger from the fumes of the gasoline, but he dared not uncover the engine. The boat was blown rapidly toward the shore, and, grabbing the emergency oars, we worked with all our might. Bones called for every man to do his best, but our strength amounted to little against the gale. We realized our boat would be demolished if we were blown against the icebound shore, and we were now so close to it we could hear the broken ice grinding against the shore ice and granite rocks. We called to Gene, and, raising his head from beneath the canvas, he saw the fate that awaited us, and dived back under to his task. Holding our breath, we prepared for the worst. Our fate seemed inevitable when suddenly we felt the impulse of the engine, followed by the familiar "put put put." Mr. Snyder grabbed the steering wheel and righted the boat about just in time to keep it from striking the shore ice which extended out from the crags. The boat was then run to the middle of the lake where we were willing to remain.

The wind increased and the water became rougher. We saw that it would be necessary to transfer some of the weight to the dory, as our boat continued to ship much water, but it was impossible to do so at that time. Gene said that our only chance was to keep the water bailed out until we reached Destruction Bay, a few miles ahead, where we would have shelter from the wind and could make a landing. After some time the bay was reached and within its shelter we were able to land. We built a small fire on the shore and made tea; then, after bailing all the water out of both boats, we transferred a portion of the ice-covered luggage to the dory and started again. The gale subsided for a little while and we made fairly good progress, but soon it began blowing harder than ever, and several times the engine stopped. We were far out in the lake, however, and Gene was able to start the engine each time before we were blown to the shore.

Far in the distance that afternoon we watched Frank Sketch and Al Voss winding their way over the rough trail, which sometimes ran low on the mountain side and at other times high up over the cliffs. Voss rode in front and Sketch in the rear, with the other twenty horses traveling between them—their noses almost to the ground, as usual, and each one in his accustomed place in the line. Frequently we had grown very tired of the long overland trip with the horses and looked forward to the pleasure of crossing Kluane Lake in a gasoline boat, but now we wished we were with those trusty cayuses. At one time when the engine stopped and we were again blown toward the shore, we caught the familiar sound of the men's voices as they cursed the horses and urged them on. Presently they saw us and halting, watched us battling the waves for a little while; but unable to render any assistance, they moved on.

I will not dwell on the perils or discomforts of that evening. Darkness found us about ten miles from our destination, and Bones proposed that we go to a sheltered bay nearby and spend the night in an old cabin which we would find there. Snyder objected, insisting that we should proceed, but Bones overruled, declaring it to be too dangerous an undertaking to continue in the darkness, and turned the boat toward the bay. This was no doubt a wise decision, as it is difficult to keep one's course on the water at night. Furthermore, we could not have saved ourselves had the boat wrecked, as we were dressed in our heaviest clothing. We had worn woolen underwear since August first. I had on heavy woolen trousers, shirt and overshirt; a a sweater, a new moose skin coat I had purchased from one of the Indians the night before; a heavy mackinaw coat; one pair of light woolen and four pairs of heavy woolen socks, and shoe-pacs. The others were similarly dressed with the exception of moose skin coats, but each wore two suits of woolen underwear. Thus dressed, we were able to endure the cold, piercing wind on the lake that day. Since we had not anticipated such a delay and had brought only the lunch with us, we were without food for supper and breakfast. I found that my blankets had been soaked with water and were frozen stiff, making it necessary to build a fire to thaw them out. I had always been averse to camping or sleeping in old houses or cabins, usually preferring the out-of-doors. This cabin held no attraction for me, so I cut some spruce boughs and made my bed outside on the snow.

The wind continued to blow across Kluane Lake the next morning and it was noon when we reached Bones' place, having been on the water a day and a half. We found he had a comfortable log house, with one large room in front and a small room in the rear. A square place in the center of the floor was cut out and filled with earth, and on it a large wood burning stove rested. In the rear room was a cooking range large enough for a small hotel. We were surprised to find the floor covered with a very good looking carpet. The log walls were almost covered with heads, horns, pictures and curios, making the place look like a small museum. In one corner of the room stood a bookcase containing a good selection of books by well known authors. On a crude stand in a corner was a small Victrola and many records. There was a large accumulation of unread newspapers, as Bones subscribed to London, San Francisco and Seattle papers. He seldom had an opportunity to get mail except when making trips to White Horse, or "to town" as he termed it.

The temperature in the interior of the Yukon and Alaska sometimes falls to sixty or seventy degrees below zero. I was told that eighty-three below was the record. At such times these men of the North spend no more time out-of-doors than is absolutely necessary; in fact, it is then dangerous to venture very far from shelter. During the short days of winter there is daylight from about nine-thirty until three-thirty; and during this period Bones spent much of the time reading his accumulated newspapers. It was evident that he cared for the better things of life as shown by his books, magazines and Victrola records.

A man by the name of "Al" Supneck, who was in charge of Bones' foxes during his absence, prepared a lunch for us. He said he was almost out of food, and had expected Bones to return from White Horse with winter supplies before this time.

Bones busied himself during the afternoon making preparations for the last lap of our journey. There had been a gold strike in that locality a few years before, at which time the Canadian Government had established a narrow wagon road from White Horse to Kluane Lake, a distance of exactly one hundred and fifty miles, and Bones planned to cover this distance with his wagon.

Doctor, Mr. Snyder and I found much to interest us, which included a visit to the fox pens where we found several varieties—silvers, blacks, reds and crosses—some individuals having a value of five or six hundred dollars. Bones expected the pelts of the ones which he intended to kill that winter to bring about three thousand dollars.

Bones had felt much apprehension concerning the Indians being able to cross Slims River on account of the ice, but they arrived shortly before dark and reported they had not experienced any serious difficulty.

We sat down to an excellent meal that Sunday evening—with a cloth on the table, and three or four coal oil lamps burning. How modern they appeared after using candles so long! After supper we enjoyed the music of the Victrola until bedtime. Removed from civilization, one becomes hungry for music just as he becomes hungry for food. Being very deaf, Supneck did not engage in the conversation with us but spent much of the time reading. There was something about his face that attracted our attention. He apparently took no notice of the music until we began playing the better selections, when he laid down his book and moved closer to the instrument, listening attentively. I had never seen a man's face reveal the sensations produced by music more than did his. He interested us so much that we asked Bones to tell us something of his history, but he replied that he knew little about him. Of this man more will be said later.

CONTINUED HARDSHIPS

Next morning the wagon was loaded; four horses were hitched to it, and we were ready to start at daylight. Doctor and Mr. Snyder made places for themselves among the caribou and sheep skins in the rear, while I sat on the seat by the side of Bones. It was a heavy wagon with broad tires, and a seat so high that it reminded me of a circus wagon. Again we bade Gene goodbye and started, but the cayuses evidently did not like the abrupt change from carrying packs to being harnessed and required to pull. One of them reared and plunged until it looked as though another horse would have to be substituted, but perched on the high seat, with reins in hand and the brake at his command, Bones was equal to the occasion and finally subdued him.

It was Monday morning, October thirteenth, and we hoped to reach White Horse by Friday afternoon. We expected to make Bear Creek—thirty-three miles distant—that night, where we would find a comfortable roadhouse. It was fifty-three miles from Bear Creek to the next roadhouse at Champagne Landing; and as this would require two days' travel, it would be necessary for us to camp out Tuesday night. Bones said if we could cover forty-two miles Thursday, by Friday we should reach the Tahkeena River, where we would find another roadhouse; and from this place drive twenty-two miles to White Horse.

We crossed Boutelier Mountain in the forenoon and Bear Creek Mountain in the afternoon, where we encountered deep snow. Perched as I was on the high seat, it was a hair-raising experience as the horses trotted down the steep five-mile grade that night. Bones dared not use the brake to any extent, because to do so locked the wheels and caused the smooth tires to slide—like sled runners—on the ice and snow. Skillful driving was necessary to keep the wagon from skidding out of the road or crowding the horses down the steep mountain. I breathed much easier when we arrived at Bear Creek at nine o'clock.

The roadhouse was operated by Joe Beauchamp, a Frenchman, who traded with the Indians. It had been established by him for the convenience of the occasional prospector or trapper who passed that way. Joe had gone to White Horse for his winter supplies, so we were greeted by Mrs. Beauchamp, the first white woman we had seen since early in August; and the only white woman in that section of the country. The large one-story log house was banked with earth around the sides, which made it very warm. Included in the menu for supper were eggs which had been purchased at White Horse at a cost of a dollar and fifty cents per dozen. Notwithstanding the scarcity of food and its high cost, Mrs. Beauchamp appeared very much pleased to see us eat so heartily.

We were delighted to find Louie Jacquot spending the night there on his return from White Horse. He was anxious to hear about his brother, Gene, and the success of our hunt—cursing in his broken language when we told him about our bad luck. He had a load of fifty-five hundred pounds on a wagon drawn by six strong horses, and two thousand pounds on a lighter wagon drawn by two horses and driven by an Indian. I thought of the many hungry Indians at Jacquot's place who were waiting to trade their furs for this food. It would take him two more days to reach Bones' place, where he would leave his wagons; and at least another day to cross the lake in the boats, while the horses would be sent around the lake to Jacquot's.

It was easy to understand why it was necessary to charge high prices for supplies that had to be freighted one hundred and eighty-five miles under such conditions. The price of coal oil was one dollar and sixty cents a gallon, although little used. Salt and flour were twenty-four dollars a hundred; bacon a dollar and twenty-five cents a pound, and other supplies equally high. Meals at the Bear Creek roadhouse were two dollars, which we considered very reasonable. Two dollars was charged for a bunk with bed clothing, or one dollar if the traveler used his own blankets. Bones expected to obtain from this roadhouse food for our use during the next two days; but as they were also short of supplies, it was possible to purchase only two loaves of bread, at a cost of one dollar.

The next night we reached the canyon of the Alseck River, having covered twenty-seven miles. Joe Beauchamp had erected there a small log stable which he used as shelter when traveling to and from White Horse, and Mrs. Beauchamp had suggested that we stop there for the night. After the horses were placed inside, Doctor, Mr. Snyder and Bones spread their beds on bunks directly back of the horses and within reach of their heels, but I decided to sleep outside on top of the loaded wagon.

It was almost dark the next evening when we drove into Champagne Landing—an Indian Village—having covered twenty-

CONTINUED HARDSHIPS

five miles. We had traveled this distance with difficulty as the horses were becoming very weak. We stayed that night with a man by the name of "Shorty" Chambers, where we had food and a comfortable place to sleep. "Shorty" had a squaw wife and nine half-breed children. Men who marry squaws are referred to as "squaw men," and this one proved very interesting and intelligent. His Indian wife spent most of her time making beaded gloves and moccasins, and I purchased from her a pair of caribou gloves. We were unable to secure any food from them to take with us, as two of their boys were then at White Horse after supplies.

We were up at four-thirty the next morning and left the Indian Village long before daylight. If we were able to cover forty-two miles that day, we would stay all night at Jimmie Adams' roadhouse on the Tahkeena River; if not, we would be obliged to camp out with nothing to eat. A drive of that distance is a long one, even for grain-fed horses, but ours had subsisted largely by browsing, and were badly worked down. Furthermore, our wagon was heavy and was pulled with difficulty through the snow. I had no hope whatever of our being able to cover the distance. Mr. Snyder was very anxious to reach White Horse Friday night as there would be a train leaving Saturday morning, and he hoped to spend Sunday with his family at Skagway. If we missed this train, there would not be another for three days, and we would have to stay over that length of time.

After going six or eight miles it was discovered that Doctor Evans' large bear skin had fallen out of the wagon. Bones said inasmuch as he had rescued it from the sinking scow and brought it thus far, it would not do to lose it now, so he would go back and try to find it. Two hours later he returned with the skin which had fallen out almost four miles back.

All along the route we saw signs of Louie Jacquot's skill as a teamster. Before starting down a mountain he would cut a spruce tree, and with the lead horses, haul it to the wagon and chain it to the rear axle. The tree with the branches left on acted as a brake as it trailed behind the heavy wagon. At the bottom of every steep grade a fresh spruce tree was seen at the side of the road.

By noon it was necessary for Bones to whip the horses constantly to keep them going. Little is accomplished, however, by whipping a tired horse, and by four o'clock we were obliged to stop. Only twenty-one miles had been made, or one-half the contemplated day's travel; but we had reached a small cabin erected by "Shorty" Chambers. We fed the horses the one feed of oats that we had with us for use in case of emergency, as there was nothing for them to browse upon. A small package of hardtack was found between the logs of the cabin, and, as we were without food, Bones appropriated it with the assertion that he would leave another package in its place on his return. We made tea in which we soaked the hardtack before attempting to eat it. Bones then declared that it was useless to try to go farther until the horses had rested, so we decided to remain there until midnight, and by five o'clock we were in our blankets.

At eleven o'clock Mr. Snyder came to the wagon and awakened me, and after making tea and eating the remainder of the hardtack, we started at exactly midnight. It was very dark until the moon arose at one-thirty, and during that time it was an uncomfortable feeling riding on the high seat over the dangerous icy roads, as often the wagon almost skidded over the high banks. The night was extremely cold—so cold that I became drowsy and found it impossible to stay fully awake. When I dozed for brief intervals, beautiful strains of music came to my ears, but for a few moments only; and arousing myself to consciousness, I realized it was the musical tones produced by the wagon tires grinding over the dry frozen snow. Presently I found it impossible to endure the cold, exposed as I was on the high seat; so, getting off, I walked up the six or eight-mile grade of the mountain that lay before us, in an effort to keep warm. Continuing I left the tired horses far behind, and at daylight stopped and waited for them. After catching up with me we did not go far until our narrow, rough road converged with the government road from White Horse to Dawson. Over this road the Canadian Royal Mail, as well as express and passengers, is carried during the winter months when the Yukon River is not navigable on account of ice.

It was almost nine o'clock when we drove down to the Tahkeena River and signaled Jimmie Adams—a typical Scotchman, who operated the government ferry and roadhouse, to ferry us over. After crossing, it was not long until we were sitting by a comfortable fire, while the Scotchman was preparing breakfast. We could hardly wait until the meal was ready as we had had nothing to eat but the hardtack since five o'clock the morning before.

CONTINUED HARDSHIPS

When descending to the river we had noticed two men in a sled drawn by two horses leaving the roadhouse, and Mr. Snyder had called in an effort to attract their attention, but was unable to do so. He desired them to take him to White Horse, so he might communicate at the earliest possible moment with his family. The Scotchman said they were government men who had been sent to the roadhouse to make some repairs, and having completed their work, were returning to White Horse.

After breakfast Bones said it would be necessary to let the horses rest until afternoon. The distance to White Horse was twenty-two miles and he thought by giving them a few hours' rest, we might arrive there that night. I suggested remaining at the roadhouse until the following morning, where we would have food and shelter, but Mr. Snyder insisted we should undertake the trip; so about one o'clock we started up the six or seven-mile grade of the last mountain we would have to cross. I felt certain we would be obliged to lay out again that night and tried to buy some food from the Scotchman, but could not induce him to sell us any as he, too, was short of supplies. Before leaving, however, he gave each of us an orange, which was a rare treat.

We had gone but a short distance when it was evident that the horses were again tired out. We tried to help them along by all of us walking up the mountain, but even so they could make only one or two miles an hour, and it was some time after dark when we reached the summit. Finally, Bones declared we could not reach White Horse that night as the horses were completely exhausted. It was now slightly down grade and he thought he could urge them to an old cabin two miles farther on. Taking the axe I went ahead for the purpose of having a fire ready. The others arrived an hour later and the horses were turned out to browse. We examined the old cabin and found it had no floor and the roof had fallen in, except one corner. Under this Doctor, Mr. Snyder and Bones slept, while I again slept on the wagon.

It seemed unfortunate that we had to again camp out, without supper or breakfast, when only twelve miles from our destination. But we had come thirty-five miles, from midnight of the night before, until eight o'clock that night, with only four hours' rest for the horses; so they could do no more. I had walked all of this distance except eight miles. We had then been on the road five days since leaving Kluane Lake, and had been obliged to camp out three nights. One would naturally expect to find occasional trading posts or small stores where canned goods or crackers might be obtained; but aside from the small Indian village, there was not an improvement of any kind, except the roadhouse at Bear Creek and the one at Tahkeena River.

With his usual regularity, Snyder aroused Bones at four o'clock, after which Bones came to the wagon—a hundred yards from the cabin—and called me. I found myself covered with three or four inches of fresh snow, and then understood why I had slept so comfortably. In addition to my blankets this covering supplied by Mother Nature had provided sufficient protection to enable me to sleep without once being awakened by the cold.

Bones searched for sometime before he could hear the sound of the horses' bells. After returning with the horses, they were harnessed and hitched to the wagon; and the last lap of our journey started long before daylight. The horses had found little to eat during the night, and we made no better progress than we had the day before, notwithstanding the greater portion of the distance was down grade. During the forenoon we met a sled drawn by four spirited, bright bay horses, their mounted harness glistening in the morning sunlight. Recognizing the driver, Bones stopped him, and after a few minutes' conversation, introduced us. He was the driver of the Canadian Royal Mail and was starting on his long trip over the winter trail from White Horse to Dawson. Beside him was a woman, the only passenger carried. He told us there was much alarm at White Horse on our account, and that the Canadian Royal Mounted Police were making preparations to start in search of us the following morning. While we conversed, the beautiful horses pawed the snow, anxious to be on their way, and we contrasted these well-fed and well-groomed government horses with our half-starved, worn out cayuses. All the way to Dawson roadhouses are located at convenient distances apart where horses are changed. Here passengers are supplied with comfortable accommodations.

As we descended this last mountain, White Horse could be seen far in the distance; and as we approached the town, I wondered what news awaited us. A peculiar sense of uneasiness came over me. Our minds had been occupied with the effort to get back to civilization and when not thus engaged the thoughts of food and shelter were uppermost. Now that we would soon be able to communicate with the outside world, my thoughts were centered on the news we would receive from our homes. I had visions of what

CONTINUED HARDSHIPS

might have happened during our absence—members of my family might have died and been buried; my business establishment or my home might have burned; or our country might have suffered some great calamity. I thought of the admonition Bones had given me before we left McCarthy—". . . whoever was sick would likely be dead and buried or would be up and around again, so, as I have stated, you had just as well write and tell them to forget it." This had necessitated my writing home, advising that regardless of what might happen, it would be useless for them to try to communicate with me.

Chapter XXII

JOURNEY'S END

"The winter! the brightness that blinds you,
  The white land locked tight as a drum,
The cold fear that follows and finds you,
  The silence that bludgeons you dumb.
The snows that are older than history,
  The woods where the weird shadows slant;
The stillness, the moonlight, the mystery,
  I've bade 'em good-by—but I can't."

IT WAS almost Saturday noon when we drew up in front of a small hotel in White Horse. At last we had won in our battle to get back to civilization. Since the wreck of the scow and our rescue, we had suffered almost endless hardships. Most of the time we had been without food—for six days we had had but five meals, and less than a dozen square meals in the past nineteen days. We had been obliged to lie on beds of snow under frozen, icy blankets, suffering the pangs of hunger. Sometimes it had looked as if we would be obliged to surrender, but we had fought on with all our might, and at last we had won. A ride of a hundred and ten miles by rail to Skagway lay before us; then a voyage of five or six days by water, followed by a four or five days' trip across the continent—in all between four and five thousand miles—yet it seemed our journey was almost ended. Such was the feeling experienced on reaching the border of civilization.

Everyone knew Bones, and a crowd quickly gathered about him manifesting great interest in our return. We were told a message had been received at police headquarters concerning our contemplated trip down the White River; but as we had not yet reached the Yukon, it was thought we had met with disaster.

When Doctor Evans arrived at White Horse in May he had presented a letter of credit to the Canadian Bank of Commerce and had deposited in that bank a substantial sum of money with instructions that in case of accident or death this money, or any portion of it that might be required, should be used in getting him or his body out from the interior. We later found that the officials of the bank had become somewhat alarmed when we

JOURNEY'S END

did not arrive soon after October first—especially after the cold weather set in, and the Yukon River froze over. They had conferred with the Yukon government authorities, and when the message was received at police headquarters, it was definitely decided that two of their men—with six weeks' supply of rations—should be detailed to make the trip in our behalf. Preparations were made to start on the morning of our arrival in White Horse; but two men had come in from the Tahkeena roadhouse the evening before and reported that as they were leaving they had seen a wagon, drawn by four horses, approaching the ferry on the opposite side of the river. From the description they gave the officers thought it might be our party, and that we might have made some change in our plans. They decided to await the arrival of this wagon; then if it should prove to be someone else, they would start the following morning. These two men were the ones Mr. Snyder had tried to hail for the purpose of coming in with them. We did not receive this information, however, from the Mounted Police; nor did we elicit any comments from them concerning this expedition when we made their acquaintance later on—but were informed by other reliable sources.

We had heard much about the Royal Canadian Mounted Police, but not until now did we appreciate their good service. From what we learned of them the same interest and prompt action would have been taken in our behalf—or for the relief of anyone in need of assistance, even though there had been no influence brought to bear on the situation. Volumes have been written describing the deeds of these brave men, and no doubt many volumes more could be written to their credit. They are perhaps unequalled by any other organization of their kind in the world. It is to be regretted that our government does not maintain such an organization in Alaska where, it appeared to me, little attention was given to the enforcement of the law, or to the welfare of the residents of the interior—as compared to that given by the Canadian government.

Mr. Snyder communicated by telephone with his family at Skagway; while Doctor Evans and I sent messages to our homes from the government wireless station, requesting that replies be sent to Skagway. A restaurant was then visited as we had not had any food or nourishment since the morning of the previous day.

ALASKAN-YUKON TROPHIES

We made inquiry concerning the Baxter party, and were surprised to learn they had not yet arrived, but were then on a steamer bound from Dawson to White Horse. The weather had moderated somewhat which resulted in the ice breaking up on the Yukon, and the steamer was expected the following evening.

That afternoon Doctor, Mr. Snyder and I cast lots to determine the order in which each should have access to the one bath tub in the hotel. As it fell to my lot to wait until the others had finished, I went out to look for a baker's shop and succeeded in buying a large sackful of doughnuts to eat between meals.

The steamer arrived from Dawson the evening of the following day carrying hundreds of passengers, as it was the last trip of the season. Many men are engaged in mining in the Dawson area and other nearby points along the Yukon River. During the summer months the families of some of these men join them and remain until late in the fall, or until the last trip of the river steamers, after which they go "outside" for the winter months.

The small hotels of White Horse were unable to take care of the crowd that arrived on the steamer. Some slept on the floor of the public dance hall; others in the offices of the railroad and steamship company; while a considerable number spent the night in the chairs of the hotel lobbies.

Baxter and his party were among the ship's passengers, and we were much interested in hearing an account of their experiences. On starting down the White River they had encountered many difficulties; and notwithstanding Baxter had an experienced river man, nine days had been required to reach the mouth of the river instead of five days as planned. Their greatest trouble had been to keep their boat off the numerous sandbars when getting into networks of channels. They had run out of food and had subsisted on condensed milk during the last two days of their trip. Reaching the mouth of the White River they found the Yukon frozen and no steamers running. They secured shelter and food at a trapper's cabin close by, where they remained several days, as they expected our party to arrive daily. Fortunately the ice broke up on the Yukon River and a steamer that had been icebound only a short distance above them, passed down on its way to Dawson. They signalled it and secured passage to Dawson where they remained until it started on its return trip up the river to White Horse. They expected to find our party at the mouth of the White River as they returned; therefore, made ar-

JOURNEY'S END

rangements with the captain to take us on. Baxter was greatly alarmed when they did not find us there. He reasoned that we must have met with some disaster, as it was almost three weeks since we were to have started down the White River. Even though we should finally reach the Yukon, there would not be another steamer out that winter. He knew we would be without food long before this time and probably in need of assistance, so concluded to notify the officers. On reaching a government wireless station, located farther up the river, Baxter sent a message to Dawson from which point it was sent to the authorities at White Horse. Unfortunately, this information was sent from Dawson to the Associated Press, and western newspapers published accounts of our plight, with the statement that we had probably perished. However, the telegrams which we had sent by Mike Knowles reached our homes before these newspaper reports were brought to the attention of our families.

There was no train out until Tuesday so a good portion of Monday was required in crating our trophies and arranging with game wardens, customs officials and the United States Consul for the export of our few trophies and hunting outfit from British Territory. We now regretted we had not requested answers to our telegrams sent to White Horse instead of Skagway. We made settlement with Bones for the full amount of our contract price. The agreement was that he would deliver us with our trophies to White Horse; and although he had failed, in so far as the trophies were concerned, he had done all that any man could possibly do under the circumstances, and we paid him in full. He promised, however, he would return to the White River soon after the first of the year, when it would be frozen solid, and sink holes in the ice where the boat had gone down, with the hope of finding the heavier trophies and the guns.

Passage on the narrow gauge railway train to Skagway cost us twenty-four cents a mile. In conversation with Indian Johnnie one day, he had referred to a visit to White Horse and a trip he had made over this railroad to Skagway, and had spoken of the remarkable speed of this train. He said, "All same you get on train; soon him start; soon him go fast, then him go faster and faster; soon him go faster than bull moose can run." I concluded before we had gone very far that it would be a very decrepit old moose that could not outrun this train; but even so, our progress seemed very great compared to that of pack horses.

Notwithstanding the hardships we had undergone, I could not help experiencing a feeling of regret as we turned our backs on that majestic wilderness.

The passengers were in high spirits, and I made the acquaintance of a number of those two-fisted, big-hearted men with broad-rimmed hats. Some of them had traveled extensively—having large interests throughout the world and doing business on a big scale. There were ladies, who after a summer and fall with their husbands or fathers, were returning to the bright lights and the conventionalities of the cities.

At four in the evening the passengers began cheering, and looking out of the window I saw the ocean far below—apparently only a few minutes away. It was a welcome sight, for some of the passengers had not been "outside" for several years. However, it took an hour for the train to wind its way down the mountain to the depot at Skagway, where we were met by Mrs. Snyder and her daughters. She handed me a telegram and I nervously opened it. It was a message from my wife expressing her delight to know of our safety; and with the advice that all was well at home, which was welcome news indeed.

The hotels of Skagway were as crowded that night as those of White Horse had been the night before. Mrs. Snyder had secured hotel accommodations for us and also passage on the steamer *Alaska* which, we were pleased to hear, would depart at six the next morning. Many people were obliged to wait for the next southbound steamer, as the *Alaska* was booked to her limit.

On the return trip it was too cold to remain on the deck very long, as we had taken off our heavy clothing, so I spent the time reading or conversing with the San Francisco party, who had secured passage on the ship. Doctor Evans and I occupied a stateroom together. For sometime past the effect of the hardships he had undergone were quite visible, and he had not appeared well. On the voyage south he was confined to his berth in the stateroom much of the time. We saw little of Mr. Snyder as he remained in his stateroom relaxing from the long strain we had undergone.

My ravenous appetite had not left me, and it was not long after eating a hearty meal until I was again hungry. I had purchased doughnuts in Skagway to eat between meals, and replenished my supply when we landed at Juneau, and again at

JOURNEY'S END

Seattle; but they did not taste like those made by Gene. Having tried to eat them at home, I have concluded that real doughnuts cannot be made south of the sixty-second parallel of latitude.

The mountains along the coast, which had appeared so lofty on our voyage north, looked like hills in contrast with the great mountains of the interior.

Doctor Evans, Mr. Snyder and I bade each other goodbye quite reluctantly when we separated at Seattle, as we were all returning to our homes by different routes. We had become acquainted under very unusual and somewhat romantic circumstances, and our associations with each other had been pleasant in every respect. It was agreed we would arrange for a meeting at some future time, to live over our experiences; but this was not to be. Doctor had shown some improvement before reaching Seattle, and I thought he would soon recover from the effects of the unusual hardships. However, it was not long after reaching our homes until Mr. Snyder and I received messages telling us of Doctor's serious illness, followed later by the distressing news of his death. His family wrote us that during the last days of his illness he spoke frequently of our pleasant associations together.

Chapter XXIII

A PROMISE FULFILLED

"There's a land where the mountains are nameless,
And the rivers all run God knows where;
There are lives that are erring and aimless,
And deaths that just hang by a hair;
There are hardships that nobody reckons;
There are valleys unpeopled and still;
There's a land—oh, it beckons and beckons,
And I want to go back—and I will."

IT WAS four months to the day from the time I had left my home, until I returned. Three months later I received from Jonas Brothers, Denver, the three trophies which I had sent to be mounted, consisting of the two caribou and one sheep head—the last one I had shot, when the wolverine was close by.

We were interested in hearing from Bones as to whether he had undertaken the trip to the White River to search for the lost trophies. We had only his word that he would do so, if he found it possible, but there were many things to be considered. He had no one to leave in charge of his foxes; we had already made settlement with him in full, and he was to receive no additional compensation for the trip, so what inducement was there for him to undertake it? On the other hand, he had said he would go, if it were possible, and he was known to be a man of his word. Personally I thought it far more probable that he would try to live up to his conditional promise than there was any likelihood of his obtaining the trophies, should he attempt it. I did think, however, that he might find the two guns.

In May we received a letter from Bones stating that he and Gene Jacquot had made the trip, and that it had been a complete failure. Gene had taken his camera with him and they were able to substantiate their report by the pictures. These are included in this volume as they are of more than ordinary interest. An account of their experiences can best be given by reproducing the letter received from Bones:

"Lake Kluane, Yukon Territory:—Well, Mr. Young, I wish I were able to write you a more pleasant letter; one telling you

A PROMISE FULFILLED

Above: Bones and Eugene Jacquot starting for the White River. The dog Jumbo is in the center. Right: Bones finds the sweep protruding above the ice, three months after leaving it, and starts to excavate. Photos by Eugene Jacquot.

I had recovered all of your trophies, but not so. I only tried in vein. Eugene and I went in on the White and spent thirty-three days encluding going and coming and did not find a single thing.

"The recked scow was covered about twelve feet in the ice, only a little of the blade of the ore still remained above the ice. Also the ore marking the hides were only a little exposed. All the capes were under ice. I dug down and found them but as we got none of the heads I left them where they were.

"All the driftlogs where we had the tent pitched were covered so none of them showed up. I had trouble in finding the spot as it looked so changed with the ice extending way back in the timber at the edge of the river bars. I first past by it and went a few hundred yards but the lay of the channel told me that I had past it so I went back looking verry carefull and found the exposed blade of the ore. Well we comenced to sink (a hole) in the ice. I first got in two close and came down on the drift pile. I then run a cut in towards the channel and just came acrost the down stream end of the boat. I then sank (a hole) to the bottom of the channel about twelve feet. I found no running water, in fact no water except a hole along side of the scow.

"I drifted in alongside of the boat its full length. The water hole was about twenty feet long six feet wide and about three feet deep. I raked this verry carefull thinking I would find the guns and Bear trap there but not one thing could I find. Well then we drifted down stream for quite a distance and there was a air space of near a foot between the ice and the bed of the channel; so by lying flat I could see a long distance farther but not one thing could I see.

"Well, we got out of dog feed and had to abandon the hunt. This is hard luck for you and me also as the trip over there cost me $225.00 and over a months time. I had to hire a man to stay here and look after my foxes, besides I had to hire dogs and feed them so I think that $225.00 will not cover. I would gladly of spent this money had I of got yours and Mr. Snyder's and Doctor's heads but as it is, it's a disappointment to all of us. Eugene Jacquot did not charge me anything for his service which I think verry good of him and which I appreciate verry mutch.

"I think probibly in the last of May a person might get these heads in case the water does not come down the channel, but that time I am so busy caring for the young foxes I cannot get away; and again it might be as bad or worse than it was when we were in there.

"Well, as I have nothing pleasant to write I will close. Wishing you the best of luck. Give your old cranky guide a pleasant thought it will not make him any more cranky and don't forget to send some pictures. Yours very truly, (Signed) Morley E. Bones."

I was deeply affected by this letter; also by one I received from Gene soon afterwards, enclosing the pictures he had taken at the White River. His letter in substance was the same; except he referred incidentally to the extremely cold weather which reached fifty degrees below zero, and of which Bones had not spoken.

The course taken by these men came vividly to my mind—the great tundras of Burwash Mountain and the piercing winds that continually sweep over it; the ride down the valley of the Donjeck; up the Wolverine, down Harris Creek and the Generc River; then down the wind-swept ice-covered valley of the White River and through the long canyon to the place where the scow was wrecked. Only a portion of the distance could be covered on ice, and nowhere had they a broken trail to follow. They had left the warmth and comfort of their cabins, and for thirty-three nights, during that bleak, cold weather, they had slept in their tents; and for what? Simply because Bones had made a promise and was determined to live up to that promise, while Gene was willing to do his part and share the hardships of the trip with

A PROMISE FULFILLED

The attempt to recover trophies and equipment. Left: The ice had glaciered about five feet above the previously exposed corner of the scow, which is here seen protruding at Bones' shoulder. Right: After more difficult digging, Bones stands on the scow's corner. Photos by Eugene Jacquot.

him. It is a country where little is known of written contracts; bonds are not required for the faithful performance of agreements. A man's word is his bond, and that is all that is necessary.

In a subsequent letter received from Bones, he informed us of the tragic deaths of Oley Dickson and "Al" Supneck. I quote from his letter for the purpose of substantiating some of the remarks made in this narrative concerning the dangers of ice jams forming and breaking loose in the rivers of that country; also references I have made to the dangerous and lonesome lives lived by these lone prospectors and trappers, which in this instance resulted in the untimely death of "Al" Supneck,—alone in his cabin.

"No doubt you remember of meeting Oley Dickson in White Horse, as he was 'in town' when we arrived there. He was at the Regina Hotel and I remember of you talking with him. Well, he and an Indian were out hunting last October on Wolf Creek on the Donjeck River and an ice jam broke above them and carried them down, but by mere chance the Indian reached shore, but poor Oley went with the flowing ice. His body was not found for a month later. An Indian went up the creek and seeing so many wolf and wolverine tracks, he followed them and found where they went under the ice. An investigation found Oley partly eaten.

"I miss Oley very much, as every time he went by my cabin he would stay a few days with me. He was good company and a loyal friend.

"And 'Al' Supneck, the man who cared for my foxes when I was with you, he was found dead in his cabin on Bullion Creek. According to his diary, he took sick on the 8th day of April and died about the 29th of April. His remains was not found until August. He had tied a note to his dog's neck but it was so consealed in the hare of the dog, we did not find it until after his remains was found. Poor fellow had lumbago and could not get out."

In a letter received quite recently from Charley Baxter, he also referred to Oley Dickson's death and stated that the wolves had entirely devoured the body—except his two arms. He told me of Frank Sketch's misfortune. While on his way from White Horse to Kluane Lake, with the Jacquot brothers' six-horse team, the high, crude bridge constructed of poles at the Mendenhall River, gave way and Sketch, together with the horses and a heavy load of freight, went down. The accident resulted in the loss of an eye to Sketch, and in one of the horses being drowned.

Such are the lives of these pioneers of the North; they are fraught with many dangers. Most of them went into that country with the gold rush of '98—men at that time from twenty-one to twenty-five years of age. Only the hardiest of them remained; the older men and those with families soon returned. The comparatively few who live in the interior are scattered over a wide area throughout Alaska and the Yukon Territory; yet most of them are known to each other. The majority live alone, although a small number have taken Indian wives. It will not be many years until these hardy men have passed away, and there will be few of their kind to take their places.

As I look back on the experiences related in this narrative, I consider that we were fortunate indeed, as we were free from sickness and accidents while on our expedition; and, until we undertook to run the White River, our trip was devoid of any

A PROMISE FULFILLED

unusual hardships. These hardships and discomforts have already receded in my memory, while the joys and pleasures stand out most prominently.

We had gone far beyond the beaten trail and looked upon a great wilderness undefaced by the hands of man. I trust that I may be able always to retain in my mind the picture of that wilderness; the majestic mountains and valleys; the yawning chasms; the great rivers and the monstrous glaciers which feed them; that I will always keep fresh the memory of the Northern Lights, the azure skies, the glorious sunsets, and the beautiful mountain sheep as they grazed so peacefully on plots of green, or wound their way over lofty crests. One of my greatest hopes is that I may sometime return to that country and again gaze upon its beauties and wonders.

Epilogue

WHEN I had finished reading Senator Young's manuscript "Alaskan-Yukon Trophies Won and Lost," I was possessed with the thought that this was the finest factual story of the North Country that I had yet read; the characters and incidents described in this unusual book would always live in my memory.

To my thinking, the book leaves little to be desired except for the fact that the reader becomes so vitally interested in the account of this sub-arctic adventure that, when the story is finished, he yearns for more information concerning the individual characters, and it is with the purpose of supplying that need that this epilogue has been written.

It is recalled that the hunting party consisted of Senator G. O. Young, J. C. Snyder and Dr. A. H. Evans. Of these three, Senator Young and Mr. Snyder still survive. Dr. Evans was a victim of the unusual hardships of their trip and he died not long after his return home.

Eugene Jacquot continues to reside at Kluane Lake, Yukon Territory, 185 miles from the nearest post office. A questionnaire was recently sent to him and we believe that our readers will be interested in the observations contained in his reply. He reports that game is now more scarce in the Alaskan-Yukon area than in 1919, when he guided Senator Young, and he attributes this decrease to the great number of wolves now roaming the country. He explains that the government has made a National park from some of the best hunting territory, which, he says, gives the wolves protection and opportunity to breed. Sheep are much scarcer than in former years, and this holds true also for moose and caribou. Goats are least molested, due to their precipitous habitat. Grizzly bears are the exception; they are equal in number if not more plentiful today than in 1919.

Eugene Jacquot has guided hunting parties every year since his hazardous exploits with Senator Young. He has guided General R. E. Woods, Nelson Rockefeller, "Wild Bill" Donovan, Richard K. Mellon, Jack O'Connor and many other sportsmen of equal prominence.

Jacquot was asked whether or not he thought the new Alaskan highway would have detrimental effects upon the game population of Yukon and Alaska. He answers that, if proper protective measures are set up, including twenty-mile strips closed to hunting, on either side of the highway, there is no reason why there should be an undue depopulation of game. He expresses pleasure that this highway will enable tourists and sportsmen to travel in comfort into the heart of the North Country.

The new highway crosses the Slims River near its mouth and traverses the shore of Lake Kluane, cutting through Jacquot's homestead about three hundred yards back of his trading post. The highway also crosses the White River at a point a half-mile below the Lower Canyon and about four miles above the location where the trophy-laden boat of Senator Young's party was lost. The highway does not extend up the White River, but crosses this turbulent water and keeps on in a westerly direction to Tanana and then to Fairbanks.

Jacquot informs that, so far as he knows, the party of Senator Young was the last hunting group to attempt the hazardous trip down the White River. In fact, he states, not since 1919 has anyone ever undertaken as extensive and varied a trip as was made by the Young party. Harry Boyden has brought a few parties across the glaciers to the head waters of the White River and afterwards returned to McCarthy, from which point they had been outfitted. Jacquot recommends that sportsmen contemplating a northern trip to include both Alaska and Yukon should have an American guide for the Alaskan side and a Canadian guide for the Yukon area.

Jacquot's brother, Louis, is still at Kluane Lake, but Eugene took over the outfitting responsibilities in 1937. Indian Paddie died of tubercular trouble about four years after the Young party returned home. Indian Johnny still lives and was made Chief of the Champagne Indian Tribe in the fall of 1945. Billy Slimpert was lost in the quicksands of the Nabesna River, with his horse, in an unsuccessful attempt to ford one of the treacherous channels. This happened about 1943. Frank Sketch is still living and has a trading post at Kloo Lake, twelve miles from Bear Creek. Al Voss is reported in good health and is employed as a cook at a North Woods mining camp.

Morley Bones died in 1945, after becoming seriously afflicted with stomach ulcers. Living alone and realizing the fate that was likely to overtake him if he continued to reside at Kluane Lake, thirty-five or forty miles distant from his nearest neighbor, he decided to leave the Yukon territory. He returned to his native state of California, where he located on a small ranch and devoted the last years of his life to the raising of foxes.

Charles Baxter also died in California, a year or two earlier than Bones. Mr. and Mrs. Baxter had joined their son in southern California and there Mrs. Baxter met with a serious automobile accident, but she recovered sufficiently to return to White Horse, where she entered the employ of the Sixth Service Command.

Mike Knowles, the genial Irishman, married a Seattle, Washington, girl a few years ago and now resides in that city.

Senator Young and his surviving associate, J. C. Snyder, had planned to make another trip to the North Country several years after the harrowing experiences recited in this volume, but advancing years and increased business responsibilities prevented the materializing of this dream. Senator Young has made a number of subsequent trips to Canada, but most of these excursions have been confined to hunting and fishing and were not nearly so hazardous as the Alaskan-Yukon trip. Mr. Snyder remains active in the banking business in Metamora, Illinois, a small town some fifteen miles distant from Peoria. He and his brother own the local bank, which they have successfully operated for many years. Mr. Snyder is a prominent and substantial man in his home community and, in addition to his banking business, he owns and operates several large farms, aggregating more than a thousand acres. Like the author, he survived the great ordeal of their Alaskan-Yukon hunting trip and has lived to enjoy many fruitful years. But outstanding in his experiences will always be the trip North in 1919.

Senator G. O. Young, our capable author, is still living at his home in Buckhannon, West Virginia, and enjoys splendid health, carrying most gracefully the weight of his years. He was born December 26, 1873 in Fairmont, West Virginia, the son of a Methodist minister. He was educated in the public schools, graduating in pharmacy in 1896 from Scio College, Scio, Ohio, which school was later merged with the University of Pittsburgh. He has long been identified with the drug business as a pharmacist, as a representative of large drug companies, and as owner of the largest retail drug company in West Virginia. He was married March 28, 1895 to Emma Windom, who died in October, 1942.

Senator Young has been known in national pharmaceutical circles for many years and has served as director and member of the executive committee of the American Druggists' Fire Insurance Company, in which capacity he was one of a committee of three which planned the construction of the company's seventeen-story office building in Cincinnati. He is now vice-president of the organization. The Senator has been successful also in banking and numerous other business enterprises.

Young was the first chairman of the West Virginia Game and Fishing Commission and has been consistently active in all wild life conservation projects. A bronze memorial has been erected by the State of West Virginia in appreciation of his efforts in behalf of the conservation of outdoor life.

In 1934, the author was elected to the West Virginia State Senate on the Republican ticket to represent the 13th Senatorial District and he was re-elected without opposition, either in the primary or general election, to represent the newly created 15th Senatorial District, in 1938. He was re-elected, without opposition, in the general election, to represent the same district in 1942, which office he held until his recent voluntary retirement from politics.

Notwithstanding the fact that his successfully-conducted business affairs have required long hours and incessant labor, Senator Young has found frequent opportunity to give of his time and effort to various civic, educational and political enterprises which have had for their purpose the betterment of his state and its people.

Senator Young's hobbies have always been identified with the "great open spaces," and it has been his good fortune to make thirty-three annual trips to the North Country. He has traversed the Canadian wilderness from the Maritime Provinces of the Atlantic to the sub-arctic regions of Alaska and the Yukon. He is an ardent fisherman as well as a successful big game hunter. He admits to the writer that in recent years he has carried with him to the North Woods a camera in preference to a big game rifle, explaining that he has, for some years, enjoyed photographing big game animals quite as much as he formerly enjoyed bringing them to earth with a well-aimed bullet. In this respect, Senator Young has followed the footsteps and philosophy of many hunters and outdoorsmen who, after they had their share of shooting, have become ardent conservationists and express more interest in propagating wild life than in destroying it; who find greater compensation in seeing big game through a camera lens than through the hunting scope mounted on a high-powered rifle.

I should add that, in writing Alaskan-Yukon Trophies Won and Lost, the author disclaims any effort to become literary and he has studiously refrained from embellishing the account of his memorable trip. He kept voluminous notes during the trip and this intriguing story was written spontaneously shortly after he returned to his home; it is, perhaps, because of this fact that the story is so gripping and realistic in its detailed description. Every word in this book is written as fact and not one sentence of fiction or superficial glamour has been injected to enhance the power of the tale that he tells.

We stand upon the threshold of a new era of interest and activity in Alaska and the Yukon Territory. The recent war and air travel have brought this great North Country nearer to the sportsmen of the United States and Canada, and their close interest is further invited by the building of the new Alaskan highway.

Many readers of this book will possibly make the trek to some of the same spots visited by Senator Young and his party, but it is doubtful whether any big game hunters of the present or the future will ever live to tell the tale of a more exciting journey than that recorded in these pages.

True it is that fact can oftentimes be more exciting than fiction and I believe that the book which you hold in your hands is a case in point. Few of us can ever hope to indulge in the arduous adventure of the kind which led these courageous men into the untamed arctic wilds, but, at least, it is our privilege to live with this little group in the pages of this book. For this privilege, I think all sportsmen will give thanks and pay honor to the intrepid souls who had the courage to face and conquer the dangers that met them — and especially to Senator Young, who had the forethought to record these experiences so accurately and graphically for our pleasure.

Herman P. Dean

Huntington, West Virginia
February 1, 1947

www.ingramcontent.com/pod-product-compliance
Lightning Source LLC
Chambersburg PA
CBHW082111230426
43671CB00015B/2669